Key Visual and Online Features

DOCUMENT DESIGN

College essay format, 10

Typefaces, color, lists, and headings (with sample brochure and PowerPoint slide), 12

Tables and graphs (with 1 table and 6 graphs), 13

Images and text (with 3 images), 19

Interactive multimedia (with illustration of a multimedia visual argument), 22

RESEARCH ONLINE

Web caution!, 25

Search engines and keyword searching, 25

Indexes, databases, and Web sites, 27

Scholarly articles online, 40

Evaluating online sources, 41

How to read a Web site (with sample site), 44

WRITING IN THE DISCIPLINES

Sources in 27 subject areas, 28

CITING AND DOCUMENTING ONLINE SOURCES

Indicating the boundaries of an online citation with no page numbers, 49

MLA style: Italics, not underlining, for titles when writing online, 69

MLA: Citing Internet sources, 77

MLA: What to cite (with screenshots of full-text database screens), 80

APA style, 102

Chicago style, 112

CBE/CSE style, 119

PUNCTUATION AND MECHANICS ONLINE

Punctuation in URLS, 198

Underlining and italics online, 198

Five Ways to Use
Pocket Keys for Writers

Pocket Keys for Writers makes it easy for you to find information quickly. Here are five convenient ways to locate the information you need:

1. Color-Coded Pages

- **Red sections** cover "whole paper" issues such as the writing process and working with sources.
- **Blue sections** cover sentence-level concerns such as style, grammar, punctuation, and mechanics.

2. Contents

- **The Key to the Book** (inside front cover) is a directory to the book's nine parts.
- **Detailed Tables of Contents** (on the back of each part divider) allow you to scan easily for the exact topic you are seeking.
- **Complete Table of Contents** (inside back cover) shows the book at a glance.

3. Indexes

- **The Main Index** (p. 231) provides a complete alphabetical list of topics, terms, and words such as *I* and *me*, *who* and *whom*.
- **Specialized Indexes for MLA** (p. 60) **and APA** (p. 91) include detailed coverage of documenting electronic sources.

4. Lists

- **List of Key Visual and Online Features** (p. i) details visual- and digital-related coverage in the book.
- **Key Points Boxes** (see list on p. 250) give quick answers to quick questions.
- **Useful Sources in 27 Subject Areas** (p. 28) is a list of starting points for research across the curriculum.
- **Correction and Editing Marks** (p. 251) shows common symbols, with cross references to related coverage in the book.

5. Glossaries

- **Glossary of Usage** (p. 212) clarifies the use of commonly confused words such as *affect/effect* and *lie/lay*.
- **Glossary of Grammatical Terms** (p. 221) defines helpful terms and provides cross references to related coverage in the book.

Pocket Keys for Writers

Second Edition

Ann Raimes

Hunter College,
City University of New York

Houghton Mifflin Company   Boston New York

Publisher: Patricia A. Coryell
Executive Editor: Suzanne Phelps Weir
Senior Development Editor: Judith Fifer
Senior Project Editor: Rosemary Winfield
Editorial Assistant: Jake Perry
Art and Design Coordinator: Jill Haber
Photo Editor: Jennifer Meyer Dare
Composition Buyer: Sarah Ambrose
Designer: Henry Rachlin
Manufacturing Manager: Karen Banks
Senior Marketing Manager: Cindy Graff Cohen
Marketing Associate: Wendy Thayer

Cover: © John Wilkes

Photo credits   *Part 1:* Page 12, Horizons for Homeless
Children (formerly The Horizons Initiative), 90 Cushing Avenue,
Dorchester, MA 02125

Page 19, © Dieter Roth Foundation, Hamburg. Copyright 1961
Estate of Dieter Roth.

Page 20, Don Pierce—UVic Photo.

Page 21, <http://www.adbusters. org>.

Page 22, Institute for Multimedia Literacy, Annenberg Center for
Communication, University of Southern California, Jon Vidar, Trevor
Muirhead, Brian Olson.

Credits continue on page 230, which constitutes an extension of
the copyright page.

Printed in the U.S.A.

Library of Congress Catalog Card Number 2003115632
ISBN 0-618-44546-3

23456789-QUH-08 07 06 05

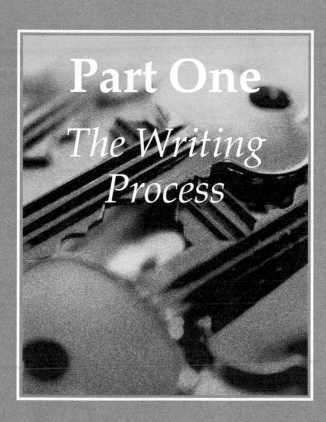

Part One
The Writing Process

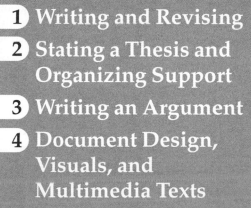

1 Writing and Revising

2 Stating a Thesis and Organizing Support

3 Writing an Argument

4 Document Design, Visuals, and Multimedia Texts

1

PART ONE   The Writing Process

1 **Writing and Revising, 2**

2 **Stating a Thesis, Organizing Support, 4**

2a From topic to thesis, 4
2b Outlining supporting points, 5

3 **Writing an Argument, 6**

3a Constructing a good argument, 7
3b Formulating an arguable claim, 7
3c Providing reasons and evidence, 8

3d Considering your audience, 9

4 **Document Design, Visuals, and Multimedia Texts, 10**

4a College essay format, 10
4b Typeface, color, lists, and headings, 12
4c Visuals for data: Tables and graphs, 13
4d Analysis of images, 18
4e The partnership of images and written text, 19
4f Interactive multimedia, 22

1   Writing and Revising

Writing and revising are parts of a larger process entailing a variety of activities: identifying your purpose, audience, and topic; generating ideas; gathering information; establishing a thesis; organizing ideas; drafting; revising; editing; and proofreading. Although virtually no one who is faced with a writing task marches neatly through a series of distinct steps, you will want to plan your time to accommodate the process. The most important features of the writing process are these:

The process is not linear.

Writing is a messy adventure; it is not done according to a formula.

Very few writers achieve perfection on the first draft.

Writing is a process of discovery, so it can be exciting.

Nonlinear as this process may be, keep in mind that generating ideas, planning, drafting, and revising are all important aspects of that process.

1. Establish clearly what the assigned task is and what you need to do to perform it well. Ask for clarification where necessary. Pay attention to requirements of

length, format, coverage, and tone. Consider whether and how you can use visuals to enhance your text.

2. Decide on your purpose for writing: Do you want to explain an idea, provide information, describe something, tell a story, record your own experience, assess cause and effect, give a definition, argue for a point of view, or persuade your reader to take action? Whatever your purpose, convey lively interest, and use an engaging voice.

3. Determine who will read what you write and what your readers will know, expect, and value. Regard a college instructor as a stand-in for a larger audience of general readers who do not know everything there is to know about your topic.

e s l **Readers' Expectations**   Readers of languages other than English may expect and appreciate obliqueness, ornate language, and digressions. Readers of English generally value simplicity and directness.   ■

4. To find a topic or explore an assigned topic, experiment with generating ideas. Try reading, discussion, brainstorming, freewriting, Web searching, and outlining

5. Establish your approach to the topic and formulate a working thesis (**2a**).

6. If necessary, consult sources and record all source information (**5**).

7. Write a rough outline of the points you will cover to support your thesis (**2b**) and then write a draft.

8. Evaluate the draft by examining each paragraph or asking someone else to read and respond: What main idea does each paragraph convey? Do details in the paragraph develop that idea? Does each paragraph's main point support the thesis of the essay or report? Does the information flow well, with no big jumps for the reader?

9. Revise as often as necessary, paying attention to content, organization, paragraph structure, transitions, and style (**14–18**).

10. Take time to give your essay a good title, one that will make the reader want to read more.

11. Check that your conclusion rounds off the essay, reinforces the thesis, and provides a frame for the essay, avoiding new points, apologies, and changes of opinion.

12. Edit for errors in grammar, sentence structure, spelling, mechanics, and punctuation (**19–36**). Use the spelling checker in your word processing program, but remember that it will not find grammatical errors such as missing plural or -*ed* endings, nor will it find a misspelled word that is actually another word (*expect* for *except,* for example). A grammar checking program will analyze what could be fixed, tightened, or polished, but be aware that the capabilities of such programs are limited.

13. Decide on the presentation of your material: format, headings, lists, visuals, and multimedia (**4**).

14. Proofread carefully to look for errors. Cover up everything below the line you are checking so that your eye cannot run ahead; read aloud to a friend, with both of you looking at a copy of your manuscript; or put your manuscript away for a day or two before you check it.

2 Stating a Thesis and Organizing Support

2a From topic to thesis

Whether you are assigned a subject or topic or are free to choose your own, make sure you consider what specific idea you want to communicate to readers. Let readers know what *you* bring to the topic, what *you* have to say about it.

Broad subject area	College admissions policies
Narrowed topic	Affirmative action in college admissions
Question	How do people perceive students accepted by colleges under affirmative action policies?
Thesis/claim (developed after considerable reading, writing, and thinking)	The public and the press act unjustly when they question the abilities of students accepted into colleges under affirmative action policies.

The statement "This essay is about affirmative action" provides no thesis. It relates only to the topic, telling readers nothing about what you bring to the topic. An authentic thesis statement, on the other hand, may lead readers to ask, "Why do you say that? What are your reasons?" and compel them to continue reading.

Although some readers may expect to find a thesis statement within the introductory paragraphs of an essay, you may not formulate your final version until you have read, written, and revised a great deal. Keep a working thesis in mind as you write, but be flexible. You are the boss as you write. You can change and narrow your thesis whenever you like. Sometimes a clear thesis may not emerge for you until the end of your first draft, pointing the way to the focus and organization of your next draft.

KEY POINTS

A Good Working Thesis

1. narrows your topic to a single main idea that you want to communicate

2. asserts your claim clearly and firmly in a sentence

3. states not simply a fact but rather an observation or opinion

4. makes a generalization that can be supported by details, facts, and examples within the assigned limitations of time and space

5. stimulates curiosity and interest in readers and prompts them to wonder, "Why do you think that?" and read on

---

For more on a thesis in an argument paper, see **3b**.

2b Outlining supporting points

Think of your essay as a structure of building blocks. At the top is the thesis, supported by your main pieces of evidence. Each piece of evidence, in turn, is supported by specific and concrete details. As you plan and begin your first draft, organize your ideas into a rough outline of numbered and lettered points, one that allows you to see the structure of your ideas and the specific examples that illustrate your ideas to your readers. Here is a student's outline of thesis, main points, and specific examples. Note the numbering system: main supporting points (I, II, and so on) and illustrative examples (A, B, and so on).

Thesis (claim): Shopping malls and superstores are damaging communities, social values, and the landscape.

I. Discount superstores, home improvement stores, and bookstore chains draw shoppers away from downtown areas, resulting in deserted town centers.
   A. Stores close in towns as malls and big chain superstores open.
      1. Example of Garden City, NY
      2. Example of Atlanta, GA
   B. Restaurants and movie theaters open in malls, further contributing to downtown decline. (Story of looking for a small lunch restaurant in Scottsdale, Arizona; being sent to a mall; getting lost in movie and restaurant crowds; and finding restaurants crowded, homogenized, and unappealing)
II. Teenagers attracted to the malls learn the ethics of consumerism.
   A. Interviews with 3 teenagers at mall
   B. Deborah's story of how she spends every Saturday
   C. *Time* magazine article
III. As megastores expand, they move into bigger buildings and bankrupt smaller businesses, leaving the concrete and asphalt of empty stores to mar the landscape.
   A. Example of Macon, GA
   B. Example of Catskill, NY

---

3 Writing an Argument

An argument in the academic sense is a reasoned, logical piece of writing designed to persuade an audience to pay attention to significant points you raise. When you write an argument, the goal is to persuade readers to appreciate or even adopt your point of view on your chosen or assigned topic.

3a Constructing a good argument

> **KEY POINTS**
> ### The Features of a Good Argument
>
> A good argument
>
> - deals with an arguable issue (**3b**)
> - is based not solely on strong personal feelings or beliefs, unsubstantiated by evidence, but also on careful analysis of readings or sources (**3b**)
> - takes a position on and makes a clear claim about the topic (**3b**)
> - supports that position with detailed and specific evidence (such as reasons, facts, examples, descriptions, and stories) (**3c**)
> - establishes common ground with listeners or readers and avoids confrontation (**3d**)
> - takes opposing views into account and either refutes them logically or shows why they may be unimportant or irrelevant (**3d**)

Try the following sites for help with writing arguments.

- *Paradigm Online Writing Assistant,* a site that began at Boise State University, at <http://www.powa.org/argument/index.html>
- The Capital Community College site on writing arguments at <http://www.ccc.commnet.edu/grammar/composition/argument.htm> with a sample annotated argument paper
- *Stephen's Guide to the Logical Fallacies* at <http://datanation.com/fallacies/>

3b Formulating an arguable claim (thesis)

The position you take on a topic constitutes your claim or your thesis (see **2a**). Make sure your claim is focused, specific, and debatable.

Here are some examples of nondebatable claims, each with a revision.

Neutral statement	There are unstated standards of beauty in the workplace.
Revised	The way we look affects the way we are treated at work and the size of our paychecks.

Too broad	This paper is about violence on TV.
Revised	TV violence must take a major part of the blame for the violence in our society.

Fact	*Plessy v. Ferguson,* a Supreme Court case that supported racial segregation, was overturned in 1954 by *Brown v. Board of Education.*
Revised	The overturning of *Plessy v. Ferguson* by *Brown v. Board of Education* has not led to significant advances in integrated education.

Truism	Bilingual education has advantages and disadvantages.
Revised	A bilingual program is more effective than an immersion program at helping students grasp the basics of science and mathematics.

Opinion based only on feeling	I think water-skiing is a dumb sport.
Revised	Water-skiing should be banned from public beaches.

3c Providing reasons and evidence

You can support a claim by telling and showing readers what reasons, statistics, facts, examples, and expert testimony bolster and explain your point of view.

Reasons Imagine a reader asking you to provide reasons for your claim. Think of a reason as something that can be attached to your claim by the word *because.*

Thesis (claim)	A large cement factory would be disastrous for the city of Hudson on the Hudson River.
Reasons	1. Drilling poses dangers to the city's water supply.
	2. A huge smokestack would emit millions of pounds of pollution a year, affecting people's health.

3. Famous views portrayed by the Hudson River school of painters would be spoiled.

Evidence You need reasons, but reasons are not enough. You also need to include specific evidence that supports, illustrates, and explains your reasons. Imagine a reader saying, after you give one of your reasons, "Tell me even more about why you say that." The details you provide are what will make your argument vivid and persuasive.

Add to the outline any items of concrete evidence you will include to illustrate and explain your reasoning. Facts, statistics, stories, examples, and testimony from experts can all be used as evidence in support of your reasons. Consider also using visual evidence: tables, graphs, images, and—for online presentations—multimedia (**4c**, **4e**, and **4f**).

3d Considering your audience

Assess who your readers are and what assumptions they may make. If you are writing for a general academic audience, include background information about the topic to orient your readers.

Type of appeal to audience The Greek philosopher Aristotle first recognized the need to appeal to readers in several ways:

- *Rational appeal,* using logic and concrete evidence as well as reasoned discussion and refutation of opposing views; often used in academic essays
- *Ethical appeal,* presenting yourself as thoughtful, knowledgeable, and objective and your sources as reliable, even-handed experts; often found in advertising, with testimony from famous people
- *Emotional appeal,* directed at gaining readers' empathy and sympathy; often used in journalism and the media

Common ground Even when you discuss views that you oppose, try to establish some common ground so as not to offend readers who hold them. Avoid extreme, confrontational, or sarcastic language; point to shared values; and acknowledge where opposing views may be valid and applicable.

4 Document Design, Visuals, and Multimedia Texts

Readers have expectations about what a particular type of document will look like. Think, for example, of what you would expect in the following: a college essay on paper or on the screen, a business letter, an e-mail message, a memo, an advertisement, a Web site or Web log (blog), a brochure, a résumé, or information displayed on presentation software.

With the recent technological explosion, the design of documents and the presentation of information have become more complex as well as more visual. Just consider the expectations of text that Internet-savvy teenagers hold compared with those of their older family members. Straight text (in words) has been joined by pictures, photographs, tables, graphs, music, and film to convey information and emotion, often more immediately and dramatically than words alone. Printed text is being replaced by "multimedia displays."

Online readers have the complex task of analyzing and evaluating the new media. They also use the texts of the new media interactively—changing photographs, adding or deleting illustrations or sound, and inserting their own contributions to a Web site, as in wikis. To the ancient art of rhetoric (the art of effective communication and persuasion in words) we now add the component of visual rhetoric, in daily life and increasingly in college and in the workplace. An important question to ask when you consider how to present your project to an audience, therefore, is this: What is the best way to meet my readers' or listeners' expectations, engage their attention, and make my points with the most impact?

4a College essay format (paper and online)

To meet the expectations of college instructors, follow these guidelines for your final draft.

PAPER   Use unlined $8\frac{1}{2}'' \times 11''$ white bond paper. Clip or staple the pages.

PRINT   Use black, letter-quality type, not draft type.

MARGINS   Leave 1" margins all around. Use a ragged right margin—that is, do not justify (set "Left" at Format/Paragraph/Alignment).

TYPE FONT AND SIZE   Use a standard font, such as Times New Roman or Arial, not a decorative font or one that looks like italic or handwriting, such as Old English Text or Brush Script. Select a regular font size of 10 or 12 points.

SPACING   For works on paper, double-space between the lines throughout the essay and list of works cited. Single-space essays online, but double-space between paragraphs.

SPACE AFTER A PERIOD   Most style manuals suggest one space after a period. Your instructor may prefer two in the text of your essay.

PARAGRAPHING   For works on paper, indent a new paragraph one-half inch from the left margin, with no additional line space between paragraphs. For online documents, begin a new paragraph at the left margin, but leave an additional line space between paragraphs.

PAGE NUMBERS   Use View/Header and Footer or Insert/Page Numbers to place a page number automatically on every page, usually in the top right margin. Use arabic numerals with no period. Do not use page numbers for essays presented online.

TITLE AND IDENTIFICATION ON THE FIRST PAGE   See page 89 for a sample of the format recommended by the Modern Language Association (MLA) for papers in the humanities.

TITLE AND IDENTIFICATION ON A SEPARATE PAGE   Include an unnumbered title page for an MLA-style paper only if your instructor requires it. Include a title page for papers in American Psychological Association (APA) style; in the style recommended by the Council of Science Editors, formerly the Council of Biology Editors (CBE/CSE); and in the *Chicago* style recommended by *The Chicago Manual of Style.* Generally, a title page will center the title (with no underlining, quotation marks, or period), your name, the course information, and the date. Section **11d** shows the format for a numbered APA-style title page with a running head.

LINKS IN ONLINE PAPERS   For citations within your paper, provide a direct link to Web pages cited. For other citations, provide a link to the work in your list of works cited.

VISUAL AND MULTIMEDIA FEATURES   See **4b–4f.**

4b Typeface, color, lists, and headings

TYPEFACE Use ornamental fonts or fonts that look like handwriting only for special effects, such as in flyers, brochures, and invitations.

FIGURE 1 Community Brochure (front)

The type has a handlettered look, adding a personal touch to the message.

The number of words is limited for maximum effect.

A CUTE KID ON TV CAN GET YOU TO SPEND $900 ON TIRES.

CAN THIS ONE GET YOU TO SPEND TWO HOURS WITH HOMELESS KIDS?

COLOR Colored type can be useful to draw attention to important points in business, community, and online documents. The entry page to the Google search engine, for instance, shows restrained but effective use of color. However, academic style guides, such as those for MLA or APA, make no mention of using colored type.

LISTS Lists are useful in technical reports and oral presentations. Bulleted or numbered lists are a feature of presentation software slides, as in student Emily Luo's outline slide for a classroom presentation of her research.

FIGURE 2   Presentation Slide

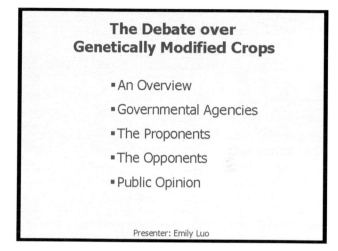

HEADINGS   Headings help readers find their way through a document. They are often used in the sciences and social sciences and in long research papers, business documents, and Web documents. Decide on the typeface and the position (centered or flush left?) of each level of heading and subheading. Keep headings parallel in typeface and grammatical form, as in this section (and see **21f**). Use headings such as *Abstract, Method, Results,* and *Discussion* for APA and CBE/CSE papers. Use bulleted lists and section headings in a résumé, too (for example, *Education, Work Experience, Special Skills,* and *References*). Note, however, that headings are not recommended for MLA-style papers. Papers posted online usually include section headings along with a table of contents linked to each section.

4c   Visuals for data: Tables and graphs

To help readers grasp data, use visuals. You can easily create professional-looking tables and graphs with your word processing program. In Microsoft Office, you can create tables, graphs, and charts in Word or Excel. In Word, for example, go to Table/Insert or to Insert/Picture/Chart, and in the Chart screen go to Chart/Chart Type. You will be able to select a type of chart (such as a pie graph or bar graph) and enter your own details, such as a title, labels for the vertical and horizontal axes of a bar graph, numbers, and data labels.

TABLE Use a table to present descriptive or numerical data.

TABLE 1 Internet Use by Educational Attainment: December 1998 to December 2002

Educational Attainment	Internet Use (as percentage of education group)			
	Dec 1998	Sept 2001	Dec 2002	Difference
Less than high school	4.2	12.8	13.4	9.2
HS diploma/GED	19.2	39.8	43.0	23.8
Some college	38.6	62.4	69.7	31.1
Bachelor's degree	58.4	80.8	76.4	18.0
Higher degree	66.4	83.7	83.3	16.9

Source: *A Nation Online: How Americans Are Expanding Their Use of the Internet,* Feb. 2002: 28. National Telecommunications and Information Administration. 1998 and 2001 data are taken from Table 2-3 on p. 28 at <http://www.ntia.doc.gov/ntiahome/dn/anationonline2.pdf>. Data were collected by the U.S. Census as part of the *Current Population Survey (CPS),* a representative sample of 137,000 adults in the United States. This table shows respondents age 25 and older. The 2002 data are calculated based on the "December 2002 Tracking Data Set" of the "Pew Internet & American Life Project" at <http://www.pewinternet.org/datasets/index.asp>.

LINE GRAPH Use a simple line graph to show changes over time or a comparative line graph to compare data over time.

FIGURE 3 Danger on the Road

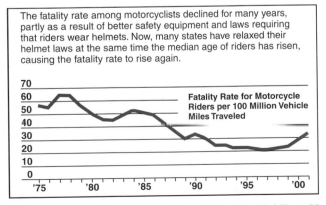

Source: Insurance Institute for Highway Safety, *New York Times,* 22 Apr. 2003: A16.

FIGURE 4 Average Tuition and Fee Charges (Enrollment-Weighted), in Constant (2002) Dollars, 1971–1972 to 2002–2003

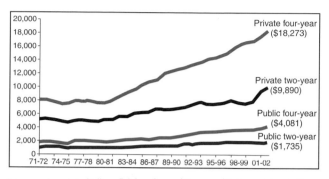

Source: *Trends in College Pricing, Annual Survey of Colleges,* The College Board, New York, 2002, 8, at <http://www.collegeboard.com/press/cost02/html/CBTrendsPricing02.pdf>. Data are based on surveys of 2,414 postsecondary institutions for the 2002–2003 academic year.

BAR GRAPH A bar graph shows comparisons and correlations and can highlight differences among groups.

FIGURE 5 Grade Inflation among Students Entering Different Types of Institutions (Percentage Earning A Averages)

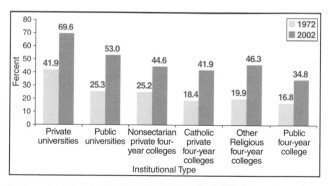

Source. L. J. Sax et al., *The American Freshman: National Norms for Fall 2002,* Los Angeles, Higher Education Research Institute, UCLA, 2003, at <http://www.gseis.ucla.edu/heri/norms.charts.pdf>. Data are from 282,549 students at 437 higher education institutions.

Student Emily Luo used a stacked bar graph to present public opinion survey data in her classroom presentation on genetically engineered food:

FIGURE 6   Public Opinion on the Labeling of Genetically Engineered Food

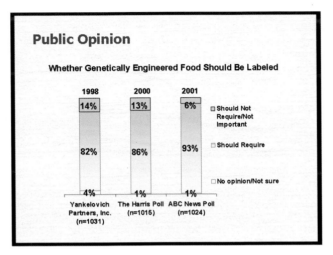

A bar graph can also be presented horizontally, which makes it easier to attach labels to the bars. Figure 7 was produced in MS Office using the data from Table 1.

FIGURE 7   Internet Use by Educational Attainment: December 1998, September 2001, and December 2002

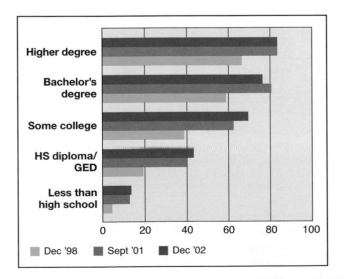

PIE GRAPH   Pie graphs (also called pie charts) show how fractions and percentages relate to one another and make up a whole.

FIGURE 8   Attitudes about Gender Roles (Responses to this statement: "It is much better for everyone involved if the man is the achiever outside the home and the woman takes care of the home and family.")

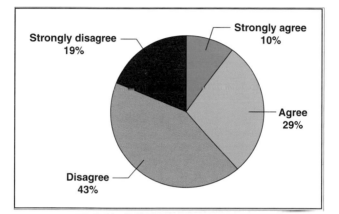

Source: General Social Survey, Inter-university Consortium for Political and Social Research, 1972–2002. Responses from 898 respondents. Details at <http://webapp.icpsr.umich.edu/cocoon/ICPSR-STUDY/03728.xml>.

KEY POINTS

Using Graphs

- Use a graph only to help make a point.
- Set up a graph so that it is self-contained and self-explanatory.
- Make sure that the items on the time axis of a line graph are proportionately spaced.
- Always provide a clear caption.
- Use precise wording for labels.
- Always give details about the source of the data or information. For source information posted online, ask for permission to reproduce a graph.
- When using percentages, make sure to include the "percentage base," the total number of all cases.

4d　Analysis of images

Analyzing written text leads readers to examine it from beginning to end, in a linear way. Narratives, descriptions, comparisons, and arguments move logically from page 1 to page 10 or page 200. Confronted with an image, however, we lose the traditional structure of linear progression. The idea of discerning purpose and audience stays with us from the analysis of written texts, but now we include a close look at the following features:

- the effect of spatial organization, in which elements of the image appear in relation to each other

- the visual focus, the part of the image that speaks to us most directly and expresses the main idea of the image

- the juxtaposition of image and written text: what does one do to and for the other?

- the connections we (along with the originator of the image) make with other visual images in our experience and memory

- our response to color, to alignment, and (with multi-media images) to the sequence and progression of the images

Think, for example, of films that reverse chronology, use fade-outs and flashbacks, and cut rapidly from one image to another. We "read" such visual texts differently from the way we read a print article or a piece of fiction.

The following work combines image and words. Its wooden frame immediately suggests "work of art," which we try to reconcile with what is positioned within the frame—two sausages. The sausages are hanging—which suggests real food, not a work of art. The images are centered in the frame; the words are centered on one of the images. Are these sausages? Why put sausages in a frame? The words on one of the images and in the caption to the work offer clues. The label on the sausage gives the names of an author and a book. And the caption gives us a clue to the artist's message: these sausages were made by chopping up a book and pressing it into a sausage shape. Are we right to surmise that the book is not a favorite literary work of the artist? Or is the artist complimenting the work by saying that it is delicious and sustaining?

FIGURE 9 Dieter Roth, Literaturwurst (Martin Walser: Halbzeit) (Literature Sausage [Martin Walser: Halftime]). Copyright 1961 Estate of Dieter Roth.

4e The partnership of images and written text

Images dominate our consciousness. We may not remember details of written accounts, but we easily recall the pictures of young John Kennedy saluting his father's coffin and of the twisted steel columns of the destroyed World Trade Center. We experience recent historical and political events through the lens of news photography. In addition, popular culture is communicated largely through visuals such as the movies, television, picture magazines, and billboards that reach millions. We come to "know" celebrities through these media—Donald Trump through his appearances on *The Apprentice* or Janet Jackson through the endlessly replayed "wardrobe malfunction" at the 2004 Superbowl.

Comics and cartoons show how images and written text work well together. The film *American Splendor* combines these media and others in novel and engaging ways.

For a college paper on hard copy or online, an oral presentation, a technical or business report, a brochure, flyer, or Web site, images do not replace but certainly enhance words. Pictures and photographs (scanned or from the Web) provide valuable, sometimes necessary, information about people, places, social issues, or works of art. They can also illustrate an idea in your paper or reinforce an argument. An essay on migrant workers could, for example, gain in impact by the addition of the searing 1930s photographs by Walker Evans or Dorothea Lange.

Lindsay Camp, the writer of the sample research paper in **10d**, recognized the power of an image. She chose to bolster her argument about what a woman has to do to be a firefighter by showing a photograph of the rigors of the test, not just describing it in words.

FIGURE 10   Preparing to Be a Firefighter

Source: Robie Liscomb, "Preparing Women for Firefighting in B.C.," *The Ring,* 6 Feb. 1998, University of Victoria Sport and Fitness Centre, <http://ring.uric.ca/98feb06/firefighting.html>.

Images not only provide evidence to inform and persuade readers; they also make a point memorable. An article "Keeping Up with Beverly Hills" by Craig Lambert at <http://www.harvardmagazine.com/issues/mj98/right .keeping.html> comments on what Juliet Schor, author of *The Overspent American,* calls the "new consumerism," a kind of "competitive spending." The image of a parody Tommy Hilfiger advertisement—here called "Tommy Hilfinger"— certainly adds a visual punch to the argument, reminding us that we consumers follow each other like sheep. (The spoof ad comes from *Adbusters,* an ecological magazine that dedicates itself to "examining the relationship between human beings and their physical and mental environment.")

FIGURE 11   Spoof Advertisement: Follow the Flock

Source: Adbusters.com at <http://adbusters.org/spoofads/fashion/tommy/>.

KEY POINTS
On Using Visuals

1. Decide which type of visual presentation best fits your data and where you should place your visuals—within your text or in an appendix.

2. When you include a visual from the Web in your own online document, make sure that the image file is not so large that it will take a long time for readers to download.

3. Whenever you place a visual in your text, introduce it, and discuss it fully before readers come across it. Do not just make a perfunctory comment such as "The picture makes a good point." Rather, say something like "The spoof ad drives home the point of the contemporary consumer's tendency to follow others."

4. Do not include visuals simply to fill space or make your document look colorful. Analyze and interpret each visual so that it enhances your content and makes an interesting and relevant point.

5. Give each visual a title, number each visual if you use more than one of the same type, and credit the source.

4f Interactive multimedia: The language of words, sound, and images

Technology allows writers to use new ways to express ideas. They are no longer limited to using type or visuals printed on a page. Writers today can use screens to present an interaction of words, drawings, photographs, animation, film, video, and audio to make a point.

In preparing a live or online multimedia presentation, consider the effectiveness of positioning images near your words and of conveying emotion and meaning through pictures. Imagine, for instance, how you might present an argument against genetic engineering of food crops to classmates or colleagues. In addition to your well-formed argument, you could show graphs of public opinion data on the issue, pictures of chemicals that are used on crops and of the way they are applied, and a movie clip of interviews with shoppers as they read labels and buy produce. If you use media imaginatively, you can do what writing teachers have long advised for printed essays: Show, don't just tell.

For an example of a multimedia visual argument created by students, go to <http://www.iml.annenberg.edu/projects/>. "The City of Troy" project was created by undergraduates at the University of Southern California for a course in Near Eastern and Mediterranean Archeology. Using excavation records, archeological finds, and texts of Homer's *The Illiad* and *The Odyssey* (as well as architectural modeling software, audio, and virtual-reality techniques), the students reconstructed "the citadel as it may have appeared at the time of the Trojan War in the 13th Century B.C."

FIGURE 12 **"The City of Troy" Project**

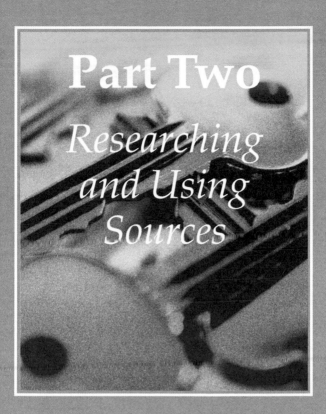

Part Two
Researching and Using Sources

5 Searching for Sources

6 Recognizing a Scholarly Article

7 Evaluating Sources

23

PART TWO   Researching and Using Sources

5 Searching for Sources, 24

5a Sources and field research, 24
5b Print and online sources, 25
5c Online sources: Caution!, 25
5d Search engines and keyword searching, 25
5e Basic sources, indexes, databases, and Web sites, 27
5f Sources in 27 subject areas, 28

5g Keeping track of sources, 38

6 Recognizing a Scholarly Article, 39

6a Print articles, 39
6b Articles accessed online, 40

7 Evaluating Sources, 40

7a Works originating in print, 40
7b Online sources, 41
7c How to read a Web site, 44

Doing research involves looking for or creating information on a topic in order to develop and refine your own views. When doing research for an academic paper, you gather information that you evaluate as responsible and relevant. Then you cite the research in your essay to add weight to your argument. But no matter how many sources you find and use, you should still present *your* ideas. Avoid the danger of letting an abundance of sources take the place of your own voice and opinions. Your research paper should not be simply a listing of what experts have said. Rather, let it present you in interaction with your topic and with the ways in which others have addressed that topic.

5 Searching for Sources

5a Finding source material and doing field research

Finding source material and creating it are two approaches to research, each providing support for a thesis. You may choose to find and read what others have written about your topic, or you can actively create your own source material, as scientists do when they initiate their own experiments. Field research can include firsthand ethnographic observations, scientific laboratory experiments, questionnaires, surveys, and interviews. Even though preparing your own source material to support a thesis can be valuable, field research needs careful planning. You need to set up a system for collecting relevant data, taking notes, and allowing for follow-up. Surveys and questionnaires, for instance, involve complex sampling, construction, and analysis of data. Ask your instructor for guidance.

5b Finding print and online sources

Use all of the following resources to find materials:

- the Internet: informational Web sites, library catalogs, online books and journals, databases of abstracts or full texts of articles
- your college library: its catalog, reference materials, CD-ROMs, bound volumes or microforms of articles published in print before 1980
- librarians: trained professionals who can help you locate and evaluate materials

5c Online sources: Caution!

Researchers find a proliferation of information online, such as databases with abstracts and full texts of articles readily available for saving or printing. Be aware, however, that some dangers accompany the benefits of using online sources.

- You limit your research by sitting at your computer for everything. Books and many articles (especially those published before 1980) probably will not be available in databases but will only be on your library shelves or on microform.
- The ease of copying and pasting may lead to inadvertent plagiarism (**8b, 8d**) if your record-keeping and note-taking (**5g**) are not as meticulous as they should be.
- Web sites provide vast amounts of information, but much of it is unreliable and untested. Surfing the Web can lead you into sites unsuitable for academic use. It's easy to get sidetracked. Evaluate all Web sites with great care (**7b**).

5d Search engines and keyword searching

Search engines help you find relevant material for your topic by searching millions of Web sites and organizing or ranking the results. Reliable, commonly used search engines include Google at <http://www.google.com>, AltaVista at <http://www.altavista.com>, and Hotbot at <http://www.hotbot.com>. Web directories, such as those operated by Google or Yahoo! (at <http://www.yahoo.com>), classify Web sites into searchable subject areas. Meta search engines, such as MetaCrawler at <http://metacrawler.com> and Dogpile at <http://www.dogpile.com>, make use of several search engines to search the Web. Use keywords to find source material in these general search engines, as well as in specialized databases, academic directories, and library sites (**5e**).

KEY POINTS
Keyword Searching

1. *Know the system of the database or search engine.* Use Search or Help to learn how to conduct a search. Many searches operate on the Boolean principle; that is, they use the "operators" *AND, OR,* and *NOT* in combination with keywords to define what you want the search to include and exclude. Imagine that you want to find out how music can affect intelligence. A search for "music AND intelligence" would find sources in the database that include both the word *music* and the word *intelligence.* A search for "music AND (intelligence OR learning)" would expand the search. You would find sources, in the database, that included both the word *music* and the word *intelligence* or the word *learning.* Some search engines let you use terms such as *NEAR* and *ADJ* (adjacent to) to find phrases close to each other in the searched text. Not all search engines use the Boolean system. In Google, for instance, you need simply to add words to narrow the search: *music Mozart intelligence.*

2. *Use a wildcard character (* or ?) to truncate a word or to provide optional spellings.* For example, *lab?r* will search for *labor* or *labour;* the truncation *music** will find instances of *music, musical, musicale, musician(s),* and *musicology.*

3. *Require or prohibit a term.* Many search engines allow you to use a symbol such as + before a term that must be included in the indexed document; a − symbol prohibits a term: *−Lincoln + battle* limits the results for *Gettysburg* alone by 86 percent in a search on Google.

(Continued)

(Continued)

4. *Narrow a search by grouping words.* Often you can use parentheses or double quotation marks to surround a search term and group the words into a phrase. Entering the book title *Flight Out of Time* into Google produces more than seven million hits, including many related to airlines and flight training schools. Entering the words as the phrase *"Flight Out of Time"* produces 405 hits, most of which are related to the book title.

5. *Narrow a search by limiting the dates or the URL (Uniform Resource Locator) domain.* Some search engines make it possible to search for sources published within a specific time frame, such as the last month or the last year, or within a specific URL domain, such as *.gov* or *.edu.*

6. *Be flexible.* If your search results in no hits, or an overwhelming number of hits, try again. Limit or expand the search. Use different terms. Try variant spellings, too: *Chaikovsky, Tchaikovsky, Tschaikovsky.*

7. *Use the results to help tailor your search.* If your search produces only one useful source, look at the terms used in that one source and its subject headings and search again, using those terms.

5e Basic sources, indexes, databases, and Web sites

To begin research in a subject area that is new to you, go first to general reference sources, indexes, databases, and, when appropriate, informational Web sites. These sources will give you a sense of the field and the issues. Many reference works and indexes are available online—some accessible on the Internet, some available only by subscription. Always check to learn which general reference works and databases your library or Internet Service Provider subscribes to. For specialized works in twenty-seven subject areas, see **5f.**

- *Encyclopedias, both general and specialized by subject matter* Encyclopedias are useful for background information, but do not consider a general encyclopedia a major source for your research. Go beyond it to more specialized sources. Examples: *Encyclopaedia Britannica; Columbia Encyclopedia;* specialized works such as *Encyclopedia of Psychology,* and *Encyclopedia of American History*

- *Dictionaries, general and specialized* Examples: *Oxford English Dictionary; American Heritage Dictionary of the English Language;* specialized dictionaries such as *Dictionary of Literary Terms* and *Dictionary of Economics*

- *General reference works* Examples: *Oxford Companion to African American Literature; Contemporary Literary Criticism; Oxford Companion to Art*

- *Bibliographies* (titles of books and articles on a specific subject) Examples: *Foreign Affairs Bibliography; MLA International Bibliography of Books and Articles on the Modern Languages and Literature*

- *Geographical reference sources* Examples: *Countries of the World; Columbia-Lippincott Gazetteer of the World*

- *Government documents* Examples: *Statistical Abstract of the United States; Handbook of Labor Statistics; U.S. Census Bureau* at <http://www.census.gov>; *Bureau of Labor Statistics* at <http://www.bls.gov>; *Thomas Legislative Information on the Internet* at <http://thomas.loc.gov>

- *Indexes and databases* Databases collect published abstracts and full text articles. Indexes, often on CD-ROM or available online by library subscription, provide information about books and articles published in periodicals. Both are best accessed by keyword searching (**5d**). Ask librarians about specialized indexes, too. Examples: *Readers' Guide to Periodical Literature; InfoTrac; FirstSearch; LexisNexis; New York Times on the Web* at <http://www.nytimes.com>; *ERIC* (education index); *PsycINFO* (psychology index); *Art Index*

- *Academic directories and library sites* Many sites contain worthwhile information and links. Bookmark those you find useful. Examples: *The WWW Virtual Library* at <http://vlib.org/Overview.html>; *Research Quickstart* at the University of Minnesota at <http://research.lib.umn.edu>; *Internet Public Library* at <http://www.ipl.org>; *Librarians' Index to the Internet* at <http://www.lii.org>; *Library of Congress* at <http://www.loc.gov>; *Infomine* at <http://infomine.ucr.edu>; *Public Agenda Online* at <http://www.publicagenda.org>

5f **Useful sources for research in twenty-seven subject areas**

This list of frequently used reference works in print, print and electronic indexes, and Web sites gives you starting points for further research. See the *Keys* Web site at

<http://www.college.hmco.com/keys.html> for an expanded version of this list, with links to all the nonsubscription online reference sites.

Art and architecture

American Museum of Photography: <http://www
.photographymuseum.com>

Art Abstracts

Art History Resources on the Web: <http://witcombe
.sbc.edu/ARTHLinks.html>

Art Index

Arts and Humanities Citation Index

Avery Index to Architectural Periodicals

Bibliography of the History of Art

Contemporary Artists

Dictionary of Art (known as *Grove's*)

Getty Institute: <http://www.getty.edu>

Lives of the Painters

Metropolitan Museum of Art Time Line: <http://www
.metmuseum.org/toah/splash.htm>

Mother of All Art and Art History Links: <http://www
.art-design.umich.edu/mother/>

Oxford Companion to Art

World Wide Arts Resources: <http://wwar.com>

Biology

Bio Network: <http://www.pasteur.fr/recherche/BNB/
bnb-en.html>

Biological Abstracts: BIOSIS (print and online)

Biological and Agricultural Index (print and online)

Biology Browser: <http://www.biologybrowser.org>

BioView.com: <http://www.biolinks.com>

Cell and Molecular Biology Online: <http://www.cellbio.com>

Gray's Anatomy

Henderson's Dictionary of Biological Terms

Tufts University Biology Research Guide: <http://www.library
.tufts.edu/tisch/subject/biology.htm>.

WWW Virtual Library: Biosciences: <http://www.mcb
.harvard.edu/Biolinks.html>

Business

ABI Inform Index (online)

Bureau of Labor Statistics: <http://www.bls.gov>

Business Abstracts (online, full text)

Business and Industry (database with full texts of articles; available in library subscriptions)

Business Dateline (database of full-text articles from business journals)

Business Periodicals Index (print and online)

Gale Business and Company Resource Center: <http://www.galegroup.com>

Hoover's Handbook of World Business

Monthly Labor Review

MSU-Ciber International Business Resources on the WWW (Michigan State University): <http://ciber.bus.msu.edu>

Prentice Hall Encyclopedic Dictionary of Business Terms

Ward's Business Directory of U.S. Private and Public Companies

Chemistry

American Chemical Society Website: <http://www.chemistry.org>

Beilstein Handbook of Organic Chemistry

Chemical Abstracts (online from the American Chemical Society)

Chemicool Periodic Table: <http://www-tech.mit.edu/Chemicool/index.html>

ChemInfo (Chemical Information Sources): <http://www.indiana.edu/~cheminfo>

Chemistry Virtual Library Resources: Links for Chemists: <http://www.liv.ac.uk/Chemistry/Links/links.html>

CRC Handbook of Chemistry and Physics

Kirk-Othmer Encyclopedia of Chemical Technology

NIST (National Institute of Standards and Technology) *Webbook* (physical properties for thousands of substances): <http://webbook.nist.gov>

Ullman's Encyclopedia of Industrial Chemistry

Classics

Chronology of the Ancient World

Classical Scholarship: An Annotated Bibliography

Concise Oxford Companion to Classical Literature

DCB: Database of Classical Bibliography

Internet Classics Archive: <http://classics.mit.edu>

Library of Congress Websites for Classical and Medieval History: <http://www.loc.gov/rr/main/alcove9/classics.html>

Perseus Digital Library: <http://www.perseus.tuf*

Communications and media

ABC-CLIO Companion to the Media in America

American Communication Association: <http://www.uark.edu/~aca>

ComAbstracts (print and online)

ComIndex (print and CD-ROM index of articles)

Encyclopedia of Rhetoric and Composition

International Women's Media Foundation. <http://www.iwmf.org>

Kidon Media-Link: <http://www.kidon.com/media-link/index.shtml>

Webster's New World Dictionary of Media and Communications

WWW Virtual Library: Communications and Media: <http://vlib.org/Communication.html>

Computer science

ACM Guide to Computing Literature (print and online)

Association for Computing Machinery: <http://www.acm.org>

Computer Abstracts

History of the Internet: A Chronology, 1843 to the Present (ed. Christos Moschovitis)

Information Resources for Computer Science: <http://www.library.ucsb.edu/subj/computer.html>

Microcomputer Abstracts (online by subscription)

MIT Laboratory for Computer Science: <http://www.lcs
.mit.edu>

Virtual Computer Library: <http://www.utexas.edu/
computer/vcl>

WWW Virtual Library: Computing: <http://vlib.org/
Computing.html>

Economics

Dictionary of Economics

Econlit (online by subscription)

Gale Encyclopedia of U.S. Economic History (ed. Thomas
Carson)

PAIS (Public Affairs Information Service) database (print
and online)

Prentice Hall Encyclopedic Dictionary of Business Terms

Social Sciences Citation Index: <http://www.hwwilson.com>

WWW Virtual Library: Economics: <http://hkkk.fi/
EconVLib.html>

Education

Educator's Reference Desk: <http://www.eduref.org>

Educational Resources Information Center: <http://www
.eric.ed.gov>

Dictionary of Education

Education Index: <http://www.educationindex.com>

Education Virtual Library: <http://www.csu.edu.au/
education/library.html>

Higher Education Research Institute, UCLA:
<http://www.gseis.ucla.edu/heri/heri.html>

Michigan Electronic Library: Education:
<http://mel.org/index.jsp.html>

National Center for Education Statistics:
<http://nces.ed.gov>

U.S. Department of Education: Other Educational Resources:
<http://www.ed.gov/about/contacts/gen/othersites/
index.html>

Engineering

Applied Science and Technology Index (print and online)

Compendex/Engineering Index (online by subscription)

Engineering Library at Cornell University: <http://www
.englib.cornell.edu>

WWW Virtual Library: Engineering: <http://vlib.org/
Engineering.html>

Environmental studies

Environmental Science: Working with the Earth

Facts on File Dictionary of Environmental Science

National Library for the Environment: <http://www
.cnie.org/nle>

Scripps Institution of Oceanography: <http://www.sio
.ucsd.edu>

*Sourcebook on the Environment: A Guide to the
Literature*

Toxic Air Pollution Handbook

United Nations Environment Programme: <http://www
.unep.org>

U.S. Environmental Protection Agency: <http://www
.epa.gov/>

WWW Virtual Library: Earth Science: <http://vlib
.org/EarthScience.html>

Ethnic studies

Chicano Scholars and Writers

Encyclopedia of Asian History

Harvard Encyclopedia of American Ethnic Groups

Historical and Cultural Atlas of African Americans

Native Web: <http://www.nativeweb.org>

Oxford Companion to African American Literature

WWW Virtual Library: Migration and Ethnic Relations:
<http://www.ercomer.org/wwwvl>

Geography

Companion Encyclopedia of Geography

Geographical Abstracts (online)

Geography Web Ring: <http://www.zephryus.demon.co.uk/
education/webring>

U.S. Census Bureau: U.S. Gazetteer: <http://www.census
.gov/cgi-bin/gazetteer>

Geology

AGI (American Geological Institute): <http://www
   .agiweb.org>

GeoRef: <http://www.agiweb.org/georef>

Glossary of Geology and Earth Sciences

Macmillan Encyclopedia of Earth Sciences

New Penguin Dictionary of Geology

USGS (United States Geological Survey): <http://www
   .usgs.gov>

USGS Library: <http://www.usgs.gov/library>

History

Dictionary of Medieval History (Scribner)

Don Mabry's Historical Text Archive:
   <http://historicaltextarchive.com/>

Great Events from History series

*Historical Abstracts and America: History and Life
   from ABC-CLIO:* <http://www.abc-clio.com>

WWW Virtual Library: History Central Catalogue:
   <http://www.ukans.edu/history/VL>

Linguistics

Cambridge Encyclopedia of the English Language (ed. David
   Crystal)

Center for Applied Linguistics: <http://www.cal.org>

Linguistics: A Guide to the Reference Literature (ed. Anna L.
   DeMiller)

Oxford Companion to the English Language (ed. Tom
   McArthur)

WWW Virtual Library: Applied Linguistics: <http://alt
   .venus.co.uk/VL/AppLingBBK/welcome.html>

Literature

Complete Works of Shakespeare: <http://the-tech.mit
   .edu/Shakespeare>

Dictionary of Literary Biography

*MLA International Bibliography of Books and Articles on the
   Modern Languages and Literature* (online)

New Cambridge Bibliography of English Literature

Oxford Companion to Contemporary Authors

Project Bartleby (complete texts of books no longer in copyright): <http://www.bartleby.com>

Victorian Women Writers Project: <http://www.indiana.edu/~letrs/vwwp>

Voice of the Shuttle: <http://vos.ucsb.edu>

Mathematics and statistics

American Mathematical Society MathSciNet (index and abstracts of articles): <http://www.ams.org/mathscinet>

HarperCollins Dictionary of Mathematics

Mathematical Reviews (print and online)

Statistical Abstract of the United States (Government Printing Office: print and online): <http://www.census.gov/statab/www>

University of Tennessee Math Archives: <http://archives.math.utk.edu>

WWW Virtual Library: Statistics: <http://www.stat.ufl.edu/vlib/statistics.html>

Music

Baker's Biographical Dictionary of Musicians

Classical USA: <http://classicalusa.com>

Indiana University Worldwide Internet Music Resources: <http://www.music.indiana.edu/music_resources>

International Index to Music Periodicals

New Grove Dictionary of Music and Musicians

New Harvard Dictionary of Music

New Oxford History of Music

RILM Abstracts of Musical Literature (online)

Thematic Catalogues in Music: An Annotated Bibliography Including Printed, Manuscript, and In-Preparation Catalogues

The Music Index

WWW Virtual Library: Classical Music: <http://www.gprep.org/classical/>

WWW Virtual Library: Music: <http://www.vl-music.com>

Nursing

Allnurses.com: <http://allnurses.com>

American Nurses Association Nursing World: <http://www.nursingworld.org>

Cambridge World History of Human Disease

Culture and Nursing Care

Dorland's Illustrated Medical Dictionary

Gray's Anatomy

Health Web: <http://healthweb.org/>

National Institute of Nursing Research: <http://www.nih
.gov/ninr>

Philosophy

American Philosophical Association: <http://www.apa
.udel.edu/apa/index.html>

Cambridge Dictionary of Philosophy

Handbook of Western Philosophy

Internet Encyclopedia of Philosophy: <http://www.utm.edu/
research/iep>

Oxford Companion to Philosophy

Philosopher's Index

Philosophy in Cyberspace: <http://www-personal.monash
.edu.au/~dey/phil>

Routledge History of Philosophy

Physics

American Institute of Physics: <http://www.aip.org>

American Physical Society: <http://www.aps.org>

Physics Abstracts (online)

Physics Today: <http://www.physicstoday.org>

WWW Virtual Library: Physics: <http://vlib.org/
Physics.html>

Political science

American Statistics Index

Congressional Quarterly Weekly Reports

International Political Science Abstracts

PAIS (Public Affairs Information Service) database (online
and CD-ROM)

Political Handbook of the World (annual)

Political Science Links: <http://www.loyola.edu/dept/
politics/polilink.html>

Political Science Resources on the Web: <http://www.lib
.umich.edu/govdocs/polisci.html>

The White House: <http://www.whitehouse.gov>

THOMAS: Legislative Information on the Internet: <http://thomas.loc.gov>

United Nations: <http://www.un.org>

U.S. Census Bureau: The Official Statistics: <http://www.census.gov>

Psychology

American Psychological Association: <http://www.apa.org>

CyberPsychLink: <http://cctr.umkc.edu/user/dmartin/psych2.html>

Handbook of Practical Psychology

Psychological Abstracts

PsycINFO (database of online abstracts)

The Social Psychology Network, Wesleyan University: <http://www.socialpsychology.org>

WWW Virtual Library: Psychology: <http://www.clas.ufl.edu/users/gthursby/psi/>

Religion

Academic Info: Religious Studies: <http://www.academicinfo.net/Religion.html>

Anchor Bible Dictionary

ATLA Religion Database

Encyclopedia of the American Religious Experience

Encyclopedia of World Religions

New Interpreter's Bible

Religion Index

Wabash Center Guide to Internet Resources for Teaching and Learning in Theology and Religion: <http://www.wabashcenter.wabash.edu/Internet/front.htm>

Sociology

CIA Factbook: <http://www.odci.gov/cia/publications/factbook/index.html>

Data on the Net: <http://odwin.ucsd.edu/idata>

Firstgov (U.S. Government site): <http://www.firstgov.gov>

Handbook of Sociology (ed. Neil Smelser)

International Encyclopedia of the Social and Behavioral Sciences (print and online)

Public Agenda (public opinion data): <http://www
.publicagenda.org/>

Social Sciences Abstracts (print and online)

Sociological Abstracts (print and online)

Sociological Tour through Cyberspace: <http://www
.trinity.edu/~mkearl/index.html>

State and County QuickFacts:
<http://quickfacts.census.gov/qfd>

Statistical Abstract of the United States: <http://www
.census.gov/statab/www/>

Statistical Resources on the Web: <http://www.lib
.umich.edu/govdocs/stats.html>

WWW Virtual Library: Sociology: <http://socserv2
.mcmaster.ca/w3virtsoclib/>

Women's studies

ABC-CLIO Guide to Women's Progress in America

Encyclopedia of Feminism

Feminism and Women's Studies: <http://eserver.org/
feminism/index.html>

Handbook of American Women's History

Notable American Women

Voice of the Shuttle Gender Studies Page:
<http://vos.ucsb.edu/browse.asp?id=2711>

Women in the World

WWW Virtual Library: Women's History: <http://www
.iisg.nl/~womhist/vivalink.html>

5g Keeping track of sources

Once you find good sources, whether in print or online, you
need to record what you find accurately so that you can provide full documentation if you end up using the source in
your paper.

KEY POINTS
Recording the Information You Need

1. Keep a working bibliography. Make a bibliography
   card (one for each source; use one side only), fill out a
   bibliographical database on your computer, or keep
   printouts from a library catalog or database listing.
   Record all the relevant information for each source

(Continued)

(Continued)

you read and intend to use, including reference works. Record inclusive page numbers for all print sources. You can also use the templates provided on our Web site at <http://college.hmco.com/keys.html> (click on Downloadable Forms).

2. Make copies of print material you know you will use. Make sure to copy complete journal or magazine articles and the periodical's table of contents (which will provide date and volume number); with book chapters, copy the title page and copyright page of the book. You will need this information for your list of works cited.

3. Save material you find online by printing it out, e-mailing it to yourself, or saving it on a disk, making sure you use a special font to distinguish material you have copied and saved. Record complete document information (address, author, date posted or updated, if available), along with the date you access the material. Use Copy and Paste to copy the URL exactly. Bookmark all the useful sites you visit so that you can easily find them again.

4. Take careful notes, relating what you read to your paper topic. Give each note a heading.

5. Distinguish exact quotations from summaries and paraphrases (**9a, 9b**), and record all exact page numbers or sections of electronic sources.

6 Recognizing a Scholarly Article

6a Recognizing a scholarly article in print

A scholarly article is not something you are likely to find in a magazine in a dentist's office. A scholarly article does the following—the first point being the most important:

- refers to the work of other scholars (look for in-text citations and a bibliographical list of works cited, footnotes, or endnotes)
- names the author and usually describes the author's credentials
- includes notes, references, or a bibliography
- deals with a serious issue in depth
- uses academic or technical language for informed readers

- appears in journals that do not include colorful advertisements or eye-catching pictures (any appearance of stunning models is an indication that you are not looking at a scholarly article)

6b Recognizing a scholarly article online

Online articles in databases do not necessarily provide the immediate signals of color, illustrations, and varied advertisements that would identify nonscholarly work in print publications. Online scholarly articles may have few immediately distinguishing features, so examine such articles with care, using the following guidelines:

- Always scroll to the end of the Web page to look for a list of references.
- Follow links from the author's name to find a résumé and more information.
- Do a Google search of the author's name to find out about credentials and publications, and do a reverse lookup using the Google toolbar to find out which reputable sites link to the article you have under consideration.
- Examine any article you find in an online database as you would a print article. In addition, do a search for the title of the periodical in which the article appears to find out that periodical's purpose and its requirements for submitting and publishing articles. In some databases, you can limit your search to articles that are "refereed" or "peer-reviewed"; that is, they are read by experts and approved for publication.

For more on distinguishing the types of periodicals, go to <http://www.library.cornell.edu/okuref/research/skill20.html>.

7 Evaluating Sources

7a Evaluating works originating in print

Before taking detailed notes from a print source, make sure it addresses your research question. Then use the following guidelines to assess its usefulness.

A book

- Check the date of publication, notes about the author, table of contents, and index.

- Skim the preface, introduction, chapter headings, and summaries to get an idea of the information contained in the book and of its theoretical basis and perspective.
- Do not waste time taking detailed notes from an out-of-date book (unless your purpose is to discuss and critique its perspective) or a book that deals only tangentially with your topic.

An article

- Check the date of publication.
- Evaluate the type of periodical the article appears in (popular or scholarly? See **6**).
- Avoid periodicals devoted to gossip, advertising, or propaganda.
- Note any information given about the author or about the stated purpose of the publication: Is the article likely to contain an unbiased examination of any controversial issues? Look up the author in Google for more information.

7b Evaluating online sources

Online searching will vastly increase the quantity of sources you are likely to find on your topic. However, it is never advisable to let quantity take precedence over quality. Only sources that are credible, detailed, relevant, and timely are worth using.

Conventional library sources made available online Subscription databases such as *LexisNexis, EBSCO,* and *InfoTrac* have made available online the full texts of articles published since 1980 in a variety of newspapers and print periodicals. For these, use the criteria for evaluating print works (**7a**), and remember to record any print publication information that appears on the screen, as well as the database information. Make sure that any electronic version of a literary book is based on a reliable, authoritative edition of the text. Usually you can safely assume the reliability of conventional sources accessible online in databases such as those sponsored by professional institutions or government agencies—*ERIC* for education, for instance.

Web-based journals and magazines Articles in Web-based journals appear only on the Web, not in print. Some of the journals, such as *Early Modern Literary Studies,* are refereed as selectively as print journals; others, such as *Slate,* are more akin to popular magazines.

Postings found in e-mail discussion lists and blogs Discussion list postings and blogs (individuals' Web logs) will often appear in a list of a search engine's findings. Postings in Usenet newsgroups (available at <http://groups.google.com>) are open and unmonitored but may contain ideas to stimulate thinking or illustrate current concerns on a topic. Many professionally moderated lists and other targeted discussion lists can be useful sources of information, though quality can vary considerably. Treat with caution postings in e-mail bulletin boards, newsgroups, blogs, or synchronous (real-time) communications such as those in buddy lists, chat rooms, MOOs (multiuser domains, object-oriented) or MUDs (multiuser domains). With moderated e-mail discussion lists and blogs, find out what you can about the sponsor and purpose of the communication and the credentials and credibility of the author (try doing a Google search of the author's name, for instance), and assess the logic and soundness of the argument.

Web sites What makes the Internet so fascinating is that it is wide open, free, and democratic. Individuals on a rant, as well as serious government or research agencies, can establish a site. Anyone can "publish" anything, and thousands or millions can read it. For scholars looking for information and well-presented, informed opinions, therefore, evaluating Web pages can pose a challenge.

Whether you find sites by surfing or by using a search engine, use the strategies in the Key Points box to answer the question "Should I use this site as a source to refer to, quote from, and include in my bibliography?" and to separate good information from junk. Section **7c** provides help for locating the information you need on a Web site.

> **KEY POINTS**
> **Developing Your Junk Antennae for Web Sites**
>
> 1. *Scrutinize the domain name of the URL.* Informational Web sites tend to come from *.gov* and *.edu* addresses, which will have used a review process. Nonprofit organizations (*.org*) may provide informative mission statements about the purpose of the site. With *.com* ("dot-com") sources, always assess whether the source is informational or is basically an advertisement or self-promotion.
>
> 2. *Assess the originator of an .edu source.* Is the educational institution or a branch of it sponsoring the site?
>
> *(Continued)*

(Continued)

A tilde (~) followed by a name in the URL indicates an individual posting from an academic source. Try to ascertain whether the individual is a faculty member or a student. Increasingly, though, individuals are setting up Web sites under their own domain name.

3. *Investigate the purposes of a Web site author or sponsor.* Objectivity and rationality are not necessarily features of all Web pages. You may come across propaganda, hate sites, individuals purporting to have psychic powers, religious enthusiasts, and extreme political groups. The owner of a site may want to persuade, convert, or sell. Always go to the site's home page and "About" and to its linked sites. In addition, note any postal or e-mail address or phone number you can use to get more information about the page and the sponsor. Even if the message is not pointedly biased and extreme, be aware that most authors write from some sense of conviction or purpose. (Note, though, that a Web site can be oriented toward a specific view without necessarily being irresponsible.)

4. *Evaluate the quality of the writing.* A Web site filled with spelling and grammatical errors should not inspire confidence. If the language has not been checked, the ideas probably haven't been given much time and thought, either. Don't use such a site as a source.

5. *Follow the links.* See whether the links in a site take you to authoritative sources. If the links no longer work (you'll get a 404 message: "Site Not Found"), the home page with the links has not been updated in a while—not a good sign.

6. *Check for dates, updates, ways to respond, and ease of navigation.* A recent date of posting or recent updating; information about the author; ways to reach the author by e-mail, regular mail, or phone; a clearly organized site; easy navigation; and up-to-date links to responsible sites are all indications that the site is well managed and current.

For more on evaluating Web sites, go to *Thinking Critically about World Wide Web Resources* at <http://www.library.ucla.edu/libraries/college/help/critical/index.htm> and *Evaluating Web Resources* at <http://www2.widencr.edu/Wolfgram-Memorial-Library/webevaluation/webeval.htm>.

7c How to read a Web site

Using the chart Use the chart that runs across pages 44–45 to find on a Web site the information that will help you evaluate its content. In addition, if you record the information for every accessed site that you might refer to or quote from in your paper, you will then be able to construct your citation without

How to Read a Web Site

What to look for and record; where and how to find it

1. Name of author

Look at the top or bottom of the page. For Web documents with no author named, look for an organization, government agency, or business that serves as the author.

2. Title of document

Find it at the top of the page. Note, though, that some sites will contain documents with titles, and some will not.

3. Name of site

If it is not visible at the top or bottom of the page, go to "Home" or "About." Or delete the URL progressively back to each single slash, and click to see which part of the site you access.

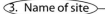

4. Your date of access

Because Web sites come and go and change, always record the exact date on which you access the site.

5. URL

Copy and paste this from your browser into your working bibliography.

retracing your steps. (Templates for recording source information are available on the *Pocket Keys* Web site.) Although different styles of documentation, such as MLA and APA, ask for different chunks of information in different configurations, the five items listed in the chart are common to most of them. Read this chart with the accompanying annotated screenshot on page 46.

Additional things you may need to do

- Follow any links on the document page to a résumé, publications, purpose statement, or home page.
- Do a Google search for details about the author, whether an individual, institution, organization, business, or government agency.
- Do not confuse the Web site manager or the person maintaining the site with the author of the information.
- If you cannot find an author, look on the "Home" or "About" page, or go to #2, "Title."

- For online sources previously in print form, record any print publication details provided.
- Record page numbers only for *.pdf* documents, in which page numbers appear on the screen.
- Record the name of the document section in which relevant information appears (e.g., Introduction).
- Record paragraph numbers *only* when they are part of the document and appear on the screen.

Also record what you can of the following, if available:
- name of the organization in charge of the content of the site (owner or sponsor)—usually indicated in the root domain of the URL (before the first single slash)
- for an online journal, the volume and issue numbers
- the date when material was posted online or updated (often not available)

Save any page that provides you with crucial information or is likely to update or change its content, such as blogs or files ending with *.php*.

If a page is divided into sections (called "frames"), and you want to refer to one frame only, right-click in the frame, and select "Save (or Add) as Favorite"; then retrieve the material in the frame with its own URL.

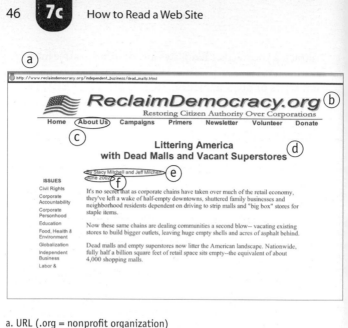

a. URL (.org = nonprofit organization)
b. Owner and name of site
c. Information about purpose of site
d. Title of document
e. Authors' names: Bio data appear at bottom of page
f. Date of posting online

Recognizing the difficulties   Note that on many sites, you may have difficulty finding a date of posting, a document title as well as a Web site name, or an exact identification of the author of the material, whether an individual or an organization. Just record whatever you can find on a thorough search of the site. Try using the root domain of the URL—the material just before the dot preceding the first single slash (as in <http://www.library.ucla.edu/>)—to identify the owner, also referred to as the *publisher* or *sponsor,* of the site, who is responsible for its content. If the "Home" and "About" links provide no useful information, consider whether you should use a source if you are unsure about the identity of the author, the author's credentials, or the owner and purpose of the site.

The URL   For more on recording URLs and using them in your paper and citations, see **10c**, item 30, and **33a**.

Part Three

Steering Clear of Plagiarism

8 Avoiding Even the Suspicion of Plagiarism

9 Using and Integrating Source Material

8 Avoiding Even the
Suspicion of
Plagiarism, 48

8a What is plagiarism?, 48
8b Knowing what to cite,
49
8c Indicating the
boundaries of a
citation, 49
8d Checklist: Ways to
avoid plagiarizing,
51

9 Using and
Integrating Source
Material, 52

9a Summarizing and
paraphrasing, 52
9b Quoting, 53
9c Introducing and
integrating cited
material, 55
9d Driving the
organization with
ideas, not sources, 56
9e Documenting to fit
your discipline, 57

8 Avoiding Even the Suspicion of Plagiarism

8a What is plagiarism?

The word *plagiarize* is derived from the Latin verb meaning "to kidnap," and kidnapping or stealing someone else's words or ideas and presenting them as your own is a serious offense in Western academic culture and public life. Any of the following are regarded as plagiarizing:

- presenting the work of another person as your own work

- downloading chunks of material from the Internet without acknowledgment

- using words you find in a print or online source without acknowledging where the words come from

- forgetting to add a citation to ideas that you use from a source, even if you put those ideas in your own words (paraphrase)

- thinking that the source of a fact or point does not need to be cited when it does

- thinking that one citation is enough to cover a long paraphrase or many instances of your referring to the same source

Some famous public figures and authors, such as Stephen Ambrose, Joseph J. Ellis, and Doris Kearns Goodwin, have been accused of plagiarism and have had their reputations tarnished, their research standards questioned, and their careers damaged. In college, too, the consequences of cheating by plagiarizing can be severe, ranging from a failing grade for an assignment or for the whole course, to disciplinary hearings, to dismissal from school.

8b Knowing what to cite

Intentionally presenting another person's work as your own may be the most deceptive kind of plagiarism, but the effect is the same if you neglect to acknowledge your sources because of sloppy research and writing practices—readers will not be able to discern which ideas are yours and which are not. Always provide full documentation for everything mentioned in the Key Points box on what to cite. (See Part Four for the recommendations of several style manuals about how to cite sources and document them.)

KEY POINTS
What to Cite

1. exact words from a source, enclosed in quotation marks
2. somebody else's ideas and opinions, even if you restate them in your own words in a summary or paraphrase
3. each sentence in a long paraphrase if it is not clear that all the sentences paraphrase the same source
4. all facts and statistics, unless they are common knowledge and available in many sources (such as the dates of the Civil War, birth and death dates and chronological events in the lives of authors and public figures, or allusions to nursery rhymes or folktales handed down through the ages)

8c Indicating the boundaries of a citation

Naming an author or title in your text tells readers that you are citing ideas from a source, and citing a page number at the end of a summary or paraphrase lets them know where your citation ends. However, for one-page print articles and for Internet sources, a page citation is not necessary, so indicating where your comments about a source end is harder to do. You always need to indicate clearly where your summary or paraphrase ends and where your own comments take over. Convey the shift to readers by commenting on the source in a way that clearly announces a statement of your own views. Use expressions such as *it follows that, X's explanation shows that, as a result, evidently, obviously,* or *clearly* to signal the shift.

Unclear citation boundary

According to a Sony Web site, <u>Mozart Makes You Smarter</u>, the company has decided to release a cassette on the strength of research indicating that listening to Mozart improves IQ. The product shows the ingenuity of commercial enterprise while taking the researchers' conclusions in new directions.

[Does only the first sentence refer to material on the Web page, or do both sentences?]

Revised citation, with source boundary indicated

According to a Sony Web site, <u>Mozart Makes You Smarter</u>, the company has decided to release a cassette on the strength of research indicating that listening to Mozart improves IQ. Clearly, Sony's plan demonstrates the ingenuity of commercial enterprise, but it cannot reflect what the researchers intended when they published their conclusions.

Another way to indicate the end of your citation is to include the author's or authors' name(s) at the end of the citation instead of (or even in addition to) introducing the citation with the name.

Unclear citation boundary

For people who hate shopping, Web shopping may be the perfect solution. Jerome and Taylor's exploration of "holiday hell" reminds us that we get more choice from online vendors than we do when we browse at our local mall because the online sellers, unlike mall owners, do not have to rent space to display their goods. In addition, one can buy almost anything online, from CDs, cell phones, and books to cars and real estate.

Revised citation, with source boundary indicated

For people who hate shopping, Web shopping may be the perfect solution. An article exploring the "holiday hell" of shopping reminds us that we get more choice from online vendors than we do when we browse at our local mall because the online sellers, unlike mall owners, do not have to rent space to display their goods (Jerome and Taylor). In addition, one can buy almost anything online, from CDs, cell phones, and books to cars and real estate.

8d Checklist: Ways to avoid plagiarizing

Clear documentation opens a channel of communication between you and your readers. They learn what your views are and what has influenced those views. They will assume that anything not documented is your original idea and your wording. If you even accidentally present someone else's words or ideas as if they were your own, readers may suspect you of plagiarizing.

KEY POINTS

Ways to Avoid Plagiarizing

1. Set up a working bibliography, making a record of each source, so that you have all the information you need for appropriate documentation (**5g**).

2. When you take notes from sources, use a systematic method of indicating quotation, summary, paraphrase, and your own comments. For example, use quotation marks around quoted words, phrases, sentences, and passages; introduce a summary or a paraphrase with a tag, such as "Stalker makes the point that . . ."; in your notes about a source, write your own comments in a different color. Then, later, you will see immediately which ideas are yours and which come from your source.

3. Never include in your own essay a passage or an identifiable phrase that you have copied from someone else's work without using quotation marks and citing the source.

(Continued)

(Continued)

4. Use your own sentence structure, sequence of ideas, and organization of argument when you write about the ideas in a documented source. Readers should not find your text disturbingly similar to your source.

5. Always cite the source of any summary or paraphrase. Credit ideas as well as exact words.

6. Do not substitute synonyms for a few words in the source or move only a few words around. Using such strategies will not help you avoid plagiarism.

7. Never—but never—"borrow," buy, copy, download, or receive a paper or a section of a paper that you turn in as your own work.

e s l **Ownership Rights across Cultures** The Western view takes seriously the ownership of words and text. Copyright laws define and protect the boundaries of intellectual property. In some cultures, however, memorization and the use of classic texts in writing are common. And worldwide, the ownership of language, texts, and ideas is currently being called into question by the democratic, interactive nature of the Internet. Although the concept of plagiarism is not something universally agreed upon, in Western academic culture the advice given in **8d** is very much in effect.

9 Using and Integrating Source Material

9a Summarizing and paraphrasing

A *summary* presents in your own words and sentences the main idea of a source. A summary should be more objective than evaluative. Above all, it should be brief.

A *paraphrase,* in contrast, is similar in length to the original material. It presents the details of the author's argument and logic, but *it does not use the author's exact words or sentence structure.* (See **8d** on avoiding plagiarism.) If you keep the source out of sight as you write a paraphrase, you will not be tempted to use any of the sentence patterns or phrases of the original. Even if you are careful to cite your source, your writing may still be regarded as plagiarized if your paraphrase resembles the original too closely in wording or sentence structure. You can use common words and expressions without quotation marks, but if you use longer or more unusual expressions from the source, always enclose them in quotation marks.

Original source

We cannot legislate the language of the home, the street, the bar, the club, unless we are willing to set up a cadre of language police who will ticket and arrest us if we speak something other than English.

—James C. Stalker, "Official English or English Only," *English Journal 77* (Mar. 1988): 21.

The first paraphrase that follows uses words and structures (highlighted) that are distinctly reminiscent of the original. Even though it cites the author and page accurately, it could still be considered plagiarized.

Paraphrase too similar to the original

As Stalker points out, we cannot pass legislation about the language we speak at home, on the street, in bars, or in restaurants, unless we are willing to have a cadre of special police who will take us off to jail if they hear us not speaking English (21).

Revised paraphrase

Stalker points out that in a democracy like the United States, it is not feasible to have laws against the use of language, and it certainly would not be possible to enforce such laws in homes and public places (21).

Even when you are careful to use your own words in a summary or paraphrase, you must still inform readers of the source of the information.

9b Quoting

Deciding what and when to quote   Quote sparingly and only when the original words express the exact point you want to make and express it succinctly and well. Ask yourself: Which point of mine does the quotation illustrate? Why am I considering quoting this particular passage rather than paraphrasing it? What do I need to tell my readers about the author of the quotation?

Quoting the exact words of the original Any words you use from a source must be included in quotation marks and quoted exactly as they appear in the original, with the same punctuation marks and capital letters. Do not change pronouns or tenses to fit your own purpose unless you enclose changes in square brackets (**29d**).

Omitting words in the middle of a quotation If you omit as irrelevant to your purpose any words or passages from the middle of a quotation, use the ellipsis mark, three dots separated by spaces. If you omit the end of the source's sentence at the end of your own sentence, use three ellipsis dots following the sentence period—four dots in all. Use three dots after a period if you omit a complete sentence (or more) when the omission is preceded and followed by a complete sentence (**29e**).

Adding or changing words If you add any comments or explanations in your own words or if you change a word of the original to fit it grammatically into your sentence or to spell it correctly, enclose the added or changed material in square brackets (**29d**). However, do not overuse this strategy.

The following example shows how a student integrates some exact words from the passage by Stalker on page 53 into her own writing, introduces the author of the quotation, indicates that she omits some words, and adds both a comment and a grammatical adjustment to make the quotation fit into her own sentence:

Educator James C. Stalker points out that passing laws against the use of any one particular language would mean "set[ting] up a cadre of language police who will . . . arrest us if we speak [and maybe also write] something other than English" (21).

Quoting longer passages If you quote more than three lines of poetry or four typed lines of prose, do not use quotation marks. Instead, indent the quotation one inch or ten spaces from the left margin in MLA style or five spaces for APA style. Double-space throughout. Do not indent from the right margin. Establish the context for a long quotation and name its author in your introductory statement.

Stalker also explains why, in the United States, democracy requires that all people must have the freedom to use any language they choose:

> If any language group, Spanish or other, chooses to maintain its language, there is precious little that we can do about it, legally or otherwise, and still maintain that we are a free country. (21)

NOTE: With a long indented quotation, the period goes before the parenthetical citation, not after it.

Avoiding a string of quotations   Use quotations, especially long ones, sparingly and only when they help you make a good argument. Readers do not want a collection of passages from other writers; they could read the original works for that. Rather, they want your analysis of your sources and the conclusions you draw from your research. Quotations should not appear in a string, one after the other. If they do, your readers will wonder what purpose the quotations serve and will search for your voice in the paper.

9c   Introducing and integrating cited material

Introduce quotations, summaries, and paraphrases and integrate them into the flow of your writing. They should not just pop up with no lead-in.

Source not introduced and integrated

Our ability to use whatever language we choose is necessary in a free democracy. "We cannot legislate the language of the home, the street, the bar, the club, unless we are willing to set up a cadre of language police who will ticket and arrest us if we speak something other than English" (Stalker 21).

Source introduced and integrated

In an article critical of the English-only movement, educator James C. Stalker points out that we, as citizens of a free democratic country, "cannot legislate the language of the home, the street, the bar, the club, unless we are willing to set up a cadre of language police who will ticket and arrest us if we speak something other than English" (21).

Inserting a part of a quoted sentence into your own sentence helps ensure that you introduce and integrate the quotation.

Naming the author (Modern Language Assocation style)
If you quote, paraphrase, or summarize a section of another work, introduce the reference by providing in an introductory phrase the author's full name (for the first reference to an author) and a brief mention of his or her expertise or credentials, as in the example above. For subsequent citations, the last name is sufficient. Then, for a book or print article, give the page number in parentheses at the end of the quotation, followed by the sentence period.

Varying the introductory phrase   Avoid always introducing a quotation with a form of the verb *say* or *write.* Explore alternatives such as the following:

In fact, educational researcher James Stalker also claims . . .

James Stalker, an educational researcher, makes the following observation: . . .

Verbs like the following are often useful alternatives to *say* and *write: acknowledge, agree, argue, assert, believe, claim, comment, contend, declare, deny, emphasize, explain, insist, note, point out, propose, suggest.*

9d Driving the organization with ideas, not sources

Let your ideas, not your sources, drive your paper. Large amounts of information and a large number of sources are no substitute for a thesis with relevant, organized evidence. Resist the temptation to organize your paper in the following way:

1. What points Smith makes
2. What points Jones makes
3. What points Fuentes makes
4. What points Jackson and Hayes make in opposition
5. What I think

That organization is driven by your sources, with the bulk of the paper a stringing together of the views of Smith, Jones, and the rest. Instead, synthesize the information and relate it to your thesis:

1. First point of support: what ideas I have to support my thesis and what evidence Fuentes and Jones provide
2. Second point of support: what ideas I have to support my thesis and what evidence Smith and Fuentes provide
3. Third point of support: what ideas I have to support my thesis and what evidence Jones provides
4. Opposing viewpoints of Jackson and Hayes
5. Common ground and refutation of those viewpoints
6. Synthesis

To avoid producing an essay that reads like a serial listing of summaries or references ("Crabbe says this," "Tyger says that," "Tyger also says this"), spend time reviewing your notes and synthesizing what you find into a coherent and convincing statement of what you know and believe.

- Make lists of good ideas your sources raise about your topic.
- Look for the connections among those ideas: comparisons and contrasts.
- Find links in content, examples, and statistics.
- Note connections between the information in your sources and what you know from your own experience.

If you do these things, you will take control of your material instead of letting it take control of you.

9e Documenting to fit your discipline

Documentation is an integral part of the writing process. Conventions vary from discipline to discipline, but the various styles of documentation are not entirely arbitrary. These styles reflect what each discipline values and what readers need to know.

In the humanities, for instance, many research findings offer interpretation and speculation, so they may be relevant for years, decades, or centuries. Publication dates in the MLA (Modern Language Association) style, therefore, occur only in the works-cited list and do not make an appearance in the in-text citation. Such a practice also serves to minimize interruptions to the text.

The endnote system of *The Chicago Manual of Style* goes further. It requires only a small superscript number in the text.

In the sciences and social sciences, however, in APA and CBE/CSE styles, the dates of the works are put at the forefront because timeliness of research is an issue in the fields. Abbreviations used in a style such as CBE/CSE reflect the fact that scientists are expected to be aware of the major sources in their field.

See Part Four for more details on MLA, APA, *Chicago*, and CBE/CSE documentation styles.

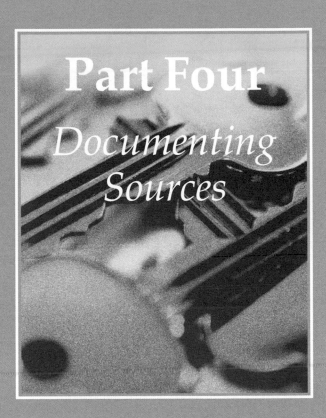

Part Four
Documenting Sources

10 MLA Style

11 APA Style

12 *The Chicago Manual of Style*

13 CBE/CSE Style (Sciences and Mathematics)

10 MLA Style, 60
10a   Basic features, 62
10b   In-text citations, 63
10c   MLA list of works cited, 68
10d   MLA student paper: Sample pages, 88

11 APA Style, 91
11a   Basic features, 92
11b   In-text citations, 93
11c   APA list of references, 96
11d   APA student paper: Sample pages, 105

12 The Chicago Manual of Style, 108
12a   Basic features, 108
12b   In-text citations, 108

12c   *Chicago* endnotes, 108
12d   *Chicago* bibliography, 114
12e   *Chicago* student paper: Sample pages, 115

13 CBE/CSE Style, 116
13a   Basic features, 117
13b   In-text citations, 117
13c   CBE/CSE sequential list of references, 117
13d   CBE/CSE student paper: Sample list of references, 120

10 MLA Style

At a Glance: Index of MLA Style Features

SAMPLES OF MLA IN-TEXT CITATIONS (**10b**), 63

Citing a work with individual authors

A. One author quoted or mentioned in your text, 63
B. Author cited in parentheses, 63
C. Work written by more than one author, 63
D. Work by author with more than one work cited, 64
E. Two authors with same last name, 64
F. Author of work in an edited anthology, 64
G. Author of work quoted in another source, 64
H. More than one work in one citation, 65

Citing a work with no individual author

I. Corporation, government agency, or organization as author, 65
J. No author or editor named, 65
K. Unauthored entry in dictionary or encyclopedia, 66

Citing a work with page numbers not available or relevant

L. Reference to an entire work, 66
M. Work only one page long, 66
N. Internet and electronic sources with no page numbers, 66

Citing special types of sources

O. Multimedia or nonprint source, 67
P. Multivolume work, 67
Q. Lecture, speech, personal communication, interview, 67
R. Literary works, 67
S. The Bible and other sacred texts, 68
T. Historical or legal document, 68

MLA LIST OF WORKS CITED (10c), 68

Print Books and Parts of Books

1. One author, 70
2. Two or more authors, 70
3. Book with editor, 70
4. Author and editor, 70
5. One work in an anthology (original or reprinted), 71
6. More than one work in an anthology, cross-referenced, 71
7. Entry in a reference book, 71
8. No author named, 72
9. Corporation, organization, or government agency as author, 72
10. Translation, 72
11. Multivolume work, 72
12. Book in a series, 72
13. Publisher and imprint, 73
14. Foreword, preface, introduction, or afterword, 73
15. Republished book, 73
16. Book not in first edition, 73
17. Title including a title, 73
18. The Bible and other sacred texts, 74
19. Dissertation, 74

Print Articles

20. Scholarly journal, paged by volume, 75
21. Scholarly journal, paged by issue, 75
22. Magazine article, 75
23. Newspaper article, 75
24. Article that skips pages, 76
25. Review, 76
26. Unsigned editorial or article, 76
27. Letter to the editor, 76
28. Abstract in an abstracts journal, 76
29. Article on microform, 76

Internet and Other Electronic Sources

30. Information to include, 77
31. Work in an online database or subscription service, 79
32. Online book, 81
33. Online poem, 82
34. Article in a reference database, 82
35. Article in an online journal,
36. Article in an online magazine, 82
37. Article in an online newspaper, 83
38. Online review, editorial, abstract, or letter, 83
39. Scholarly project, 83
40. Professional site, 83
41. Online government publication, 83
42. Personal Web page, 84
43. Course page, 84
44. Online posting on a discussion list or blog, 84
45. Synchronous communication, 85
46. Personal e-mail message, 85
47. CD-ROM, 85

Multimedia and Miscellaneous Sources

48. Online versions of multimedia and other sources, 85

49. Lecture, speech, personal communication, interview, 86
50. Published or broadcast interview, 86
51. Map or chart, 86
52. Film or video, 86
53. Television or radio program, 87
54. Sound recording, 87
55. Live performance, 87
56. Work of art, slide, or photograph, 87
57. Cartoon, 88
58. Advertisement, 88
59. Legal source, 88

10a   Basic features of MLA style

MLA (Modern Language Association) style for the humanities is recommended in Joseph Gibaldi, *MLA Handbook for Writers of Research Papers*, 6th ed. (New York: MLA, 2003) and on the MLA Web site at <http://www.mla.org>.

KEY POINTS
Two Basic Features of MLA Style

1. *In your paper,* include an author/page citation for each source:

   the **last name(s)** of the author (or authors)

   the **page number(s)** where the information is located (unless the source is online or only one page long) but without the word *page* or *pages* or the abbreviation *p.* or *pp.*

2. *At the end of your paper,* include a list, alphabetized by authors' last names or by title if the author is not known, of all the sources you refer to in the paper. Begin the list on a new page with the title *Works Cited.* See **10c**.

NOTE: Use endnotes (at the end of the paper) or footnotes (at the bottom of each page or at the end of each chapter) only for supplementary comments and information, not for regular source citations.[1] (See the sample footnote below.) Number information notes consecutively in your text with a raised (superscript) numeral as in the previous sentence. Indent the first line of each numbered note. The following double-spaced endnote example corresponds to the superscript number above:

[1]Both MLA and The Chicago Manual of Style describe systems that make use of footnotes or endnotes for citing sources.

10b **Samples of MLA in-text citations**

CITING A WORK WITH INDIVIDUAL AUTHOR(S) (MLA)

A. One author quoted or mentioned in your text For the first mention of an author, use the full name and any relevant credentials. After that, use only the last name. Generally, use the present tense to cite an author.

┌─────────── author and credentials ───────────┐
National Book Award winner Paul Fussell points out that even people in low-paying jobs show "all but universal pride in a uniform of any kind" (5).
                                                    └page number

When a quotation includes a question mark or an exclamation point, use an additional period only if you provide a parenthetical citation.

Fussell reminds us of our equating uniforms with seriousness of purpose when he begins a chapter by asking, "Would you get on an airplane with two pilots who are wearing cut-off jeans?" (85).

For a quotation longer than four lines, see **9b**.

B. Author cited in parentheses As an alternative to naming the author in your text, especially if you have referred to the author previously or if you are citing statistics, simply include the author's last name before the page number within the final parentheses, with no comma between them.

The army retreated from Boston in disarray, making the victors realize that they had defeated "the greatest military power on earth" (McCullough 76).

Note that with a long indented quotation, when no quotation marks are necessary, the final period comes before the citation within parentheses. See **9b**.

C. Work written by more than one author For a work with two or three authors, include all the names, either in your text sentence or in parentheses.

(Lakoff and Johnson 42).

(Hare, Moran, and Koepke 226–28).

For a work with four or more authors, use only the first author's last name followed by "et al." (The Latin words *et alii* mean "and others.") See **10c**, items 2 and 11, for how to list several authors in a works-cited list.

D. Work by author with more than one work cited Include the author and title of the work in your introductory text.

Alice Walker, in her book In Search of Our Mothers' Gardens, describes learning about Flannery O'Connor (43–59).

If you do not mention the author in your text, include in your parenthetical reference the author's last name, followed by a comma; an abbreviated form of the title, not followed by a comma; and the page number.

O'Connor's house still stands and is looked after by a caretaker (Walker, In Search 57).

To list more than one work by the same author in your works-cited list, see item 9 in the Key Points box on page 69.

E. Two authors with the same last name Include each author's first initial, or if the initials are the same, include the whole first name.

A writer can be seen as both "author" and "secretary," and the two roles can be seen as competitive (F. Smith 19).

F. Author of work in an edited anthology Cite the author of the included or reprinted work and the page numbers of the work included in the anthology. Mention the editor of the anthology only in the entry in the works-cited list (as shown in **10c**, items 5 and 6).

Des Pres asserts that "heroism is not necessarily a romantic notion" (20).

G. Author of work quoted in another source Use "qtd. in" (for "quoted in") in your parenthetical citation, followed by the last name of the author of the source in which you find the quotation (the indirect source) and the page number if it is a print source. List the indirect source in your list of works cited. In the following example, *Smith* would be included in the list, not *Britton*.

The words we use simply appear, as James Britton says, "at the point of utterance" (qtd. in Smith 108).

H. More than one work in one citation   Include all the citations, separated by semicolons. Avoid making the list too long.

The links between a name and ancestry have occupied many writers and researchers (Waters 65; Antin 188).

CITING A WORK WITH NO INDIVIDUAL AUTHOR (MLA)

I. Corporation, government agency, or organization as author   Sometimes you will use material authored not by an individual but by a corporation, government agency, or organization. (See **7c** on finding the author of a Web site.) Cite the organization as the author, making sure it corresponds with the alphabetized entry in your works-cited list (shown in **10c**, item 41). Use the complete name in your text or a shortened form in parentheses. The following examples cite a Web site, so page numbers are not included.

```
┌───────────── full name ─────────────┐
```
The United States Department of Education projected an enrollment of 69.2 million people in schools and colleges in 2002.

An enrollment of 69.2 million people in schools and
```
                       ┌─shortened name─┐
```
colleges was predicted for 2002 (US Dept. of Educ.).

J. No author or editor named   If there is no stated author of a source, refer to the book (underlined) or article (within quotation marks) by its title. Within a parenthetical citation, shorten the title to the first word alphabetized in the works-cited list (**10c**, item 8).

According to The Chicago Manual of Style, writers should always "break or bend" rules when necessary (xiii).

Writers should always "break or bend" rules when necessary (Chicago xiii).

If you need help in determining the author of an Internet source, see **7c**. For a site with no author indicated, use the name of the site.

K. Unauthored entry in dictionary or encyclopedia For an unsigned entry, give the title of the entry; a page number is not necessary for an alphabetized work. Begin the entry in the works-cited list with the title of the alphabetized entry (see **10c**, item 7).

Drypoint differs from etching in that it does not use acid ("Etching").

CITING A WORK WITH PAGE NUMBERS NOT AVAILABLE OR RELEVANT (MLA)

L. Reference to an entire work and not to one specific idea or page Use the author's name alone, with no page number.

Diaries tell about people's everyday lives and the worlds they create (Mallon).

M. Work only one page long If a print article is only one page long, you may mention the author's name alone in your text, but be sure to include the page number in your works-cited list (**10c**, item 22). However, a page reference indicates where a citation ends, so you may prefer to include it in your text (**8c**).

N. Author or title only for Internet and electronic sources with no page numbers Electronic database material and Web sources, which appear on a screen, have no stable page numbers that apply across systems or when printed unless you access them in PDF (page document format) files. If your source on the screen includes no visible numbered pages or numbered paragraphs, provide only the author's name or the title if no author is named. With no page number to indicate where your citation ends, be careful to define where the citation ends and your commentary takes over. See **8c**.

Science writer Stephen Hart describes how researchers Edward Taub and Thomas Ebert conclude that for musicians, practicing "remaps the brain."

Provide page or paragraph numbers only if they appear on the screen as part of the document. See **10c**, item 35.

Hatchuel discusses how film editing "can change points of view and turn objectivity into subjectivity" (par. 6).

You may also locate the information according to an internal heading of the document, such as *Introduction, Chapter,* or *Section.*

CITING SPECIAL TYPES OF SOURCES (MLA)

O. Multimedia or nonprint source   For radio or TV programs, interviews, live performances, films, computer software, recordings, works of art, or other nonprint sources, include only the author (or producer, actor, director, and so on) or title. Make sure your text reference corresponds to the first element of the information you provide in your works-cited list. See **10c**, item 55.

It takes an extraordinary actor to keep an audience enthralled by visits to a chiropodist (Redgrave).

P. Multivolume work   Indicate the volume number, followed by a colon, a space, and the page number (Richardson 1: 25). Give the total number of volumes in your works-cited list (**10c**, item 11).

Q. Lecture, speech, personal communication, or interview
Give the name of the person delivering the communication. In your works-cited list, state the type of communication after the author's name (**10c**, items 49 and 50).

According to George Kane, Vice President of Infoplease.com, students of all ages increasingly turn first to the Internet when conducting research.

R. Literary works: fiction, poetry, and drama   For a short story or novel with no divisions or chapters, simply give the author's name and page number. For other works, particularly classic works appearing in many editions, using the following guidelines will allow readers to find your reference in any edition. Include details about the edition you use in your works-cited list.

NOVELS Give a chapter or section number in addition to the page number: (104; ch. 5).

POEMS Give line numbers, not page numbers: (lines 62–68). Omit the word *lines* in subsequent line references. See **29d** and **29e** for more on how to quote poetry.

CLASSIC POEMS WITH DIVISIONS INTO BOOKS OR PARTS Give the book or part, followed (no space) by line numbers, not page numbers: (8.21–25).

CLASSIC VERSE PLAYS Give act, scene, and line numbers, in Arabic numerals. For classic works by Chaucer, Homer, Wordsworth, Shakespeare, and others, titles such as

A Midsummer Night's Dream can be abbreviated in parentheses: (*MND* 1.1.133–36)

S. The Bible and other sacred texts   Give book, chapter, and verse(s) in your text—Genesis 27.29—or abbreviate the book in a parenthetical citation (New Jerusalem Bible, Gen. 27.29). Give the edition of the Bible or other sacred text in your works-cited list.

T. Historical or legal document   Cite any article and section number of a familiar historical document, such as the Constitution in parentheses in your text (US Const., art. 2, sec. 4), with no entry in the works-cited list. Underline the name of a court case (Roe v. Wade), but do not underline laws and acts. List cases and acts in your works-cited list (see **10c**, item 59).

10c The MLA list of works cited

The references you make in your text to sources are brief—usually only the author's last name and a page number—so they allow readers to continue reading without interruption. For complete information about the source, readers can use the in-text citation as a guide to the full reference in your list of works cited.

KEY POINTS
Setting Up the MLA List of Works Cited

1. *What to list*   List only works you actually cited in the text of your paper, not works you read but did not mention, unless your instructor requires you to include all the works you consulted as well as those mentioned in your text.

2. *Format of the list*   Begin the list on a new numbered page after the last page of the paper or any endnotes. Center the heading (Works Cited) without quotation marks, underlining, or a period. Double-space throughout the list.

3. *Organization*   Do not number the entries. List works alphabetically by author's last name. List works with no stated author by the first main word of the title (**10c**, items 8 and 26).

(Continued)

(Continued)

4. *Indentation*   To help readers find an author's name and to clearly differentiate one entry from another, indent all lines of each entry—except the first—one-half inch (or five spaces). A word processor can provide these "hanging indents" (Format/Paragraph/ Special).

      If you intend to publish on the Internet, it is often preferable to use no indentation at all (HTML does not support hanging indents well). Instead, follow each bibliographical entry with a line space.

5. *Periods*   Separate the main parts of each entry—author, title, publishing information—with a period followed by one space.

6. *Capitals*   Capitalize the first letter of all words in titles of books and articles except *a, an, the,* coordinating conjunctions, *to* in an infinitive, and prepositions (such as *in, to, for, with, without, against*) unless they begin or end the title or subtitle.

7. *Underlining or italics*   Underline the titles of books and the names of journals and magazines as in the examples in this section. You may use italics instead if your instructor approves and if your printer makes a clear distinction from regular type.

      If you write for publication on a World Wide Web site, do not underline titles of books and journals, because underlining is a signal for a hypertext link. Use italics, or consult your instructor or editor.

8. *Page numbers*   Give inclusive page numbers for print articles and sections of books. Do not use *p.* (or *pp.*) or the word *page* (or *pages*) before page numbers in any reference. For page citations over 100 and sharing the same first number, use only the last two digits for the second number (for instance, 683–89, but 798–805). For an unpaginated work, write "n. pag."

9. *Several works by one author*   After the first entry, use three hyphens and a period in place of the author's name. List the works alphabetically by title.

PRINT BOOKS AND PARTS OF BOOKS (MLA)

Find the necessary information for an entry on the title page of a book and on the copyright page. Use the most recent copyright date and list only the first city on the title page.

Use a shortened form of the publisher's name; usually one word is sufficient: *Houghton,* not Houghton Mifflin; *Basic,* not Basic Books. For university presses, use the abbreviations "U" and "P" with no periods.

1. Book with one author

Fussell, Paul. <u>Uniforms: Why We Are What We Wear</u>.
→Boston: Houghton, 2002.

McCullough, David. <u>John Adams</u>. New York: Simon, 2001.

2. Book with two or more authors
Separate the names with commas. Reverse the order of only the first author's name.

Lakoff, George, and Mark Johnson. <u>Metaphors We Live By</u>.
Chicago: U of Chicago P, 1980.

With four or more authors, either list all the names or use only the first author's name followed by "et al." (Latin for "and others").

Bellah, Robert N., et al. <u>Habits of the Heart:
Individualism and Commitment in American Life</u>.
Berkeley: U of California P, 1985.

3. Book with editor or editors
Include the abbreviation "ed." or "eds."

Gates, Henry Louis, Jr., ed. <u>Classic Slave Narratives</u>. New York: NAL, 1987.

With four or more editors, use the name of only the first, followed by a comma and "et al."

4. Author and editor
When an editor has prepared an author's work for publication, list the book under the author's name(s) if you cite the author's work. Then, in your listing, include the name(s) of the editor or editors after the title, introduced by "Ed." ("edited by") for one or more editors.

Bishop, Elizabeth. <u>One Art: Letters</u>. Ed. Robert Giroux.
New York: Farrar, 1994.

If you cite a section written by the editor, such as a chapter introduction or a note, list the source under the name of the editor.

Giroux, Robert, ed. <u>One Art: Letters</u>. By Elizabeth Bishop. New York: Farrar, 1994.

5. One work in an anthology (original or reprinted) For a work included in an anthology, first list the author and title of the included work. Follow this with the title of the anthology, the name of the editor(s), publication information (place, publisher, date) for the anthology, and then the pages in the anthology covered by the work you refer to.

Alvarez, Julia. "Grounds for Fiction." <u>The Riverside Reader</u>. 8th ed. Ed. Joseph Trimmer and Maxine Hairston. Boston: Houghton, 2005. 125–39.

If the work in the anthology is a reprint of a previously published scholarly article, supply the complete information for both the original publication and the reprint in the anthology.

Gates, Henry Louis, Jr. "The Fire Last Time." <u>New Republic</u> 1 June 1992: 37–43. Rpt. in <u>Contemporary Literary Criticism</u>. Ed. Jeffrey W. Hunter. Vol. 127. Detroit: Gale, 2000. 113–19.

6. More than one work in an anthology, cross-referenced If you refer to more than one work from the same anthology, list the anthology separately, and list each essay with a cross-reference to the anthology.

Des Pres, Terrence. "Poetry and Politics." Gibbons 17–29.

Gibbons, Reginald, ed. <u>The Writer in Our World</u>. Boston: Atlantic Monthly, 1986.

Walcott, Derek. "A Colonial's-Eye View of America." Gibbons 73–77.

7. Entry in a reference book For a well-known reference book, give only the edition number and the year of publication. When entries are arranged alphabetically, omit any volume and page numbers.

"Etching." <u>The Columbia Encyclopedia</u>. 6th ed. 2000.

8. *Book with no author named* Put the title first. Do not consider the words *A*, *An*, and *The* in alphabetizing the entries. The following entry would be alphabetized under *C*.

The Chicago Manual of Style. 15th ed. Chicago: U of
    Chicago P, 2003.

9. *Book written by a corporation, organization, or government agency* Alphabetize by the name of the corporate author or branch of government. If the publisher is the same as the author, include the name again as publisher.

College Board. Trends in College Pricing: Annual Survey
    of Colleges. New York: College Entrance Examination
    Board, 2002.

If no author is named for a government publication, begin the entry with the name of the federal, state, or local government, followed by the agency.

United States. Department of Labor. Bureau of Labor
    Statistics. Occupational Outlook Handbook
    2004–2005. Indianapolis. JIST, 2004.

10. *Translated book* After the title, include "Trans." followed by the name of the translator, not in inverted order.

Grass, Günter. Novemberland: Selected Poems,
    1956–1993. Trans. Michael Hamburger. San Diego:
    Harcourt, 1996.

11. *Multivolume work* If you refer to more than one volume of a multivolume work, give the number of volumes ("vols.") after the title.

Barr, Avon, and Edward A. Feigenbaum. The Handbook of
    Artificial Intelligence. 4 vols. Reading: Addison-
    Wesley, 1981–86.

If you refer to only one volume, limit the information in the entry to that one volume.

Richardson, John. A Life of Picasso. Vol. 2. New York:
    Random, 1996.

12. Book in a series Give the name of the series after the book title.

Connor, Ulla. <u>Contrastive Rhetoric: Cross-Cultural Aspects of Second Language Writing</u>. The Cambridge Applied Linguistics Ser. New York: Cambridge UP, 1996.

13. Book published under a publisher's imprint State the names of both the imprint (the publisher within a larger publishing enterprise) and the larger publishing house, separated by a hyphen.

Atwood, Margaret. <u>Negotiation with the Dead: A Writer on Writing</u>. New York: Anchor-Doubleday, 2003.

14. Foreword, preface, introduction, or afterword List the name of the author of the book element cited, followed by the name of the element, with no quotation marks. Give the title of the work; then use "By" to introduce the name of the author(s) of the book (first name first). After the publication information, give inclusive page numbers for the book element cited.

Hemenway, Robert. Introduction. <u>Dust Tracks on a Road: An Autobiography</u>. By Zora Neale Hurston. Urbana: U of Illinois P, 1984. ix–xxxix.

15. Republished book Give the original date of publication after the title and the reprint date at the end.

Walker, Alice. <u>The Color Purple</u>. 1982. New York: Pocket, 1985.

16. Book not in first edition Give the edition number ("ed.") after the title.

Raimes, Ann. <u>Keys for Writers</u>. 4th ed. Boston: Houghton, 2005.

17. Book title including a title Do not underline a book title included in the title you list. (However, if the title of a short work, such as a poem or short story, is included, enclose it in quotation marks.)

Hays, Kevin J., ed. <u>The Critical Response to Herman Melville's</u> Moby Dick. Westport: Greenwood, 1994.

18. *The Bible and other sacred texts* Give the usual bibliographical details for a book, including the name of a translator.

Koran. Trans. George Sales. London: Warne, n.d.

(*n.d.* means no date is given.)

The New Testament in Modern English. Trans. J. B.
> Phillips. New York: Macmillan, 1972.

19. *Dissertation* For an unpublished dissertation, follow the title (in quotation marks) with "Diss." and the university and date.

Hidalgo, Stephen Paul. "Vietnam War Poetry: A Genre of
> Witness." Diss. U of Notre Dame, 1995.

Cite a published dissertation as you would a book, with place of publication, publisher, and date, but also include dissertation information after the title (for example, "Diss. U of California, 1998.").

If the dissertation is published by University Microfilms International (UMI), underline the title and include "Ann Arbor: UMI," the date, and the order number at the end of the entry.

Diaz-Greenberg, Rosario. The Emergence of Voice in
> Latino High School Students. Diss. U of San Francisco,
> 1996. Ann Arbor: UMI, 1996. 9611612.

If you cite an abstract published in *Dissertation Abstracts International*, give the relevant volume number and page number.

Hidalgo, Stephen Paul. "Vietnam War Poetry: A Genre of
> Witness." Diss. U of Notre Dame, 1995. DAI 56
> (1995): 0931A.

PRINT ARTICLES IN PERIODICALS (MLA)

The conventions for listing articles differ according to the type of publication in which they appear: newspapers, popular magazines, or scholarly journals. For distinguishing scholarly journals from other periodicals, see **6**. In all cases, omit from your citation any introductory *A*, *An*, or *The* in the name of a newspaper, magazine, or scholarly journal. Always provide the range of page numbers for the article.

20. Article in a scholarly journal, continuously paged by volume For journal volumes with continuous pagination (for example, the first issue ends with page 174 and the next issue begins with page 175), give the volume number, the year in parentheses followed by a colon, and page numbers.

first name   title of article,
last name   /   in quotation marks
Hesse, Douglas. "The Place of Creative Nonfiction."
        period
title of journal,
underlined   volume number
College English 65 (2003): 237–41.
        year   colon inclusive page numbers

21. Article in a scholarly journal, paged by issue For journals in which each issue begins with page 1, include the issue number after the volume number, separated by a period. (Include the issue number alone if no volume number is given.)

Ginat, Rami. "The Soviet Union and the Syrian Ba'th

Regime: From Hesitation to *Rapprochement*."

Middle Eastern Studies 36.2 (2000): 150–71.

22. Article in a magazine Give the complete date (day, month, and year, in that order, with no commas between them) for a weekly or biweekly magazine. For a monthly or bimonthly magazine, give only the month and year (as in item 27). In either case, do not include volume and issue numbers. If the article is on only one page, give that page number. If the article covers two or more consecutive pages, list inclusive page numbers.

Scahill, Jeremy. "Inside Baghdad." Nation / Apr. 2003:

11–13.

Tyrangiel, Josh. "A *Source* of Discomfort." Time 12 Jan.

2004: 74.

23. Article in a newspaper After the newspaper title (omit the word *The*), give the date. For a newspaper that uses letters to designate sections, give the letter before the page number: "A23." For a numbered section, write, for example, "sec. 2: 23." See **10c**, item 37, for the online version of the entry for the following article.

Smith, Dinitia. "Critic at the Mercy of His Own Kind."

New York Times 24 May 2003: B9.

24. *Article that skips pages* When an article does not appear on consecutive pages (the one by Kilgannon begins on page B1 and skips to page B6), give only the first page number followed by a plus sign.

Kilgannon, Corey. "Get That Oak an Accountant."
New York Times 12 May 2003: B1+.

25. *Review* Begin with the name of the reviewer and the title of the review article if these are available. After "Rev. of," provide the title and author of the work reviewed, followed by publication information for the review.

Hollander, Anne. "Men in Tights." Rev. of Why We Are
What We Wear, by Paul Fussell. New Republic 10 Feb.
2003: 33–36.

26. *Unsigned editorial or article* Begin with the title. For an editorial, include the label "Editorial" after the title. In alphabetizing, ignore an initial *A, An,* or *The.*

"Santorum and Tolerance." Editorial. Wall Street Journal
25 Apr. 2003: A8.

27. *Letter to the editor* Write "Letter" or "Reply to letter of . . ." after the name of the author.

Ronk, Chris. Letter. Harper's May 2003: 5–6.

28. *Abstract in an abstracts journal* Provide exact information for the original work and add information about your source for the abstract: the title of the abstract journal, volume number, year, and item number or page number. (For dissertation abstracts, see item 19.)

Van Dyke, Jan. "Gender and Success in the American
Dance World." Women's Studies International
Forum 19 (1996): 535–43. Studies on Women
Abstracts 15 (1997): item 97W/081.

29. *Article on microform (microfilm and microfiche)* Many articles published before 1980 are available only on microfiche or microfilm. Provide as much print publication information as is available along with the name of the microfilm or microfiche and any identifying features.

"War with Japan." Editorial. New York Times 8 Dec. 1941:
22. UMI University Microfilm .

INTERNET AND OTHER ELECTRONIC SOURCES (MLA)

30. Information to include   With whatever system of documentation you use, the basic question is "What information do readers need to access the same site and find the same information I found?" The chart on "How to Read a Web Site" in **7c**, with its accompanying sample Web page, shows how and where to find the information you need. The following chart refers to the Web site on page 46 and shows you how to provide and format the information in an MLA list of works cited.

The Basics for Citing Internet Sources, MLA Style

1. **Author**
   Last name, First name, Middle initial, if available. Names of more than one author begin with first name. (Author may also be name of corporation, business, institution, or government agency.)

   Mitchell, Stacy, and Jeff Milchen.

2. **Document title + details of any print publication** "Title of Online Article, Story, Poem, or Posting to Discussion List."

   "Littering America with Dead Malls and Vacant Superstores."

3. **Name of site + date of posting or update, whatever is available, and name of sponsor if available**
   Name of Web Site, Project, Online Periodical, Book, or Name of Database. Date of posting. Sponsor.

   ReclaimDemocracy.org. June 2002. ReclaimDemocracy.org.

4. **Date of access**
   Day Month (abbrev.) Year (no period after year)

   28 Feb. 2004

5. **URL**
   Enclosed in angle brackets, followed by period. Line split only after a slash. No spaces or hyphens inserted. All underscoring is included.

   <http://www.reclaimdemocracy.org/independent_business/dead_malls.html>.

FORMAT OF MLA CITATION:

Mitchell, Stacy, and Jeff Milchen. "Littering America
    with Dead Malls and Vacant Superstores."
    ReclaimDemocracy.org . June 2002.
    ReclaimDemocracy.org. 28 Feb. 2004
    <http://www.reclaimdemocracy.org/
    independent_business/dead_malls.html>.

Many complex sites need more information: see the "Special
Considerations" Key Points box (below) and the sample
entries in items 31–48 for variations.

KEY POINTS

**Beyond the Basics: Special Considerations of
Online Documentation in an MLA List of
Works Cited**

1. *Author*   If no individual author or organizational
   author is evident, list the source by title of document
   or name of site, whichever is available. Evaluate a
   source with no author especially carefully before you
   use it. See **7b** and **7c**.

2. *Document title*   Sometimes you may find it difficult
   to differentiate a document title from the name of a
   Web site. Examining the home page and the structure
   of the site carefully will often help (**7c**). Include after
   the title any available print publication information
   or online journal details such as the journal name,
   volume number of a scholarly journal, date, and
   whatever information is provided about the page
   numbers in a print publication or a PDF document.

3. *Name of site*   Underline the name of a Web site or
   project, an online periodical or book, or the name of
   a database. Provide, if you can, the date of the online
   posting and the name of the owner or sponsor of the
   site, if available. Abbreviations such as *Assn.*, *Lib.*,
   and *Dept.* are acceptable. *Note:* A Webmaster is not
   the owner of the site.

4. *Dates*   The last date in your source reference,
   immediately before the URL or keyword path,
   should be the date when you accessed the material.

(Continued)

(Continued)

Two dates might appear next to each other, as in items 36 and 37, but both are necessary; the first is the date when the work was posted or updated; the second is the date when you found the material.

5. *URL*   Copy and paste a URL whenever possible to avoid transcription errors. Do not split a protocol (http://) across lines. See also **33a** on how to include angle brackets with a URL.

31. Work in an online database or subscription service
Libraries subscribe to large information services (such as *InfoTrac, FirstSearch, EBSCO, SilverPlatter, Dialog, SIRS,* and *LexisNexis*) to gain access to extensive databases of online articles, as well as to specialized databases (such as *ERIC, Contemporary Literary Criticism,* and *PsycINFO*). You can use these databases to locate abstracts and full texts of thousands of articles.

The URLs used to access databases are useful only to those accessing them through a subscribing organization such as a college library or a public library. In addition, database URLs tend not to remain stable, changing day by day, so providing a URL at the end of your citation will not be helpful to your readers unless you know it will be persistent. So include the URL of the document only if it is persistent and not impossibly long; otherwise, give the URL of the search page or home page—or no URL at all.

The examples that follow show citations of a magazine article, a scholarly article, and a newspaper article, accessed from different databases.

print publication information

Gray, Katti. "The Whistle Blower." <u>Essence</u> Feb. 2001:

starting page of article   database service

148–. <u>Academic Search Premier</u>. EBSCO. City U of

date
library   of access

New York Lib. 18 Feb. 2004 <http://

EBSCO database provides a persistent URL

search.epnet.com/direct.asp?an=4011390&db=aph>.

The screenshots below show pertinent information.

Full text of article

a. URL is not persistent and is too long for a citation.
b. Online service
c. Name of library system
d. Clicking here gives a short, persistent URL. See next screenshot.
e. Print information needed for documentation
f. Database
g. The full text of the article begins here.

Information in "Citation" link

a. Subject terms useful for searching
b.–c. Print information to include
c. Number of first page of 8-page article
d.–e. Online information to include

Lowe, Michelle S. "Britain's Regional Shopping

volume and issue number for print version of scholarly article
Centres: New Urban Forms?" Urban Studies 37.2
(2000): 261– . Academic Search Premier. EBSCO.

Brooklyn Public Lib., Brooklyn, NY. 1 July 2004
<http://search.epnet.com/
direct.asp?an=2832704&db=aph>.

Weeks, Linton. "History Repeating Itself; Instead of
Describing Our Country's Past, Two Famous Scholars
Find Themselves Examining Their Own."
Washington Post 24 Mar. 2002: F01– . Academic
Universe: News. LexisNexis. City U of New York Lib.

<─────── URL of home page ───────┐
27 June 2004 <http://web.lexis-nexis.com/>.

If the service provider supplies a direct link to a licensed
database without displaying the URL of the accessed database, give the name of the database, the name of the subscription service or library, and your date of access.
Specify any path or keywords that you used to access the
source.

"Parthenon." The Columbia Encyclopedia. 6th ed. 2000.
America Online. 12 Nov. 2003. Keywords: Reference;
Encyclopedias; Encyclopedia.com; Bartleby.com;
Columbia Encyclopedia 6th ed.

32. Online book   Give whatever is available of the following: author, title, editor or translator, print publication information, electronic publication information and
date, date of access, and complete electronic address
(URL).

┌─ author ─┐ ┌──── title of work ────┐ ┌──────
Darwin, Charles. The Voyage of the Beagle. London:

print publication
──── information ───┐ ┌─ title of database ─┐
John Murray, 1859. Oxford Text Archive.

date of
electronic
┌ publication ┐ ┌──── name of sponsor of site ────┐
28 Mar. 2000. Arts and Humanities Data Service.

date of   electronic address enclosed
┌── access ──┐ ┌──── in angle brackets ────┐
14 Feb. 2004 <http://ota.ahds.ac.uk>.

33. *Online poem*

```
                          title of              print
      ┌── author ──┐    ┌── poem ──┐        ┌── source ──┐  ┌──────
      Levine, Philip. "What Work Is." What Work Is. New
```

```
      print publication
      ──── information ──┐   ┌──── title of database ────┐
      York: Knopf, 1991. Internet Poetry Archive.
```

```
      date of electronic          sponsor                date of
      ┌─updating─┐      ┌────── of site ──────┐       ┌── access ──┐
      4 Apr. 2000. U of North Carolina P. 17 Feb. 2004
```

```
                        electronic address (URL)
      ┌───────── enclosed in angle brackets ─────────┐
      <http://www.ibiblio.org/ipa/levine/work.html>.
```

34. *Article in a reference database*

```
      ┌── title of article ──┐       ┌────── title of database ──────┐
      "Bloomsbury Group." Columbia Encyclopedia 6th ed.
```

```
      date of electronic                    date of
      ┌─updating─┐  ┌─sponsor─┐           ┌── access ──┐
      7 July 2003. Bartleby.com. 15 Feb. 2004
      <http://www.hartleby.com/65/bl/
      Bloomsbury.html>.
```

35. *Article in an online journal*   Give the author, title of
article, title of journal, volume and issue numbers, and date
of issue. Include the page number or the number of paragraphs only if pages or paragraphs are numbered in the
source. End with the date of access and URL.

```
      ┌── author ──┐    ┌────────── title of article ──────────
      Hatchuel, Sarah. "Leading the Gaze: From Showing to
```

```
      ┌──────────────────────────────────────────────────────┐
      Telling in Kenneth Branagh's Henry V and Hamlet."
                        name of              volume and
              ┌──── online journal ────┐   issue number
      Early Modern Literary Studies 6.1 (2000):
                                                date of online
      number of paragraphs   date of          publication
      (numbered in the text)  access
          22 pars. 12 Feb. 2004 <http://www.shu.ac.uk/
          emls/06–1/hatchbra.htm>.
```

36. *Article in an online magazine*

Charoenying, Timothy. "Jazz at the Crossroads." Atlantic
    Online 26 Feb. 2003. 30 Jan. 2004 <http://
    www.theatlantic.com/unbound/flashbks/jazz.htm>.

37. *Article in an online newspaper*

Smith, Dinitia. "Critic at the Mercy of His Own Kind."

New York Times on the Web 24 May 2003. 25 May

2003 <http://www.nytimes.com/2003/05/24/

books/24WOOD.html>.

38. *Online review, editorial, abstract, or letter* After author and title, identify the type of text: "Letter," "Editorial," "Abstract," or "Rev. of … by …" (see **10c**, items 25–28). Continue with details of the electronic source.

39. *Scholarly project online*

title of scholarly
┌─────── project ───────┐   ┌────── editor ──────┐
Perseus Digital Library. Ed. Gregory Crane.

date of electronic
┌─publication─┐   ┌────────── sponsor ──────────┐
Updated daily. Dept. of Classics, Tufts U.

                date of
        ┌──── access ────┐
17 June 2004 <http://www.perseus.tufts.edu>.

40. *Professional site online*

                                    date of
┌──────── title of professional site ────────┐ ┌─update─┐
MLA: Modern Language Association. 30 Jan. 2004.

                            date of
┌────────── sponsor ──────────┐ ┌─access─┐
Mod. Lang. Assn. of Amer. 28 June 2004 <http://

www.mla.org>.

41. *Online government publication* Begin with the government, agency, and title of the work. Include the place and date of print publication, if available. Follow this with the date of electronic posting or update, the date of access, and the URL.

United States. Dept. of Educ. Natl. Center for Educ.

Statistics. Digest of Education Statistics, 2002.

16 Feb. 2004 <http://nces.ed.gov/programs/

digest/d02>.

42. Personal Web page If a personal Web page has a title, supply it, underlined. Otherwise, use the designation "Home page."

date of
⌐update⌐
Gilpatrick, Eleanor. Home page. June 2004.

    28 June 2004 <http://www.gilpatrickart.com>.

43. Course page For a course home page, give the name of the instructor and the course, the words *Course home page*, the dates of the course, the department and the institution, and then your access date and the URL.

Raimes, Ann. Expository Writing. Course home page. Aug.

    2004–Dec. 2004. Dept. of English, Hunter Coll. 18

    Aug. 2004 <http://bb.hunter.cuny.edu>.

44. Online posting on a discussion list, blog, Web forum, bulletin board service, or Usenet Give the author's name, the document (as written in the subject line), the label "Online posting," and the date of posting. Follow this with the name of the forum or the title of the Web log (blog), date of access, and URL or address of the list. For a Usenet newsgroup, give the name and address of the group, beginning with the prefix *news:*.

Desai, Satish. "FCC's Limited Authority." Online posting.

    15 Feb. 2004. Explainer Forum in "The Fray" in Slate.

    18 Feb. 2004 <http://fray.slate.msn.com/

    ?id=3936&m=9834327>.

Cromm, Oliver. "Crossers of the Atlantic." Online

    posting. 6 May 2003. 9 May 2003

    <news:alt.usage.english>.

To make it easy for readers to find a posting, refer whenever possible to one stored in Web archives.

Howard, Rebecca Moore. "Institutional Pressures."

    Online posting. 16 Apr. 2003. WPA-L Archives.

    10 May 2004 <http://lists.asu.edu/cgi-bin/

    wa?A1=ind0304&L=wpa-l>.

To cite a forwarded document in an online posting, include author, title, and date, followed by "Fwd. by" and the name of the person forwarding the document. End with "Online posting," the date of the forwarding, the name of the discussion group, date of access, and address of the discussion list.

CUNY University Faculty Senate. "Chancellor Comments on
Exec. Budget." 20 Jan. 2004. Fwd. by Ken Sherrill.
Online posting. 20 Jan. 2004. Hunter–L. 5 Feb. 2004
<http://hunter.listserv.cuny.edu>.

45. *Synchronous communication* When citing a source from a chat room, a MUD (multiuser domain), or a MOO (multiuser domain, object-oriented), give the name of the person speaking or posting information, type of event, title, date, forum, date of access, and electronic address. Refer to archived material whenever possible.

Day, Michael. Discussion of e-mail and argument. C-Fest
12. 19 June 1996. LinguaMOO. 10 June 2004
<http://lingua.utdallas.edu:7000/2007/>.

46. *Personal e-mail message* Treat this like a letter (item 49).

Kane, George. "Visual Rhetoric." E-mail to the author.
17 Feb. 2004.

47. *CD-ROM* Cite material from a CD-ROM published as a single edition (that is, with no regular updating) in the same way you cite a book, but after the title add the medium of publication and any version or release number.

Keats, John. "To Autumn." Columbia Granger's World of
Poetry. CD-ROM. Rel. 3. New York: Columbia UP, 1999.

MULTIMEDIA AND MISCELLANEOUS SOURCES (MLA)

48. *Online versions of multimedia and other sources* Identify online interviews, maps, charts, films and film clips, videos, television programs, radio programs, sound recordings, works of art, cartoons, and advertisements as you would sources that are not online, with the addition of electronic publication information (such as the date and site name), your date of access, and the URL. Items 53 and 56 include sample citations of multimedia works online.

49. *Lecture, speech, personal communication, or interview* For a lecture or speech, give the author and title, if known. For a presentation with no title, include a label such as "Lecture" or "Address" after the name of the speaker.

Parry, Kate. Lecture. Hunter College, New York. 16 Apr. 2003.

For letters and personal interviews, identify the type of communication.

Rogan, Helen. Letter to the author. 3 Feb. 2003.

Gingold, Toby. Telephone interview. 5 May 2003.

Cite a published letter as you would cite a work in an anthology. Include the page numbers for the letter.

Bishop, Elizabeth. "To Robert Lowell." 26 Nov. 1951. One Art: Letters. Ed. Robert Giroux. New York: Farrar, 1994. 224–26.

50. Published or broadcast interview For interviews that have no title, include the label "Interview" after the name of the person interviewed.

Guest, Christopher. Interview. Charlie Rose. PBS. WNET, New York. 13 May 2003.

51. Map or chart Include the designation after the title.

Auvergne/Limousin. Map. Paris: Michelin, 1996.

52. Film or video List the title, director, performers, and any other pertinent information. End with the name of the distributor and the year of distribution.

Sunshine. Dir. Istvan Szabo. Perf. Ralph Fiennes. Paramount, 2000.

When you cite a videocassette or DVD, include the date of the original film, the medium, the name of the distributor of the DVD or cassette, and the year of the new release.

Casablanca. Dir. Michael Curtiz. Perf. Humphrey Bogart and Ingrid Bergman. 1943. DVD. MGM, 1998.

53. Television or radio program Give the title of the program episode; the title of the program; any pertinent information about the performers, writer, narrator, or director; the network; and the local station and date of broadcast.

"The Difference between Us." <u>Race: The Power of an
    Illusion</u>. Narr. C. C. H. Pounder. Dir. Christine Herbes-
    Sommers. PBS. WLIW, New York. 18 May 2003.

"The Fix Is In." <u>This American Life</u>. Narr. Ira Glass. WBEZ,
    Chicago. 15 Feb. 2004. 17 Feb. 2004
    <http://www.thislife.org>.

54. Sound recording   List the composer or author, the
title of the work, the names of artists, the production company, and the date. If the medium is not a compact disc,
indicate the medium, such as "Audiocassette," before the
name of the production company.

Scarlatti, Domenico. <u>Keyboard Sonatas</u>. Andras Schiff,
    piano. London, 1989.

Walker, Alice. Interview with Kay Bonetti. Audiocassette.
    Columbia: American Audio Prose Library, 1981.

55. Live performance   Give the title of the play, the
author, any pertinent information about the director and
performers, the theater, the location, and the date of the
performance. If you are citing an individual's role in the
work, begin your citation with the person's name.

<u>Talking Heads</u>. By Alan Bennett. Perf. Lynn Redgrave.
    Minetta Lane Theater, New York. 2 Apr. 2003.

Redgrave, Lynn, perf. <u>Talking Heads</u>. By Alan Bennett.
    Minetta Lane Theater, New York. 2 Apr. 2003.

56. Work of art, slide, or photograph   List the name of the
artist; the title of the work (underlined); the name of the
museum, gallery, or owner; and the location.

Johns, Jasper. <u>Racing Thoughts</u>. Whitney Museum of
    Amer. Art, New York.

Duchamp, Marcel. <u>Bicycle Wheel</u>. 1951. Museum of Mod.
    Art, New York. 17 Feb. 2004 <http://www.moma.org/
    collection/depts/paint_sculpt/blowups/
    paint_sculpt_020.html>.

For a photograph in a book, give complete publication
information, including the number of the page on which
the photograph appears.

Johns, Jasper. <u>Racing Thoughts</u>. Whitney Museum of
   Amer. Art, New York. <u>The American Century: Art and
   Culture 1950–2000</u>. By Lisa Phillips. New York:
   Norton, 1999. 311.

For a slide in a collection, include the slide number (*Slide 17*).

57. *Cartoon*   Include the label "Cartoon." Follow this with
the usual information about the source, and give the page
number.

Chast, Roz. "Cloud Chart." Cartoon. <u>New Yorker</u> 14 Apr.
   2003: 59.

58. *Advertisement*   Give the name of the product or company, followed by the label "Advertisement" and publication
information. If a page is not numbered, write "n. pag."

Scholastic. Advertisement. <u>Ebony</u> Feb. 2003: n. pag.

59. *Legal source*   For a legal case, give the name of the case
with no underlining or quotation marks, the number of the
case, the name of the court deciding the case, and the date of
the decision.

Roe v. Wade. No. 70–18. Supreme Ct. of the US. 22 Jan.
   1973.

If you mention the case in your text, underline it.

Chief Justice Burger, in <u>Roe v. Wade</u>, noted that . . .

Give the Public Law number of an act, its date, and the cata-
loging number for its Statutes at Large.

USA Patriot Act. Pub. L. 107–56. 26 Oct. 2001. Stat.
   115.272.

10d   MLA student paper: Sample pages

Student Lindsay Camp plans to become a police officer. She
examined and then chose to oppose differing standards for
men and women in police and fire department examinations. Camp included in her paper a table showing fitness
standards for men and women as well as a persuasive illustration (shown on page 20).

Camp 1

Lindsay Camp
Professor Raimes
English 120, section 129
5 December 2003

Safety First: Women and Men in Police
and Fire Departments

If any of us were caught in a fire, we would almost certainly prefer to see a man rather than a woman coming to carry us down a ladder out of the flames and smoke—though we would certainly be grateful to either. In an interview, a firefighter made precisely that point about perceptions of size and strength (Mignone). However, because society is increasingly conscious of discrimination based on gender, police and fire departments have implemented quotas to hire more women. In many cases, though, in order to meet the quotas they have used different physical standards for women and men, so women who want equality have been treated unequally, men have experienced reverse discrimination, and public safety has been threatened. To meet standards of both safety and equality, women and men should pass the same physical tests.

In order to become police officers, candidates have to pass a psychological test (Wexler) and a physical fitness test, which "assumes that being physically fit is a good predictor of job success for fire and police department personnel" (Rafilson, "Legislative"). In most departments around the country, this test consists of sit-ups, a mile-and-a-half run, bench press repetitions, and a flexibility test (Rafilson, Police Officer 39). Women are encouraged to apply, but in the tests they are judged by lower standards than men.

Page of works cited

Works Cited

Heidensohn, Frances. Women in Control? The
Role of Women in Law Enforcement. New York: Oxford
UP, 1992.

Mignone, Douglass. Telephone interview. 17 Oct. 2003.

Polisar, Joseph, and Donna Milgram. "Recruiting,
Integrating and Retaining Women Police Officers:
Strategies That Work." The Police Chief Oct. 1998.
IWITTS. Institute for Women in Trades, Technology,
and Science. 27 Oct. 2003 <http://www.iwitts.com/
html/the_police_chief.htm>.

Rafilson, Fred M. "Legislative Impact on Fire Service Physical
Fitness Testing." Fire Engineering Apr. 1995: 83- .
Academic Search Premier. EBSCO. City U of New York
Lib. 23 Oct. 2003 <http://search.epnet.com/
direct.asp?an=9505024136&db=aph>.

---. Police Officer. 15th ed. United States: Arco, 2000.

Wexler, Ann Kathryn. Gender and Ethnicity as
Predictors of Psychological Qualification
for Police Officer Candidates. Diss. California School
of Professional Psychology, Los Angeles, 1996. Ann
Arbor: UMI, 1996. 9625522.

11 APA Style

At a Glance: Index of APA Style Features

SAMPLES OF APA IN-TEXT CITATIONS (11b), 93

Citing an author or authors
A. Author mentioned in your text, 93
B. Author cited in parentheses, 93
C. Author quoted or paraphrased, 93
D. Work with more than one author, 93
E. Author of work in an edited anthology, 94
F. Author's work cited in another source, 94
G. More than one work in one citation, 94
H. Author with more than one work published in one year, 95
I. Two authors with the same last name, 95

Citing a work with no individual author
J. Corporation, government agency, or organization as author, 95
K. No author named, 95

Citing special types of sources
L. Multivolume work, 95
M. Electronic or Internet source, 96
N. Multimedia or nonprint source, 96
O. Personal communication or interview, 96
P. Classical work, 96

APA LIST OF REFERENCES (11c), 96

Print Books and Parts of Books
1. One author, 98
2. Two or more authors, 98
3. Edited book, 98
4. Work in an anthology or reference book, 98
5. No author named, 99
6. Corporation or government organization as author, 99
7. Translation, 99
8. Multivolume work, 99
9. Foreword, preface, introduction, or afterword, 99
10. Republished book, 100
11. Technical report, 100
12. Dissertation or abstract, 100

Print Articles in Periodicals
13. Scholarly journal, paged by volume, 100
14. Scholarly journal, paged by issue, 101
15. Magazine, 101
16. Newspaper, 101
17. Article that skips pages, 101
18. Review, 101
19. Unsigned article or editorial, 102
20. Letter to the editor, 102

Internet and Electronic Sources
21. Work in electronic database or information service, 102
22. Newspaper article retrieved from database or Web, 103
23. Online abstract, 103
24. Online article with a print source, 107

25. Article in online journal, no print source, 103
26. Article in online site (no author identified), 104
27. Entire Web site, 104
28. Document on Web site (no author identified), 104
29. Document on a university or government agency site, 104
30. E-mail and electronic discussion lists, 104

Multimedia and Miscellaneous Sources
31. Personal communication or interview, 105
32. Film, recording, or video, 105
33. Television or radio program, 105
34. Computer software, 105

This section gives details about the documentation style recommended for the social sciences by the *Publication Manual of the American Psychological Association,* 5th ed. (Washington, DC: Amer. Psychological Assn., 2001) and on the Web site for the *APA Publication Manual* (<http://www.apastyle.org>).

11a Basic features of APA style

KEY POINTS
Two Basic Features of APA Style

1. *In the text of your paper,* include the following information each time you cite a source: the last name(s) of the author (or authors) and the year of publication. See **11b**.

2. *At the end of the paper,* include on a new numbered page a list entitled "References," double-spaced and arranged alphabetically by authors' last names followed by initials of other names, the date in parentheses, and other bibliographical information. See **11c** for sample entries.

NOTE: Use endnotes only to amplify information in your text. Number notes consecutively with superscript numerals; after the list of references, attach a separate page containing your numbered notes and headed "Footnotes." Use notes sparingly. Include all important information in your text, not in footnotes.

11b Samples of APA in-text citations

CITING AN AUTHOR OR AUTHORS (APA)

A. Author mentioned in your text Give the author's last name when you introduce the citation. Include the year in parentheses directly after the author's name. Generally, use the past or the present perfect tense for your citation.

  author   year
Wilson (1994) has described in detail his fascination with insects.

(See **11c**, item 1, for this work in a list of references.)

B. Author cited in parentheses If you do not mention the name of the author to introduce the citation, include both the name and the year, separated by a comma, in parentheses.

The army retreated from Boston in disarray, making the rebels realize that they had achieved a great victory (McCullough, 2001).
       author comma year

C. Author quoted or paraphrased If you include a direct quotation, include in the parentheses the abbreviation "p." or "pp." followed by a space and the page number. All items within parentheses are separated by commas.

Memories are "built around a small collection of dominating images" (Wilson, 1994, p. 5).

A long quotation (more than forty words) should be indented one half inch, with no quotation marks (but double-spaced). Put the period *before* the parenthetical citation.

    You can also provide page numbers with a paraphrase or summary to help readers locate information easily.

D. A work with more than one author For a work by two authors, name both in the order in which their names appear on the work. Within parentheses use an ampersand (&) in place of *and*.

Kanazawa and Still (2000) in their analysis of a large set of data showed that the statistical likelihood of being divorced increased if one was male and a secondary school teacher or college professor.

Analysis of a large set of data showed that the statistical likelihood of being divorced increased if one was male and a secondary school teacher or college professor (Kanazawa & Still, 2000).

ampersand in parentheses

(See **11c**, item 13, for this work in a list of references.)

For a work with three to five authors or editors, identify all of them the first time you mention the work.

Jordan, Kaplan, Miller, Stiver, and Surrey (1991) have examined the idea of *self*.

In later references, use the name of the first author followed by "et al." (for "and others") in place of the other names.

Increasingly, the self is viewed as connected to other human beings (Jordan et al., 1991).

(See **11c**, item 2, for this work in a list of references.)

For six or more authors, always use "et al." after the name of the first author.

E. *Author of work in an edited anthology* In your text, refer to the author of the work itself, not to the editor of the anthology (though you will include information about the anthology in your list of references) (**11c**, item 4).

Seegmiller (1993) has provided an incisive analysis of the relationship between pregnancy and culture.

F. *Author's work cited in another source* Give the author or title of the work in which you find the reference, preceded by "as cited in" to indicate that you are referring to a citation in that work. List that secondary source in your list of references. In the following example, *Smith* will appear in the list, but *Britton* will not.

The words we use simply appear, as Britton says, "at the point of utterance" (as cited in Smith, 1982, p. 108).

G. *More than one work in one citation* List the sources in alphabetical order, separated by semicolons.

Criticisms of large-scale educational testing abound (Crouse & Trusheim, 1988; Nairn, 1978, 1980; Sacks 2003).

H. Author with more than one work published in one year
Identify each work with a lowercase letter after the year:
(Zamel, 1997a, 1997b). Separate the dates with a comma. In
the reference list, repeat the author's name in each entry,
and alphabetize by the title: Zamel, V. (1997a).

I. Two authors with the same last name Use the authors'
initials as well, even if the dates of publication differ.

F. Smith (1982) described a writer as playing the competitive roles of author and secretary.

CITING A WORK WITH NO INDIVIDUAL AUTHOR (APA)

*J. Corporation, government agency, or organization as
author* In the initial citation, use the full name of the
organization; in subsequent references, use an abbreviation
if one exists.

┌─────── first mention: full name ───────┐
A survey by the College Entrance Examination Board
(CEEB) showed that 43% of total enrollment in higher
education was in two-year public institutions.
Full-time enrollment was different, with only 24%
enrolled in two-year public schools (CEEB, 2002).
                    abbreviation in citation

See **11c**, item 6, for this work in a list of references.

K. No author named In your text, use the complete title if
it is short, with capital letters for major words. Within
parentheses, you can shorten the title. For Web sources,
search the site carefully for an author's name (**7c**).

According to *Weather* (1999), one way to estimate the
Fahrenheit temperature is to count the number of times a
cricket chirps in 14 seconds and add 40.

Increasing evidence has shown that glucosamine relieves
the symptoms of arthritis (*The PDR Family Guide,* 1999).

(See **11c**, item 5, for a reference list entry using the complete
title.)

CITING SPECIAL TYPES OF SOURCES (APA)

L. A multivolume work In your citation, give the publication date of the volume you are citing: (Barr & Feigenbaum, 1982). If you refer to more than one volume, give

inclusive dates for all volumes you cite: (Barr & Feigenbaum, 1981–1986).

See **11c**, item 8, for this work in a list of references.

M. Electronic or Internet source   Give author, if available, or title, followed by the year of electronic publication or update. Use "n.d." if no date is given. In order to locate a section of text you quote, paraphrase, or comment on in a source with no page or paragraph numbers visible on the screen, give the section heading, and indicate the paragraph within the section: (Conclusion section, para. 2). To cite an entire Web site, give the URL in your paper, not in the list of references.

N. Multimedia or nonprint source   For a film, television or radio broadcast, recording, live performance, or other nonprint source, include in your citation the name of the originator or main contributor (such as the writer, interviewer, director, performer, or producer), along with the year of production: (Berman & Pulcini, 2003). See **11c**, item 32, for this work in a list of references.

O. Personal communication (letter, conversation, e-mail) or interview   Give the last name and initial(s) of the author of the communication and an exact date. Do not include a citation in your list of references.

According to Dr. C. S. Apstein, Boston University School of Medicine, research in heart disease is critical to the well-being of society today (personal communication, January 7, 2004).

P. A classical work   If the date of publication of a classical work is not known, use in your citation "n.d." for "no date." If you use a translation, give the year of the translation, preceded by "trans." You do not need a reference list entry for the Bible or ancient classical works. Just give information about text version, book, and line numbers in your text.

11c APA list of references

KEY POINTS
Setting Up the APA List of References

1. *What to list*   List only the works you cited (quoted, summarized, paraphrased, or commented on) in the text of your paper, not every source you examined.

(Continued)

(Continued)

2. *Format* Start the list on a new numbered page after the last page of text or notes. Center the heading "References," without quotation marks, not underlined or italicized, and with no period following it. Double-space throughout the list. Place any tables and charts after the "References" list.

3. *Conventions of the list* List the works alphabetically by last names of primary authors. Do not number the entries. Begin each entry with the author's name, last name first, followed by an initial or initials. Give any authors' names after the first in the same inverted form, separated by commas. Use "et al." only for six or more authors. List works with no author by title, alphabetized by the first main word.

4. *Date* Put the year in parentheses after the authors' names. For journals, magazines, and newspapers, also include month and day, but do not abbreviate the names of the months.

5. *Periods* Use a period and one space to separate the main parts of each entry.

6. *Indentation* Use hanging indents. (Begin the first line of each entry at the left margin; indent subsequent lines one-half inch.)

7. *Capitals* In titles of books and articles, capitalize only the first word of the title or subtitle and any proper nouns or adjectives.

8. *Italics* Italicize the titles of books, but do not italicize or use quotation marks around the titles of articles. For magazines and journals, italicize the publication name, the volume number, and the comma. Italicize the names of newspapers.

9. *Page numbers* Give inclusive page numbers for articles and sections of books, using complete page spans ("251–259"). Use the abbreviation "p." or "pp." only for newspaper articles and sections of books (such as chapters or anthologized articles).

PRINT BOOKS AND PARTS OF BOOKS (APA)

You will find all the necessary information on the title page and the copyright page of a book. Use the most recent copyright date. Include the city and state of publication or the name of the major city alone. Give the publisher's name in a shortened but intelligible form, including words like *Press* but omitting *Co.* or *Inc.*

1. Book with one author   Give the author's last name first, followed by initials.

last name   initials
        comma / periods
            / /   year in
            / /   parentheses   title italicized
            / /   period   period
Wilson, E. O. (1994). *Naturalist*. Washington, DC:
⟶Island Press.   place of   colon
        publisher final period   publication
    indented

2. Book with two or more authors   Reverse the order of all the names: last name first, followed by initials. Separate all names by commas, and use an ampersand (&) before the last name. Use "et al." only if there are six or more authors.

Jordan, J. V., Kaplan, A. G., Miller, J. B., Stiver, I. P., & Surrey, J. L. (1991) *Women's growth in connection: Writings from the Stone Center.* New York: Guilford Press.

3. Edited book   Use "Ed." or "Eds." for one or more editors.

Denmark, F., & Paludi, M. (Eds.). (1993). *Psychology of women: A handbook of issues and theories.* Westport, CT: Greenwood Press.

4. Work in an anthology or reference book   List the author, the date of publication of the edited book, and the title of the work first. Follow this with the names of the editors of the book (not inverted), the title of the book, and the page numbers (preceded by "pp.") of the chapter in parentheses. End with the place of publication and the publisher. If you cite more than one article in an edited work, include full bibliographical details in each entry.

Seegmiller, B. (1993). Pregnancy. In F. Denmark & M. Paludi (Eds.), *Psychology of women: A handbook of issues and theories* (pp. 437–474). Westport, CT: Greenwood Press.

For a well-known reference book with unsigned alphabetical entries, begin with the title of the entry, and include the page number(s).

Multiculturalism. (1993). In *The Columbia Encyclopedia* (5th ed., p. 1855). New York: Columbia University Press.

5. *Book with no author named* Put the title first. Ignore *A, An*, and *The* when alphabetizing.

The PDR family guide to natural medicines and healing therapies. (1999). New York: Three Rivers-Random House.

6. *Book by a corporation or government organization* Give the name of the corporate author first. If the publisher is the same as the author, write "Author" for the name of the publisher.

College Entrance Examination Board. (2002). *Trends in college pricing: Annual survey of colleges.* New York: Author.

If no author is named for a government publication, begin with the name of the federal, state, or local government, followed by the agency.

United States. Department of Labor. (2004). *Occupational outlook handbook 2004–2005.* Indianapolis: JIST.

7. *Translation* In parentheses, give the initials and last name of the translator, followed by a comma and "Trans."

Jung, C. G. (1960). *On the nature of the psyche* (R. F. C. Hull, Trans.). Princeton, NJ: Princeton University Press.

8. *Multivolume work* Give the number of volumes after the title. The date should include the range of years of publication, if appropriate.

Barr, A., & Feigenbaum, E. A. (1981–1986). *The handbook of artificial intelligence* (Vols. 1–4). Reading, MA: Addison-Wesley.

9. *Foreword, preface, introduction, or afterword* List the name of the author of the book element cited. Follow the date with the name of the element, the title of the book, and the page number(s) for the element, preceded by "p." or "pp."

Weiss, B. (Ed.). (1982). Introduction. *American education and the European immigrant 1840–1940* (pp. xi–xxviii). Urbana: University of Illinois Press.

10. Republished book After the author's name, give the most recent date of publication. At the end, in parentheses add "Original work published" and the date. In your text citation, give both dates: (Smith, 1793/1976).

Smith, A. (1976). *An inquiry into the nature and causes of the wealth of nations.* Chicago: University of Chicago Press. (Original work published 1793)

11. Technical report Give the report number ("Rep. No.") after the title.

Morgan, R., & Maneckshana, B. (2000). *AP students in college: An investigation of their course-taking patterns and college majors* (Rep. No. SR–2000–09) Princeton, NJ: Educational Testing Service.

12. Dissertation or abstract For a manuscript source, give the university and year of the dissertation and the volume and page numbers of *DAI*.

Salzberg, A. (1992). Behavioral phenomena of homeless women in San Diego County (Doctoral dissertation, United States International University, 1992). *Dissertation Abstracts International, 52,* 4482.

For a microfilm source, also include in parentheses at the end of the entry the university microfilm number. For a CD-ROM source, include "CD-ROM" after the title; then name the electronic source of the information and the access number.

PRINT ARTICLES IN PERIODICALS (APA)

13. Article in a scholarly journal, continuously paged throughout volume Give only the volume number and year for journals that number pages sequentially for each issue in a volume. Italicize the volume number and the following comma as well as the title of the journal. Do not use "p." or "pp." with page numbers. Use capital letters only for the first word of an article title or subtitle and for proper nouns. See **6** on recognizing scholarly journals.

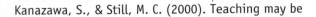

Kanazawa, S., & Still, M. C. (2000). Teaching may be

                                journal title,
   no quotation marks around   volume number,
   ———— article title ————┐ ┌— and comma italicized —
hazardous to your marriage. *Evolution and Human*

   ————┐ no "p." or "pp." before page numbers
Behavior, 21, 185–190.

14. *Article in a scholarly journal, paged by issue*   Include the issue number in parentheses (not in italics) immediately following the volume number.

Ginat, R. (2000). The Soviet Union and the Syrian
    Ba'th regime: From hesitation to *rapprochement.*
    Middle Eastern Studies, 36(2), 150–171.
                    issue number not in italics

15. *Article in a magazine*   Include the year and month and any exact date of publication in parentheses. Do not abbreviate months. Italicize the magazine title, the volume number, and the comma that follows; then give the page number or numbers.

Levy, S. (2003, April 21). The killer browser. *Newsweek,*
    141, 6–12.

16. *Article in a newspaper*   Include the month and date of publication after the year. Give the section letter or number before the page, where applicable. Use "p." and "pp." with page numbers. Do not omit *The* from the title of a newspaper.

Revkin, A. C. (2003, April 28). At the bustling North Pole,
    here today, gone tomorrow. *The New York Times,* pp.
    A1, A6.

17. *Article that skips pages*   Give all the page numbers, separated by commas, as in item 16.

18. *Review*   After the title of the article, add in brackets a description of the work reviewed and identify the medium: book, film, or video, for example.

Himmelfarb, G. (2003, March). The Victorian achievement
    [review of the book *The Victorians*]. *The Atlantic, 291,*
    113–120.

19. *Unsigned article or editorial* For a work with no author named, begin the listing with the title; for an editorial, add the word "Editorial" in brackets.

No nuke blackmail [Editorial]. (2003, April 26). *The New York Post,* p. 14.

20. *Letter to the editor* Write "Letter to the editor" in brackets after the date or the title of the letter, if it has one.

Chapman, R. C. (2003, March). [Letter to the editor]. *Natural History, 112,* 13.

INTERNET AND ELECTRONIC SOURCES (APA)

Provide enough information to enable readers to find the material you refer to. See examples of documentation at <http://www.apa.org>.

Include in your citation whatever information is available of the following: author/s; date of work; title of work; any print publication information (items 1–20, above); and identification of type of source, in square brackets (for example, "[letter to the editor]"). End with the name of an information service and document number for an online service, or "Retrieved (date) . . . from" followed by the URL for the actual document (not just the home page), with no final period. Include also any log-in instructions.

21. *Work in an electronic database or information service* Universities and libraries subscribe to large searchable databases such as *InfoTrac, EBSCO, ERIC, LexisNexis,* and *WilsonWeb,* providing access to abstracts and full-text articles. In addition to print information, provide the name of the database and the date of retrieval. Add the item number if it is provided.

Goldstein, B. S. C., & Harris, K. C. (2000). Consultant practices in two heterogeneous Latino schools. *The School Psychology Review, 29,* 368–377. Retrieved February 19, 2004, from WilsonWeb Education Full Text database (0279–6015).

For works retrieved from generally available Web databases, such as government or newspaper databases, also provide the URL.

22. Newspaper article retrieved from database or Web site
Newspaper articles, as well as journal articles, are often available from several sources, in several databases, and in a variety of formats, such as in a university online subscription database.

Wade, N. (2000, May 9). Scientists decode Down syndrome chromosome. *The New York Times,* p. F4. Retrieved January 4, 2004, from LexisNexis Academic Universe database.

Liptak, A. (2003, June 2). Internet battle raises questions about the First Amendment. *The New York Times.* Retrieved June 4, 2003, from http://www.nytimes.com/2003/06/02/national/02INTE.html

no period at end after URL

23. Online abstract

Frith, H., & Gleeson, K. (2004). Clothing and embodiment: Men managing body image and appearance. *Psychology of Men & Masculinity, 5,* 40–48. Abstract retrieved February 20, 2004, from http://www.apa.org/journals/men/104ab.html#4

24. Online article with a print source Cite an article in PDF format as you would a print article, with the addition of "[Electronic version]" after the title of the article. If information such as page numbers or figures is missing or if the document may have additions or alterations, give full retrieval information.

Jones, C. C., & Meredith, W. (2000, June). Developmental paths of psychological health from early adolescence to later adulthood. *Psychology and Aging, 15,* 351–360. Retrieved June 2, 2003, from http://www.apa.org/journals/pag/pag152351.html

25. Article in an online journal with no print source

Holtzworth-Munroe, A. (2000, June). Domestic violence: Combining scientific inquiry and advocacy. *Prevention & Treatment, 3.* Retrieved July 8, 2004, from http://journals.apa.org/prevention/volume3/pre0030022c.html

26. Article in an online site, no author identified

Division spotlight. (2003, February). *APA Monitor, 34*(2).
Retrieved June 3, 2003, from http://www.apa.org/
monitor/feb03/ds.html

27. Entire Web site Give the complete URL in the text of
your paper, not in your list of references (**11b**, item M).

28. Document on a Web site, no author identified
Italicize the title of the document (the Web page).
Alphabetize by the first major word of the title.

APAStyle.org: Electronic references. (2003). Retrieved June
24, 2004, from http://www.apastyle.org/
elecgeneral.html

29. Document on a university or government agency site
Italicize the title of the document. In the retrieval statement,
give the name of the university or government agency (and
the department or division if it is named). Follow this with a
colon and the URL.

McClintock, R. (2000, September 20). *Cities, youth, and
technology: Toward a pedagogy of autonomy.*
Retrieved February 4, 2004, from Columbia University,
Institute for Learning Technologies Web site:
http://www.ilt.columbia.edu/publications/cities/
cyt.html

30. E-mail and contributions to electronic discussion lists
Make sure that you cite only scholarly e-mail messages. Cite
a personal e-mail message in the body of your text as "personal communication," and do not include it in your list of
references (**11b**, item O).

Gracey, D. (2001, April 6). Monetary systems and a
sound economy [Msg 54]. Message posted to
http://groups.yahoo.com/group/ermail/message/54

Whenever possible, cite an archived version of a message:

Howard, R. M. (2003, April 16). Institutional pressures.
Message posted to WPA–L electronic mailing list,
archived at http://lists.asu.edu

MULTIMEDIA AND MISCELLANEOUS SOURCES (APA)

31. Personal communication (letter, telephone conversation, or interview) Cite a personal communication only in your text (**11b**, item O). Do not include it in your list of references.

32. Film, recording, or video Identify the medium in brackets after the title.

Berman, S. S., & Pulcini, R. (Directors). (2003). *American Splendor* [motion picture]. United States, Fine Line Features.

33. Television or radio program

Keach, S. (Narrator). (2000, July 9). *Storms of the century* [Television broadcast]. New York: WNET.

34. Computer software

Movie Magic Screenwriter (Version 4.5) [Computer software]. (2000). Burbank, CA: Storymind.

11d APA student paper: Sample pages

The following sample pages are from a paper written for a college course in experimental psychology. They follow APA style guidelines. Check with your instructor as he or she may want to modify the format for the title page to include course and section number in place of affiliation. APA style uses headings to indicate sections in the paper. Main headings are centered, and subheadings are flush left and italicized. Main headings include *Method, Results, Discussion,* and *Conclusions.*

Title page (APA)

Absolute Auditory Thresholds   1

Running head: ABSOLUTE AUDITORY THRESHOLDS

Absolute Auditory Thresholds in College Students

Todd Kray

Hunter College of the City University of New York

Abstract page (APA)

Absolute Auditory Thresholds   2

Abstract

Seventeen college students participated in an auditory experiment, collecting data while working in pairs. In the experiment, absolute auditory thresholds were established and compared with "normal" thresholds. This study discusses details and plots results on two graphs for one pair of students: one 20-year-old female and one 37-year-old male. While results paralleled the "norm" at many frequencies (125 Hz, 250 Hz, 500 Hz, 1000 Hz, 2 KHz, 4 KHz, and 8 KHz), strong evidence for high-frequency loss was discovered for the older of the two participants. Environmental conditions and subject fatigue were also seen to be influences on determining auditory thresholds.

First page of APA paper

Absolute Auditory Thresholds   3

Absolute Auditory Thresholds in College Students

For decades, the branch of psychophysics known as psychoacoustics has concerned itself with the minimum amount of sound pressure level (SPL) required for detection by the human ear. An early landmark study by Sivian and White (1933) examined loudness thresholds by measuring minimum audible field (MAF) and minimal audible pressure (MAP) and found that the ear was not as sensitive as had been reported in earlier studies by Wien (as cited in Sivian & White, 1933). Parker and Schneider (1980) tested Fechner's and Weber's laws, both of which concern themselves with measuring changes in physical intensity and the psychological experiences of those changes (Jahnke & Nowaczyk, 1998; Noll, 2002) and determined that loudness is a power function of intensity, which was consistent with

Fechner's assumption. In recent years, loudness thresholds have been measured under various experimental conditions, including quiet sedentary activity, exercise, and noise (Hooks-Horton, Geer, & Stuart, 2001).

An experiment was designed to utilize the method of limits, which establishes the absolute sensitivity (threshold) for a particular sound, to test auditory thresholds.

List of references (APA)

References

Gelfand, S. A. (1981). *Hearing: An introduction to psychological and physiological acoustics.* New York: Marcel Dekker.

Hooks-Horton, S., Geer, S., & Stuart, A. (2001). Effects of exercise and noise on auditory thresholds and distortion-product otoacoustic emissions. *Journal of the American Academy of Audiology, 12,* 52–58. Retrieved April 28, 2004, from EBSCO Academic Search Premier database.

Jahnke, J. C., & Nowaczyk, R. H. (1998). *Cognition.* Englewood Cliffs, NJ: Prentice Hall.

Noll, T. (2002). *Tone apperception, relativity, and Weber-Fechner's law.* Paper presented at the 2002 2nd International Conference on Understanding and Creating Music. Retrieved April 20, 2004, from http://flp.cs.tu-berlin.de/~noll/ApperceptRelativity.pdf

Parker, S., & Schneider, B. (1980). Loudness and loudness discrimination. *Perception and Psychophysics, 28,* 398–406.

Sivian, L. J., & White, S. D. (1933). Minimum audible sound fields. *The Journal of the Acoustical Society of America, 4,* 288–321.

Pages 9 and 10 of Kray's paper contain figure captions and two graphs.

12 *The Chicago Manual of Style:* System of Endnotes or Footnotes

In addition to an author-year parenthetical system of references similar to the APA system, *The Chicago Manual of Style,* 15th ed. (Chicago: U of Chicago P, 2003), also recommends documenting sources in footnotes or, preferably, endnotes. This system is used widely in the humanities, especially in history, art history, literature, and the arts. For a *Chicago*-style paper, include an unnumbered title page, and number the first page of your paper "2."

12a Basic features of the *Chicago* endnote style

> **KEY POINTS**
> **Two Basic Features of the *Chicago* Endnote Style**
>
> 1. *In your text,* place a superscript numeral at the end of the quotation or the sentence in which you mention source material; place the number after all punctuation marks except a dash.
> 2. *On a separate numbered page at the end of the paper,* list all endnotes, and number the notes sequentially, as they appear in your paper (**12c**).

12b *Chicago* in-text citations

Use the following format. Number your notes sequentially.

George Eliot thought that *Eliot* was a "good, mouth-filling, easy to pronounce word."[1]

See page 109 for the endnote to accompany this citation.

12c *Chicago* endnotes

> **KEY POINTS**
> **Setting Up *Chicago* Endnotes and Footnotes**
>
> 1. In the list of endnotes, place each number on the line (not as a superscript), followed by a period and one space. For footnotes, word-processing software will often automatically make the number a superscript
>
> *(Continued)*

(Continued)

number—just be consistent with whatever format you use.

2. Indent the first line of each entry three or five spaces. Single-space within a note and double-space between notes unless your instructor prefers double-spacing throughout.

3. Use the author's full name, not inverted, followed by a comma and the title of the work. Put quotation marks around article titles, and italicize titles of books and periodicals.

4. Capitalize all words in the titles of books, periodicals, and articles except *a, an, the,* coordinating conjunctions, *to* in an infinitive, and prepositions. Capitalize any word that begins or ends a title or subtitle.

5. Follow a book title with publishing information in parentheses (city—and state if necessary: name of publisher, year) followed by a comma and the page number(s), with no "p." or "pp." Follow an article title with the name of the periodical and pertinent publication information (volume, issue, date, page numbers where appropriate). Do not abbreviate months.

6. Separate major parts of the citation with commas, not periods.

7. For online sources, provide the URL, and for time-sensitive material, end with the date on which you last accessed the source.

First note for a source

        comma
   author's name | title italicized, all important
   ⌐in normal order⌐ | ⌐words capitalized⌐
 1. Margaret Crompton, *George Eliot: The Woman*

        comma page number
(London: Cox and Wyman, 1960), 123.

First note for a source if a bibliography is provided If your paper includes a bibliography listing all the sources cited in your notes, the note citation can be concise.

 1. Crompton, *George Eliot,* 123.

A bibliography supplies full publication details. All lines after the first are indented, and the parts of each entry are separated with periods, not commas, with no mention of page numbers in books, as in the following example:

┌── last name first ──┐
Crompton, Margaret. *George Eliot: The Woman*.
    London: Cox and Wyman, 1960.

See also the sample bibliography in **12d**.

Note referring to the immediately preceding source   Use "Ibid." (Latin *ibidem*, meaning "in the same place") only to refer to exactly the same author and work as in the preceding reference. All the details except the page number should correspond to the previous citation.

    2. Ibid., 127.

However, avoid a series of "ibid." notes. These are likely to irritate your reader. Instead, place page references within your text: *As Crompton points out (127), . . .*

Any subsequent reference to a previously cited source   For a reference to a source cited in a previous note but not in the immediately preceding note, give only the author and page number. However, if you cite more than one work by the same author, include a short title to identify the source.

    6. Crompton, 124.

PRINT BOOKS AND PARTS OF BOOKS (*CHICAGO*)

Note the indented first line, the full name of the author, the commas separating major sections of the note, and the publication details in parentheses (city: publisher, year of publication). For an edited or translated book, use "ed." or "trans." after the author's name. If you quote or refer to a specific page of the source, provide the page number following the publication details and after a comma, as in item 1. For a general reference or a reference to the work as a whole, end the note after the closing parenthesis, as in item 2.

1. Book with one author

    1. Robert A. Caro, *Master of the Senate: The Years of Lyndon Johnson* (New York: Knopf, 2002), 8.

2. Book with two or more authors

2. George Lakoff and Mark Johnson, *Metaphors We Live By* (Chicago: University of Chicago Press, 1980).

For a book with four or more authors, use the name of only the first author followed by "et al." (for "and others"): *Randolph Quirk et al.*

3. Book with no author identified

3. *Chicago Manual of Style,* 15th ed. (Chicago: University of Chicago Press, 2003).

4. Government document

4. U.S. Department of Education, Office of Educational Research and Improvement, *Digest of Education Statistics, 2000* (Washington, DC, 2002).

5. Scriptures, Greek and Latin works, classic works of literature   Provide the reference in the text or in a note. For the Bible, include the book (in abbreviated form, chapter, and verse, not a page number) and the version used. Do not include the Bible in a bibliography.

5. Gen. 27:29 (New Revised Standard Version).

For Greek and Roman works and for classic plays in English, locate by the number of book, section, and line or by act, scene, and line. Cite a classic poem by book, canto, stanza, and line, whichever is appropriate. Specify the edition used only in the first reference in a note.

6. Article in an edited volume or anthology

6. Terrence Des Pres, "Poetry and Politics," in *The Writer in Our World,* ed. Reginald Gibbons (Boston: Atlantic Monthly Press, 1986), 17-29.

PRINT ARTICLES IN PERIODICALS (*CHICAGO*)

7. Article in a scholarly journal   If journal volumes are paged continuously through issues (for example, if issue 1 ends on page 188, and issue 2 of the same volume begins with page 189), give only the volume number and year, not

the issue number. End with the page number you refer to. To cite an abstract, include the word *abstract* before the name of the journal. For more on scholarly journals, see section **6** in Part Two.

> 7. Hesse, Douglas, "The Place of Creative Nonfiction," *College English* 65 (2003): 238.

When each issue of a journal begins on page 1, include "no." for number after the volume number, and follow it with the issue number, date in parentheses, and page number(s) cited.

8. *Article in a magazine* Include the month for monthly magazines and the complete date for weekly magazines (month, day, year). Cite only a specific page number in a note (after a comma), not the range of pages. (In a bibliography, provide the range of pages of the whole article.)

> 8. Jeremy Scahill, "Inside Baghdad," *Nation,* April 7, 2003, 12.

9. *Article in a newspaper* Do not include an initial *The* in the name of a newspaper. Give the edition and any section number, but not the page number.

> 9. Dinitia Smith, "Critic at the Mercy of His Own Kind," *New York Times,* sec. B, May 24, 2003.

For editorials with no author, begin the note with the title.

10. *Letter to the editor*

> 10. Chris Ronk, letter to the editor, *Harper's,* May 2003, 5.

11. *Review of a book, play, or film*

> 11. Anne Hollander, "Men in Tights," review of *Why We Are What We Wear,* by Paul Fussell, *New Republic,* February 10, 2003, 34.

INTERNET AND ELECTRONIC SOURCES (*CHICAGO*)

12. *General principles for listing online sources* To cite an online book, poem, article, government publication, or multimedia source in *Chicago* style, provide exactly the same information as for a non-Internet source, adding the

URL at the end. To split a URL across lines, do not insert a hyphen. Make the split after a slash or before a period or any other punctuation mark. The example shows the listing for the online version of the article cited in item 9.

12. Dinitia Smith, "Critic at the Mercy of His Own Kind," *New York Times,* sec. B, May 24, 2003, http://www.nytimes .com/2003/05/24/books/24WOOD.html.

Provide a date of access in parentheses only if the information is time-sensitive (for instance, medical information) or subject to frequent updates, as shown in items 13 and 15.

13. *Online reference work*   Cite an online dictionary or an encyclopedia in a note, but do not include it in a bibliography. Because reference works are frequently updated, you need to give the date on which you access the material. Precede the title of an alphabetized article with the initials *s.v.* (Latin for *sub verbo*—"under the word").

13. *Columbia Encyclopedia,* 6th ed., s.v. "Bloomsbury group," http://www.bartleby.com/65/bl/Bloomsbury.html (accessed February 9, 2004).

14. *Article obtained through an online database*   Give the URL of the entry page of the service and other retrieval information. No date of access is necessary unless the material is time-sensitive or may exist in varying editions.

14. Geoffrey Bent, "Vermeer's Hapless Peer," *North American Review* 282 (1997), http://www.infotrac .galegroup.com/.

15. *Web page or document from a Web site*   Give the author of the content, if known; the title of the document; the owner or sponsor of the site; the URL; and your date of access if the material is frequently updated.

15. "MLA Style," Modern Language Association, http://www.mla.org (accessed May 4, 2004).

If a personal home page does not have a title, use a descriptive phrase such as "home page."

16. *E-mail communication*

16. George Kane, e-mail message to the author, July 1, 2004.

17. *Material posted on an electronic discussion list* Whenever possible, cite a URL for archived material. Otherwise, end the note after the date.

    17. Rebecca Moore Howard, e-mail to WPA-L mailing list, April 16, 2003, http://lists.asu.edu/cgi-bin/wa?A1=ind0304&L=wpa-l.

18. *CD-ROM, DVD, e-book* Indicate the medium.

    18. Ann Raimes, *Digital Keys 4.0* (Boston: Houghton Mifflin, 2005), CD-ROM.

MULTIMEDIA AND MISCELLANEOUS SOURCES (*CHICAGO*)

19. *Interview, lecture, or speech* Treat a published interview like an article or a book chapter, including the phrase "interview with." For unpublished interviews, include the type of interview and the date.

    19. Douglass Mignone, telephone interview with the author, October 19, 2003.

For a lecture or speech, also provide the location and date in parentheses: *(lecture, Hunter College, New York, April 7, 2003).*

20. *Film, filmstrip, slides, videocassette, or audiocassette* End the note with an indication of the type of medium, such as *film, filmstrip, slide, videocassette,* or *audiocassette.* For online multimedia, include the type of medium, such as *MP3 audio file.*

    20. *Citizen Kane,* produced, written, and directed by Orson Welles, 119 min., RKO, 1941, film.

12d *Chicago* sample bibliography

Check whether your instructor wants you to include a bibliography of works cited (or a bibliography of works consulted) in addition to notes. If you do, you can use the short form for notes (**12c**, p. 109).

    The following bibliography from a student's paper on the seventeenth-century Dutch painter Pieter de Hooch shows the format to use.

Bibliography

Bent, Geoffrey. "Vermeer's Hapless Peer." *North American Review* 282 (1997).
http://www.infotrac.galegroup.com/.

Botton, Alain de. "Domestic Bliss: Pieter de Hooch Exhibition." *New Statesman,* October 9, 1998, 34–35.

Franits, Wayne E. "The Depiction of Servants in Some Paintings by Pieter de Hooch." *Zeitschrift für Kunstgeschichte* 52 (1989): 559-66.

Sutton, Peter. *Pieter de Hooch: Complete Edition, with a Catalogue Raisonné.* Ithaca, NY: Cornell University Press, 1980.

12e *Chicago* student paper: Sample pages

Here is the third paragraph (along with its corresponding endnotes) of an essay by Lynn McCarthy, written for Professor Roberta Bernstein's course in modern art at the State University of New York at Albany. Page 1 of her paper was a numbered title page (see **4a**). The assignment was to analyze a work of art by Piet Mondrian. In her paper, she included a reproduction of *Trafalgar Square.*

Paragraph on third page of essay (*Chicago* style)

McCarthy 3

Trafalgar Square, an oil on canvas measuring 145.2 by 120 cm, today is housed in the Museum of Modern Art in New York City. It is interesting to discover that Mondrian planned out his compositions with colored tape before he applied any paint.[3] Some tape actually still remains on his *Victory Boogie Woogie* (1942–44), which is an unfinished work he was involved in at the time of his death. But what is even more interesting is that although Mondrian preplanned the compositions, we know from x-rays that he reworked the paint on his canvases over and over again.[4] So as methodical and mathematical as we may think Mondrian was, he still felt constant inspiration and intuitive urges to make changes along the way. It is interesting, too, to note that he worked on a flat, horizontal table rather than at an easel.[5] Maybe he did this for practical or comfort reasons, but it also can be seen as a break from the conventional way artists created their works just as their subject matter broke from tradition. I think of how an artist like Jackson Pollock takes this even further by laying his canvas on the floor and walking on and around it, dropping and splattering the paint.

Endnotes (*Chicago* style)

McCarthy   5

Notes

1. Harry Cooper and Ron Spronk, *Mondrian: The Transatlantic Paintings* (New Haven, CT: Yale University Press, 2001), 24.

2. Ibid., 24–25.

3. H. Harvard Arnason and Marla F. Prather, *History of Modern Art* (New York: Abrams, 1998), 393.

4. Cooper and Spronk, 237.

5. Arnason and Prather, 383.

6. Cooper and Spronk, 34.

7. Arnason and Prather, 233.

13 The CBE/CSE Style of Documentation in the Sciences and Mathematics

This section outlines the citation-sequence documentation style recommended by the Council of Science Editors (formerly Council of Biology Editors) for all scientific disciplines in *Scientific Style and Format: The CBE Manual for Authors, Editors, and Publishers*, 6th ed. (New York: Cambridge UP, 1994).

13a Basic features of CBE/CSE citation-sequence style

KEY POINTS
Two Basic Features of CBE/CSE Citation-Sequence Style

1. *In the text of your paper,* give each reference a super-script number in smaller type than that used for the text of your paper, or include the number on the line within parentheses. Numbers run sequentially throughout your paper.

2. *At the end of your paper,* number the items consecutively in the order in which you mention them in your paper. Do not alphabetize entries.

13b CBE/CSE in-text citations

Include a superscript number to refer readers to your list of references.

One summary of studies of the life span of the fruit fly[1] has shown that . . .

Refer to more than one entry in the reference list as follows:

Two studies of the life span of the fruit fly[1, 2] have shown that . . .

Several studies of the life span of the fruit fly[1-4] have shown that . . .

See the sample reference list in **13d**.

13c CBE/CSE sequential list of references

Use the following guidelines when preparing a list of refer-ences in CBE/CSE style.

KEY POINTS
Setting Up the CBE/CSE List of References

1. After the last page of your paper, attach the list of references, headed "References" or "Cited References."

2. Number the works consecutively in the order in which you mention them in your paper. Invert all authors' names, and use the initials of first and middle names. Use no punctuation between last names and initials, and leave no space between initials.

(Continued)

(Continued)

3. Begin each entry with the note number followed by a period and a space. Do not indent the first line of each entry; indent subsequent lines to align beneath the first letter on the previous line.

4. Do not underline or use quotation marks for the titles of articles, books, or journals and other periodicals.

5. Capitalize only the first word of a book or article title, and capitalize any proper nouns.

6. Abbreviate titles of journals and organizations.

7. Use a period between major divisions of each entry.

8. Use a semicolon and a space between the name of the publisher and the publication date of a book. Use a semicolon with no space between the date and the volume number of a journal.

9. For books, give the total number of pages, followed by a space and "p." For journal articles, give inclusive page spans, using digits in the second number that are *not* included in the first: 135–6; 287–93; 500–1.

10. For online sources, provide author, title, print publication information, date and place of online publication, your date of access, and the URL.

1. *Book with one author*

title not underlined, only first word capitalized

1. Finch CE. Longevity, senescence and the

initials with no periods between

abbreviated publishing terms semicolon

genome. Chicago: Univ Chicago Pr; 1990.

number of pages in book

922 p.

2. *Book with more than one author*

2. Ferrini AF, Ferrini RL. Health in the later years. 2nd ed. Dubuque (IA): Brown & Benchmark; 1993. 470 p.

3. *Article in a scholarly journal*

3. Kowald A, Kirkwood TB. Explaining fruit fly longevity.

no spaces

Science 1993;260:1664–5.

volume number

In a journal paginated by issue, include the issue number in parentheses after the volume number.

4. Newspaper or magazine article

4. Altman LK. Study prompts call to halt a routine eye operation. NY Times 1995 Feb 22;Sect C:10.

If no author is named, begin with "[Anonymous]." For an editorial, insert "[editorial]" after the title.

For Internet sources, CBE/CSE recommends using the formats shown on the National Library of Medicine Web site at <http://www.nlm.nih.gov/pubs/formats/internet.pdf>. Some examples follow.

5. Electronic journal article with a print source   Include the type of medium in square brackets after the journal title. Include any document number, the accession date "[cited (year, month, date)]," and an availability statement with the URL, with no period after the URL.

5. Jones CC, Meredith W. Developmental paths of psychological health from early adolescence to later adulthood. Psych Aqinq [Internet] 2000 [cited 2004 Jun 24];15(2):351–60. Available from: http://www.apa.org/journals/pag/pag152351.html

6. Electronic journal article with no print source   If no print source is available, provide an estimate, in square brackets, of the length of the document in pages, paragraphs, or screens: "[about 3 p.]," "[about 15 paragraphs]," or "[about 6 screens]."

6. Holtzworth-Munroe A. Domestic violence: Combining scientific inquiry and advocacy. Prev Treatment [serial on the Internet], 2000 June 2 [cited 2004 June 4];3 [about 6 pages]. Available from: http://journals.apa.org/prevention/volume3/pre0030022c.html

7. Article in an electronic database   After basic publication information, give the name of the database, the designation "[database on the Internet]," any date of posting or modification, or the copyright date. Follow this with the date of access, the approximate length of the article, the URL, and any accession number.

7. Mayor S. New treatment improves symptoms of Parkinson's disease. Brit Med J 2002 324(7344):997.

In: EBSCOhost Health Source: Nursing/Academic Edition [database on the Internet]; c2002 [cited 2003 Dec 1]. [about 1 screen]. Available from: http://search.epnet.com/direct.asp?an6609093&db=hch; Accession No.: 6609093.

8. *Internet home page*

8. Anemia and iron therapy [Internet]. Hinsdale (IL): Medtext, Inc.; c1995–2002 [cited 2003 Dec 2]. Available from: http://www.hdcn.com/ch/rbc/

9. *Posting to a discussion list*

9. Bishawi AH. Summary: hemangioendothelioma of the larynx. In: MEDLIB-L [discussion list on the Internet]. [Buffalo (NY): State Univ of NY]; 2002 May 6, 11:25am [cited 2002 May 15]. [about 4 screens]. Available from: MEDLIB-L@listserv.buffalo.edu

13d CBE/CSE student paper: Sample list of references

The following list of references for a paper on "Research Findings and Disputes about Fruit Fly Longevity" uses the CBE/CSE sequential numbering system. Note the use of abbreviations and punctuation.

Fruit fly longevity 17

References

1. Kowald A, Kirkwood TB. Explaining fruit fly longevity. Science 1993;260:1664-5.

2. Finch CE. Longevity, senescence and the genome. Chicago: Univ Chicago Pr; 1990. 922 p.

3. Carey JR, Liedo P, Orozco D, Vaupel JW. Slowing of mortality rates at older ages in large medfly cohorts. Science 1992;258:457.

4. Skrecky D. Fly longevity database. In Cryonet [discussion list on the Internet]. 1997 June 22. [cited 2004 May 27]. [about 12 screens]. Available from: http://www.cryonet.org/cgi-bin/dsp.cgi?msg=8339

Part Five
The 5 C's of Style

14 The First C: Cut

15 The Second C: Check for Action ("Who's Doing What?")

16 The Third C: Connect

17 The Fourth C: Commit

18 The Fifth C: Choose Vivid, Appropriate, and Inclusive Words

121

14 The First C: Cut, 122

14a Wordiness, 123
14b Formulaic phrases, 123
14c References to your intentions, 124

15 The Second C: Check for Action ("Who's Doing What?"), 124

15a "Who's doing what?" in subject and verb, 124
15b Sentences beginning with *there* or *it*, 124
15c Unnecessary passive voice, 125

16 The Third C: Connect, 125

16a Consistent subjects, 125

16b Transitional words and expressions, 126
16c Variety in connecting and combining, 126

17 The Fourth C: Commit, 127

17a Confident stance, 127
17b Consistent tone, 127

18 The Fifth C: Choose Vivid, Appropriate, and Inclusive Words, 128

18a Vivid and specific words, 128
18b Avoiding slang, regionalisms, and jargon, 129
18c Avoiding biased and exclusionary language, 130

Readers sometimes suffer from what has been called the MEGO reaction to a piece of writing—"My Eyes Glaze Over"—even when ideas are well organized. This reaction happens when readers are bored by wordiness, flatness, inappropriate word choice, clichés, and sentences constructed without interesting variations. Follow the five C's of style to prevent that glazing over.

14 The First C: Cut

When you write, do not underdevelop your ideas because you fear taxing readers' patience. Work on developing ideas and presenting material that has substance and persuasive detail. Once you have a text rich with ideas, however, scrutinize it for fumbling phrases, weak expressions, and obscurities that inevitably creep into a first draft. You can usually improve your writing if you focus on stating the essential ideas and expressing them succinctly. Examine your writing for any unnecessary material, whether ideas, sentences, phrases, or individual words.

14a Cut wordiness.

Say something only once and in the best possible place.

► The Lilly Library ~~contains many rare books. The books~~
ᶳ
~~in the library are~~ carefully preserved, ~~The library also~~
          many rare books and manuscripts
~~houses a manuscript collection~~.
                    ^
          director of
► Steven Spielberg, ~~who has directed~~ the movie ~~that has~~
  ~~been~~ described as the best war movie ever made, ~~is~~
  ~~someone who~~ knows many politicians.

► California residents have voted to abolish bilingual
  education, ~~The main reason for their voting to abolish~~
                    because
  ~~bilingual education was that~~ many children were being
  placed indiscriminately into programs and kept there
  too long.

In addition, trim words that simply repeat an idea expressed
in another word in the same phrase: *basic* essentials, *true* facts,
circle *around*, consensus *of opinion*, my *personal* opinion. Edit
redundant pairs: *various and sundry, each and every*.

► The task took ~~diligence and~~ perseverance.

          has
► His surgeon ~~is a doctor with~~ a great deal of clinical
  experience. ^

14b Cut formulaic phrases.

Replace wordy phrases with shorter or more direct expressions.

Formulaic	Not formulaic
at the present time	now
at this point in time	
in this day and age	
in today's society	
because of the fact that	because
due to the fact that	
are of the opinion that	believe
have the ability to	can
in spite of the fact that	although, despite
last but not least	finally
prior to	before
concerning the matter of	about

14c Cut references to your intentions.

Generally, your readers want to read about your topic and are not interested in learning about your thinking process. Eliminate references to the organization of your text and your own planning, such as *In this essay, I intend to prove that . . .*; or *In the next few paragraphs, I hope to show that . . .*; or *In conclusion, I have demonstrated. . . .*

15 The Second C: Check for Action ("Who's Doing What?")

Write vigorous sentences with vivid, expressive verbs rather than forms of the verb *be* (*be, am, is, are, was, were, being, been*) or verbs in the passive voice (**22g**).

15a Ask "Who's doing what?" about subject and verb.

Let the subject of your sentence perform the action.

Wordy   The mayor's approval of the new law was due to the voters' suspicion of the concealment of campaign funds by his deputy.

Ask "Who's doing what?"

Subject	Verb
the mayor	approved
the voters	suspected
his deputy	had concealed

Revised   The mayor approved the new law because the voters suspected that his deputy had concealed campaign funds.

15b Use caution in beginning a sentence with *there* or *it*.

Rewriting a sentence that begins with *there* often makes the sentence leaner and more direct. Revise by using a verb that shows action and a subject that "does" the action.

Wordy   There was a discussion of the health care system by the politicians.

Who's doing what here?

Revised   The politicians discussed the health care system.

| Wordy | It is clear that Baker admires Updike. |
| Revised | Clearly, Baker admires Updike. |

e s l **No Omitted *It* Subject**   In some languages, an *it* subject can be omitted. However, it cannot be omitted in English (see **19c**).

it
►She went to the park because ˄ was a warm day.   ■

15c Avoid unnecessary passive voice constructions.

The passive voice tells what is done to the grammatical subject of the sentence ("The turkey *was cooked* too long"). Extensive use of the passive voice can make your style dull and wordy.

| Passive | The problem will be discussed thoroughly by the committee. |
| Revised | The committee will discuss the problem thoroughly. |

The passive voice occurs frequently in scientific writing because readers are primarily interested in data, procedures, and results, not in who developed or produced them. In a scientific report, you are likely to read, for example, *The rats were fed,* not *The researchers fed the rats.* See **22g** for more on when the passive voice is appropriate.

16 The Third C: Connect

Coherent paragraphs connect information previously mentioned to new information in a smooth flow, not in a series of grasshopperlike jumps.

16a Apply the principle of consistent subjects.

Readers need to have a way to connect the ideas beginning a sentence with what has gone before. So when you move from one sentence to the next, avoid jarring shifts of subjects.

| Jarring shift | *Memoirs* are becoming increasingly popular. *Readers* all over the continent are finding them appealing. |
| Revised | *Memoirs* are becoming increasingly popular. *They* appeal to readers all over the continent. |

16b Make logical connections with transitional words and expressions.

The following expressions are useful for connecting sentences and paragraphs.

Transitional words and expressions

Adding an idea: also, in addition, further, furthermore, moreover

Contrasting: however, nevertheless, nonetheless, on the other hand, in contrast, still, on the contrary, rather, conversely

Providing an alternative: instead, alternatively, otherwise

Showing similarity: similarly, likewise

Showing order of time or order of ideas: first, second, third (and so on), then, next, later, subsequently, meanwhile, previously, finally

Showing result: as a result, consequently, therefore, thus, hence, accordingly, for this reason

Affirming: of course, in fact, certainly, obviously, to be sure, undoubtedly, indeed

Giving examples: for example, for instance

Explaining: in other words, that is

Adding an aside: incidentally, by the way, besides

Summarizing: in short, generally, overall, all in all, in conclusion, above all

For punctuation with transitional words and expressions, see **26a**.

16c Vary the ways to connect and combine ideas.

To avoid a series of short, choppy sentences, consider the logical connection between ideas. Frequently you will have several alternatives: a transition, coordination (with *and, but, or, nor, so, for,* or *yet*), or subordination (with conjunctions such as *because, if, although, while, who,* or *which*), as in the following examples. Note the punctuation in each.

▶The flight was long and cramped. The food was imaginative.

Transition: The flight was long and cramped; *however,* the food was imaginative.

The flight was long and cramped; the food, *however,* was imaginative.

Coordination:	The flight was long and cramped, *but* the food was imaginative.
Subordination:	*Although* the flight was long and cramped, the food was imaginative.
	The flight, *which* was long and cramped, provided imaginative food.

▶Brillo pads work well. I don't give them as gifts.

▶Brillo pads work well; however, I don't give them as gifts.

▶Brillo pads work well, but I don't give them as gifts.

▶Although Brillo pads work well, I don't give them as gifts.

17 The Fourth C: Commit

According to E. B. White, William Strunk, Jr., "scorned the vague, the tame, the colorless, the irresolute. He felt it was worse to be irresolute than to be wrong." Section 17 focuses on ways to be bold, colorful, and resolute.

17a Commit to a confident stance.

Use language that shows your commitment to your thesis and command of your material. When you are trying to persuade your readers to accept your point of view, avoid the language of ambivalence and indecisiveness evident in words and phrases like *maybe, perhaps, might, it could be, it could happen, it might seem,* and *it would appear.* Do not appear ambivalent or apologetic. Aim for language that reflects accountability and commitment: *as a result, consequently, of course, believe, need, demand, think, should, must.* Use the language of commitment, however, only after you have thoroughly researched your topic and found the evidence convincing.

17b Commit to an appropriate and consistent tone.

For most academic writing, commit resolutely to an objective, serious tone. Avoid sarcasm, colloquial language, name-calling, or pedantic words and structures, even in the name of variety. Make sure you dedicate a special reading of a draft to examining your tone; if you are reading along and a word or sentence strikes you as unexpected or out of place, flag it for later revision. In formal college essays, watch out especially for sudden switches to a chatty and conversational tone, as in "Nutrition plays a large part in whether people *hang on to* their own teeth as they age." (You would revise *hang on to*, changing it to *retain*.) However, maintaining an appropriate and consistent tone does not mean using big words and stuffy, pedantic language. Pretentious language makes reading difficult, as the following example shows:

▷When a female of the species ascertains that a male with whom she is acquainted exhibits considerable desire to extend their acquaintance, that female customarily will first engage in protracted discussion with her close confidantes.

Simplify your writing if you find sentences like that in your draft. Here are some words to watch out for:

Stuffy	Direct	Stuffy	Direct
ascertain	find out	optimal	best
commence	begin	prior to	before
deceased	dead	purchase	buy
endeavor	try	reside	live
finalize	finish	terminate	end
implement	carry out	utilize	use

Since tone is really a function of how you anticipate readers' expectations, ask a tutor or friend to read your writing and note any lapses in consistency of tone.

18 The Fifth C: Choose Vivid, Appropriate, and Inclusive Words

Word choice, or *diction*, contributes a great deal to the effect your writing has on a reader. Do not give readers puzzles to solve.

18a Choose vivid and specific words.

Choosing vivid words means avoiding clichés. Avoid sayings that have been heard and read too often, like *hit the nail on the head, crystal clear, better late than never,* and *easier said than done.* Use words that are vivid, descriptive, and specific. Provide details to create visual images for your readers. General words such as *area, aspect, certain* ("a certain expression," for example), *circumstance, factor, kind, manner, nature, situation, nice,* and *thing* are vague and do not give a reader much information.

Vague	**The girl in Kincaid's story "Girl" did many things often regarded as women's jobs.** [*Things* is a vague word.]
Specific	**The girl in the story did many household chores often regarded as women's work: she washed the clothes, cooked, swept, set the table, and cleared away dishes.**

18b Avoid slang, regionalisms, and jargon.

Slang   When you write college essays, your tone and diction should consistently be formal rather than colloquial. Avoid slang and colloquial expressions, such as *folks, guy, OK, okay, pretty good, hassle, kind of interesting/nice, too big of a deal, a lot of, lots of,* and *a ways away.* Do not enclose a slang expression in quotation marks to signal to your readers that you know it is inappropriate. Instead, revise.

►The working conditions were "~~gross.~~" ^disgusting^

►I did ~~great~~ ^well^ in my last job.

►The jury returned the verdict that the ~~guy~~ ^defendant^ was not guilty.

Regional language   Use regional and ethnic dialects in writing only when you are quoting someone directly: "*Your car needs fixed,*" he advised. Otherwise, use standard forms.

►I bought ~~me~~ ^myself^ a backpack.

►She used to ~~could~~ ^be able to^ run two miles, but now she's out of shape. ^

Jargon   Most areas of specialized work and study have their own technical words, which people outside those fields perceive as jargon. A sportswriter writing about baseball will, for instance, refer to *twinight doubleheaders, ERAs,* and *brushbacks.* A linguist writing about language will use terms like *phonemics, kinesics,* and *suprasegmentals.* If you know that your audience is familiar with the technical vocabulary of the field, specialized language is acceptable. Try to avoid jargon when writing for a more general audience; if you must use technical terms, provide definitions that will make sense to your audience.

18c Avoid biased and exclusionary language.

Do not use divisive terms that reinforce stereotypes or belittle other people. Do not emphasize differences by separating society into *we* to refer to people like you and *they* or *these people* to refer to people different from you. Use *we* only to be truly inclusive of yourself and all your readers. Be aware, too, of terms that are likely to offend. You don't have to be excessive in your zeal to be PC ("politically correct"), using *underachieve* for *fail,* or *vertically challenged* for *short,* but do your best to avoid alienating readers.

Gender   The writer of the following sentence edited it to avoid gender bias in the perception of women's roles and achievements.

> ▶ ~~Mrs. John~~ Andrea Harrison, ~~married to a real estate tycoon and herself~~ the bubbly, ~~blonde~~ chief executive of a successful computer company, has expanded the business overseas.

Choice of words can reveal gender bias, too.

Avoid	Use
actress	actor
chairman	chairperson
female astronaut	astronaut
forefathers	ancestors
foreman	supervisor
mailman	mail carrier
male nurse	nurse
man, mankind (meaning any human being)	person, people, our species, human beings, humanity
manmade	synthetic
policeman, policewoman	police officer
salesman	sales representative, salesclerk
veterans and their wives	veterans and their spouses

With the use of pronouns, too, avoid the stereotyping that occurs by assigning gender roles to professions, such as *he* for a doctor or lawyer, and *she* for a nurse or secretary.

or she
▶Before a surgeon can operate, he must know every detail of the patient's history.

However, often it is better to avoid the *he* or *she* issue by recasting the sentence or using a plural noun or pronoun.

▶Before operating, a surgeon must know every detail of the patient's history.

▶Before surgeons can operate, they must know every detail of the patient's history.

See **24c** for more on pronouns and gender.

Race and place   Name a person's race only when it is relevant.

▶Attending the meeting were three doctors and an ~~Asian~~ computer programmer.

Use the names people prefer for their racial or ethnic affiliation. Consider, for example, that *black* and *African American* are preferred terms; *Native American* is preferred to *American Indian; Asian* is preferred to *Oriental.* Be careful, too, with the way you refer to countries and continents; the Americas include both North and South America. Avoid stereotyping people according to where they come from. Some British people may be stiff and formal, but not all are. Not all Germans eat sausage and drink beer; not all North Americans carry cameras and wear plaid shorts.

Age   Avoid derogatory, condescending, or disrespectful terms associated with age. Refer to a person's age or condition neutrally, if at all: not *well-preserved little old lady* but *woman in her eighties* or just *woman.*

Politics   Words referring to politics are full of connotations. The word *liberal,* for instance, has been used with positive and negative connotations in various election campaigns. Take care with words like *radical, left-wing, right-wing,* and *moderate.* Are you identifying with one group and implicitly criticizing other groups?

Religion   An old edition of an encyclopedia referred to "devout Catholics" and "fanatical Muslims." The new edition refers to both Catholics and Muslims as "devout," thus eliminating biased language. Examine your use of words that sound derogatory or exclusionary, such as *cult* or *fundamentalist;* terms—such as *those people*—that emphasize difference; or even the word *we* when it implies that all your readers share (or should share) your beliefs.

Health and abilities   Avoid terms like *confined to a wheelchair* and *victim* (of a disease) so as not to focus on difference and disability. Instead, write *someone who uses a wheelchair* and *person with* (a disease). However, do not draw unnecessary attention to a disability or an illness. In particular, avoid terms such as *retarded* or *handicapped*.

Sexual orientation   Refer to a person's sexual orientation only if the information is necessary to your content. To say that someone was "defended by a homosexual lawyer" is gratuitous when describing a case of stock market fraud but may be relevant in a case of discrimination against homosexuals. Since you will not necessarily know your readers' sexual orientation, do not assume it is the same as your own, and beware of using terms and making comments that might offend.

***The word* normal**   One word to be especially careful about using is *normal*—when referring to your own health, ability, or sexual orientation. Some readers could justifiably find that offensive.

Part Six

Common Sentence Problems

19 Sentence Fragments

20 Run-ons and Comma Splices

21 Sentence Snarls

22 Verbs

23 Subject-Verb Agreement

24 Pronouns

25 Adjectives and Adverbs

133

PART SIX Common Sentence Problems

19 Sentence Fragments, 135

19a Identifying and correcting, 135
19b Dependent clause, 135
19c Phrase, 136
19d Intentional, 137

20 Run-ons and Comma Splices, 138

20a Identifying, 138
20b Correcting, 138

21 Sentence Snarls, 141

21a Tangles: Mixed constructions, faulty comparisons, and convoluted syntax, 141
21b Misplaced modifiers: *Only, even,* and split infinitives, 142
21c Dangling modifiers, 143
21d Shifts: Statements/ commands, indirect/ direct quotation, tense, and point of view, 144
21e Logical sequence after the subject, 144
21f Parallel structures, 145
21g Definitions and reasons: *Is when* and *the reason is because,* 145
21h Necessary words, 146

22 Verbs, 146

22a Verb forms, 147
22b Verb forms after auxiliaries, 151
22c Verbs commonly confused, 152
22d Tenses, 153

22e *-ed* forms, 156
22f Conditional sentences, wishes, requests, demands, and recommendations, 157
22g Passive voice, 159

23 Subject-Verb Agreement, 160

23a Basic principles, 160
23b Subject separated from verb, 160
23c Subject after verb, 161
23d Tricky subjects, 162
23e Collective nouns (*family, jury, the young*), 163
23f Compound subjects (with *and* and *or*), 163
23g Indefinite pronouns (*someone, anyone*), 164
23h Quantity words, 164
23i Relative clauses (*who, which, that*), 165

24 Pronouns, 165

24a Personal pronouns (*I* or *me, he* or *him?*), 165
24b Clear reference, 168
24c Agreement with antecedent, 169
24d Appropriate use of *you,* 170
24e Relative pronouns: *who, whom, which, that,* 170

25 Adjectives and Adverbs, 171

25a Correct forms, 171
25b Proper use, 172

25c Compound adjectives, 173

25d Double negatives, 173

25e Comparative and superlative forms, 173

25f Faulty and incomplete comparisons, 174

19 Sentence Fragments

19a Identifying and correcting fragments

An accurately formed, complete sentence is the basic building block of any written document. A complete sentence needs at least the following:

1. a capital letter at the beginning
2. an independent clause containing a subject and a complete verb
3. appropriate end punctuation: period, question mark, exclamation point, or semicolon

The elements are labeled in the following sentence:

independent clause containing

subject — verb

▶ The name *Google* comes from the word *googol*.

capital letter   end punctuation

A fragment is an incomplete sentence incorrectly punctuated as if it were a complete sentence. The following is a fragment with no independent clause:

Fragment Which is the mathematical term for a one followed by a hundred zeros.

You can often make a fragment into a complete sentence by adding or changing words or by connecting the fragment to a complete sentence.

Possible revision *Googol* is the mathematical term for a one followed by a hundred zeros.

Possible revision The name *Google* comes from the word *googol*, which is the mathematical term for a one followed by a hundred zeros.

19b Dependent clause fragments

A dependent clause beginning with a subordinating word such as *because, if, unless, when, as soon as, whenever, while, although, that, which,* or *who* (or with a question word such as *how, what,* or *why*) cannot stand alone and be punctuated as an independent clause. Choose whichever of the following two methods of repair works better.

1. Connect the dependent clause to a nearby independent clause.

   ▶The candidates agreed on most issues, ~~Until~~ ^{until} they debated on television.

2. Delete the conjunction at the beginning of the dependent clause. The dependent clause then becomes an independent clause, which can stand alone.

   ▶The author describes her family life with her

   parents and seven siblings. ~~How~~ She grew up following her parents' values.

NOTE: A subordinating conjunction at the beginning of a sentence does not always signal a fragment. A correctly punctuated sentence may begin with a subordinating conjunction introducing a dependent clause, but the sentence will also contain an independent clause.

```
          ┌──────── dependent clause ────────┐
```
▶Although scientists observe global warming,
```
          ┌──────── independent clause ───────┐
```
winters here appear to be getting colder.

19c Phrase fragments

A phrase is a group of words without a subject, a verb, or both. A phrase punctuated as if it were a complete sentence is a phrase fragment, which you need to revise.

▶*Cold Mountain* tells a universal story. ~~A story~~ of love and loss. However, many viewers felt the movie was one big cliché.

Correct phrase fragments in the following ways:

1. Delete the period and attach the phrase to a nearby independent clause to form a complete sentence. When you delete the period, you may need to add a comma or a colon to attach the former fragment to a clause.

   ▶The architect recommends solar panels. ~~To~~ ^{to} save on heating bills.

►As a child, Isabella Rossellini was diagnosed with

scoliosis. A disease of the spine.
    , a

►The space probe landed safely. Providing detailed
    , providing
geological information.

►Our schools need two basic improvements. Smaller
    : smaller
classes and better teachers.

2. Rewrite the phrase as an independent clause with its own subject and complete verb.

►Nature held many attractions for Thoreau.
Especially, the solitude nature provided.
    he valued

►Thoreau felt connected to his hometown of
Concord. For instance, returning to live there
    he returned
after college.

3. Include any missing verb or subject—especially an "it" subject (see **15b**).

►Too few people aware of the dangers of
    are
genetically engineered food.

►Doctors often point out that is wise to avoid
    it
eating salty or sugary snacks.

NOTE: One subject cannot be the subject of two verbs across two sentences. Correct a fragment beginning with *And* or *But* by removing the period and capital letter; the second verb then is attached to the subject in the independent clause, creating a compound predicate.

►After an hour, the dancers changed partners.
    and
And adapted to a different kind of music.

19d Intentional fragments

Fragments are used frequently in advertisements to keep the text short. In academic writing, writers sometimes use a fragment intentionally for emphasis, after a question, as an exclamation, or at a point of transition.

▶Did Virginia know that Tom was writing frequently at this time to Leonard asking for advice? Probably.
—Hermione Lee, *Virigina Woolf*

In college essays, use intentional fragments sparingly.

20 Run-ons and Comma Splices

20a Identifying run-on (or *fused*) sentences and comma splices

Readers expect two independent clauses to be separated—and by more than a comma alone.

Run-on error

├─────────────independent clause─────────────┤
▶Blue jeans were originally made as tough work clothes
├──────────independent clause──────────┤
they became a fashion statement in the 1970s.

Comma splice error

▶Blue jeans were originally made as tough work clothes, they became a fashion statement in the 1970s.

20b Five options for correcting run-on sentences and comma splices

KEY POINTS

Options for Editing a Run-on or Comma Splice

1. Separate the sentences. (Create two complete and separate sentences by adding either a period or a semicolon between the two or by adding a question mark, if appropriate.)

   ▶Blue jeans were originally made as tough work clothes. *They* became a fashion statement in the 1970s.

   ▶Blue jeans were originally made as tough work clothes; *they* became a fashion statement in the 1970s.

(Continued)

(Continued)

2. Include a comma, but make sure it is followed by *and, but, or, nor, so, for,* or *yet* (one of the seven coordinating conjunctions).

   ▶ Blue jeans were originally made as tough work clothes, *but* they became a fashion statement in the 1970s.

3. Separate the sentences with a period or a semicolon, followed by a transitional expression such as *however* or *therefore,* followed by a comma.

   ▶ Blue jeans were originally made as tough work clothes; *however,* they became a fashion statement in the 1970s.

4. Rewrite the sentences as one sentence by using a subordinating conjunction to make one clause dependent upon the other.

   ▶ *Although* blue jeans were originally made as tough work clothes, they became a fashion statement in the 1970s.

5. Condense or restructure the sentence.

   ▶ Blue jeans, *originally* made as tough work clothes, became a fashion statement in the 1970s.

Often several options will work grammatically. To choose the most desirable option, consider the nature of the sentences, the clause you want to emphasize, and the structure of surrounding sentences, as in the following examples.

Option 1   Separate the sentences.

- Insert a period when the two independent clauses are long.

  ▶ Sheep Meadow in Central Park actually had sheep
  . The
  grazing on it until 1934, the sheep saved the city the
  expense of mowing and fertilizing.

- Use a semicolon to separate independent clauses closely connected in meaning or indicating a contrast.

  ;
  ▶ Documentaries show us history in action, Hollywood movies force us to sort out fact from fiction.

- Use a question mark to end a clause that asks a question.

▶Why do more and more new diet fads appear, <del>people</del> **? People** should realize the value of exercise instead.

NOTE: If the second clause offers an explanation of the first, the use of a colon or a dash is possible.

▶Students frequently comment on older people's choice of words, **: T**their grandmothers say "dungarees" and "slacks" instead of "jeans" and "pants."

Option 2 Include a comma, but make sure it is followed by *and, but, or, nor, so, for,* or *yet.* This option is appropriate when the two independent clauses are not excessively long and can logically be linked to each other with one of the coordinating conjunctions.

▶A pickup truck is good for country living, **but** a sports car will get stuck in the mud.

Option 3 Separate the sentences with a period or a semicolon, followed by a transitional expression (such as *however, in addition,* or *therefore*), and then a comma. This option is appropriate when you are switching direction and want to stress the second of the two clauses.

▶Ambiguity can be an effective literary device, **; however,** <del>however</del> sometimes ambiguity is unintentionally funny.

Option 4 Rewrite the sentences as one sentence by using a subordinating conjunction to make one clause dependent on the other. This option is appropriate when one clause can be used effectively to introduce, establish a context for, or otherwise "set up" the clause containing the more notable point.

▶**When monarch** <del>Monarch</del> butterflies migrate south they sometimes travel as many as 2,000 miles.

NOTE: Do not include a comma between the two clauses if the dependent clause occurs after the independent clause.

▶Monarch butterflies sometimes travel as many as 2,000 miles when they migrate south.

Option 5 Condense or restructure the sentence. This option is a good way to eliminate wordiness and repetition and to make your prose flow more smoothly. A useful way to restructure a run-on or a comma splice is to make a clause into a phrase using an *-ing* form of a verb.

▶Engineers worked on the plans, ~~they made~~ *making* the bridge less vulnerable to an earthquake.

21 Sentence Snarls

Avoid or edit sentences with structural inconsistencies that make readers pause to untangle their meaning.

21a Tangles: Mixed constructions, faulty comparisons, and convoluted syntax

Mixed constructions A mixed construction is a sentence with parts incompatible in grammar and meaning. The sentence begins one way and then veers off in an unexpected direction. Check to ensure that the subject and verb in your sentence are clear and work together. Do not use a pronoun to restate the subject (**36a** ESL).

▶~~In the~~ *The* excerpt by Heilbrun and the story by Gould are similar.

▶~~By working~~ *Working* at night can create tension with family members.

▶Dinah Macy ~~she~~ got Lyme disease when she was ten.

When you start a sentence with a dependent clause (beginning with a word like *when, if, because,* and *since*), make sure you follow that clause with an independent clause. A dependent clause cannot serve as the subject of a verb.

▶~~Because she swims~~ *Swimming* every day does not guarantee she is healthy.

▶~~When~~ *Trading* a baseball player ~~is traded often~~ causes family problems.

Faulty comparisons   When you make comparisons, readers need to know clearly what you are comparing. See also **24a** for faulty comparisons with personal pronouns.

Faulty comparison	**Like Wallace Stevens, her job strikes readers as unexpected for a poet.** [It is not her job that is like the poet Wallace Stevens; her job is like his job.]
Revised	**Like Wallace Stevens, she holds a job that strikes readers as unexpected for a poet.**

Convoluted syntax   Revise sentences that ramble on to such an extent that they become tangled. Make sure they have clear subjects, verbs, and connections between clauses.

Tangled	**The way I feel about getting what you want is that when there is a particular position or item that you want to try to get to do your best and not give up because if you give up you have probably missed your chance of succeeding.**
Possible revision	**To get what you want, keep trying.**

21b Misplaced modifiers

Keep words, phrases, and clauses that provide adjectival or adverbial information next to the sentence elements that they modify. That is, avoid *misplaced modifiers*.

▶ Next year, everyone in the company will ~~not~~ get a raise.
                                                 ^not

[The unrevised sentence says that nobody at all will get a raise. If you move *not,* the sentence now says that although not all workers will get a raise, some will.]

Take care with words such as **only**.   Place a word such as *only, even, just, nearly, not, merely,* or *simply* immediately before the word it modifies. The meaning of a sentence can change significantly as the position of a modifier changes, so careful placement is important.

▶ *Only* the journalist began to investigate the incident.
  [no one else]

▶ The journalist *only* began to investigate the incident.
  [but didn't finish]

▶The journalist began to investigate *only* the incident. [nothing else]

Place a phrase or clause close to the word it modifies.

Misplaced   Sidel argues that young women's dreams will not always come true in her essay.

Revised   In her essay, Sidel argues that young women's dreams will not always come true.

Consider the case for splitting an infinitive.   You split an infinitive when you place a word or phrase between *to* and the verb. Avoid splitting an infinitive when the split is unnecessary or the result is clumsy, as in the following:

▶They waited for the sun to shine brightly. ~~to brightly shine.~~

▶We want ~~to honestly and in confidence inform~~ you of our plans. to inform honestly and in confidence.

    Traditionally, a split infinitive was frowned upon, but it is now much more acceptable, as in the *Star Trek* motto "To boldly go where no man has gone before. . . ." Sometimes, splitting is necessary to avoid ambiguity.

▶We had *to stop* them from talking *quickly.* [Were they talking too quickly? Did we have to stop them quickly? The meaning is ambiguous.]

▶We had *to quickly stop* them from talking. [The split infinitive clearly says that we were the ones who had to do something quickly.]

21c Dangling modifiers

A modifier beginning with *-ing* or *-ed* that is not grammatically connected to the noun or phrase it is intended to describe is said to *dangle*.

Dangling   *Driving* across the desert, the saguaro *cactus* appeared eerily human. [Who or what was driving? The cactus?]

Usually you can fix a dangling modifier by either (1) making the modifier refer to the person or thing performing the action or (2) rewriting the modifier as a dependent clause.

Possible
revisions

Driving across the desert, *the naturalists* thought the saguaro cactus appeared eerily human.

When the naturalists were driving across the desert, the saguaro cactus appeared eerily human.

21d Shifts

Do not shift abruptly from statements to commands.

They should ask
► Students need to be more aggressive. ~~Ask~~ more questions and challenge the professors.

Do not shift from indirect to direct quotation, with or without quotation marks.

asked us to
► The client told us that he wanted to sign the lease and ~~would we~~ prepare the papers.

Do not shift tenses unnecessarily.

► Some lawyers advance their careers by honest hard work. Others represent~~ed~~ famous clients.

Do not shift point of view.   Be consistent in using pronouns such as *we, you,* and *one.* Avoid using *you* to refer to people generally (**24d**).

we
► We all need a high salary to live in a city because ~~you~~ have to spend so much on rent and transportation.

21e Logical sequence after the subject

Do not use a subject and predicate (verb and object or complement) that do not make logical sense together.

Building
► ~~The decision to build~~ an elaborate extension onto the train station made all the trains arrive late. [It was not the decision that delayed the trains; building the extension did.]

► According to the guidelines, ~~people in~~ dilapidated public housing will be demolished this year. [The housing, not people, will be demolished.]

21f Parallel structures

Balance your sentences by using similar grammatical constructions in each part.

Not parallel	The results of reform were that class size decreased, more multicultural courses, and being allowed to choose a pass/fail option.
Parallel clauses after *that*	The results of reform were that class size decreased, more multicultural courses were offered, and students were allowed to choose a pass/fail option.
Parallel noun phrases	The results of reform were a decrease in class size, an increase in the number of multicultural courses, and the introduction of a pass/fail option for students.

Use parallel structures in comparisons with *as* or *than* and in lists.

To drive
▶ ~~Driving~~ to Cuernavaca is as expensive as to take the bus.

Finding
▶ ~~To find~~ a life partner is infinitely more complex than choosing a new pair of shoes.

▶ Writing well demands the following: (1) planning
your time, (2) paying attention to details, (3) ~~the need for revision,~~ revising, and (4) proofreading.

21g Definitions and reasons: Avoiding *is when* and *the reason is because*

When you write a definition of a term, use parallel structures on either side of the verb *be*. Avoid using *is when* or *is where* (or *was when, was where*).

▶ A tiebreak in tennis *is* ~~where there's~~ a final game to decide a set.

In writing about reasons, avoid *the reason is because.* . . . Grammatically, a clause beginning with *because* cannot follow the verb *be*. Instead, use *the reason is that . . .* or rewrite the sentence.

Faulty	*The reason* Andy Roddick lost *is because* his opponent won the big points.
Possible revisions	*The reason* Roddick lost *is that* his opponent won the big points.
	Roddick lost *because* his opponent won the big points.

21h Necessary words in compound structures and comparisons

Do not omit necessary words in compound structures. If you omit a verb form from a compound verb, the remaining verb form must fit into each part of the compound; otherwise, you must use the complete verb form.

                       tried
► He has always and will always try to preserve his
         ^
father's good name in the community. [*Try* fits only
with *will,* not with *has.*]

Do not omit necessary words in comparisons.

                                             as
► The debate team captain is as competitive or even more
                                            ^
competitive than her teammates. [The comparative
structures are *as competitive as* and *more competitive
than.* Do not merge them.]

Sometimes you create ambiguity for your readers if you omit the verb in the second part of a comparison See also **25f.**

                                    did
► He liked baseball more than his son. [Omitting *did*
                                  ^
implies that he liked baseball more than he liked
his son.]

22 Verbs

Identify a verb by checking to see that the base form (that is, the form found as a dictionary entry) fits one or more of these sentences with any necessary words added to complete the meaning. For example, *vary* will fit; *variety* will not.

They want to ——————. It is going to ——————.

They will ——————. It will ——————.

Verbs tell readers what people or things do and are. Changes in form and tense can convey subtle distinctions, so edit verbs with care.

22a Verb forms in Standard English

All verbs except *be* and modal verbs such as *must* and *can* (**22b**) have five forms. For *regular verbs,* the five forms follow a regular and predictable pattern. Once you know the base form, you can construct all the other forms, using the auxiliaries *be, do,* and *have.*

Base form: the form in a dictionary; used in present tense or after *do* and modal verbs (*like, expect*)

-*s* form: the third person singular form of the present tense (*interprets, tosses*)

-*ing* form: also known as the *present participle;* needs auxiliary verbs to form a complete verb phrase; can also appear in a phrase (*Looking* happy, she accepted the award) and as a noun (gerund—*Waiting* is boring)

Past tense form: forms a complete verb; used without auxiliaries (*governed, approved*)

Past participle form: needs auxiliary verbs to form a complete verb phrase (*has walked, was inspired*); can appear in a phrase (*the elected official; elected* on his war record)

For *be, do, have,* and modal verbs, see **22b**.

		Regular verbs		
Base	**-s**	**-ing present participle**	**Past tense**	**Past participle**
paint	paints	painting	painted	painted
smile	smiles	smiling	smiled	smiled

Irregular verbs do not use -*ed* to form the past tense and the past participle. See the following table for forms of irregular verbs, including the verb *be.*

Irregular verbs

Base form	Past tense	Past participle
arise	arose	arisen
be	was/were	been
bear	bore	born
beat	beat	beaten
become	became	become
begin	began	begun
bend	bent	bent
bet	bet	bet (or betted)
bind	bound	bound
bite	bit	bitten
bleed	bled	bled
blow	blew	blown
break	broke	broken
bring	brought	brought
build	built	built
burst	burst	burst
buy	bought	bought
catch	caught	caught
choose	chose	chosen
cling	clung	clung
come	came	come
cost	cost	cost
creep	crept	crept
cut	cut	cut
deal	dealt	dealt
dig	dug	dug
do	did	done
draw	drew	drawn
drink	drank	drunk
drive	drove	driven
eat	ate	eaten
fall	fell	fallen
feed	fed	fed
feel	felt	felt
fight	fought	fought
find	found	found
flee	fled	fled

Base form	Past tense	Past participle
fly	flew	flown
forbid	forbad(e)	forbidden
forget	forgot	forgotten
forgive	forgave	forgiven
freeze	froze	frozen
get	got	gotten, got
give	gave	given
go	went	gone
grind	ground	ground
grow	grew	grown
hang*	hung	hung
have	had	had
hear	heard	heard
hide	hid	hidden
hit	hit	hit
hold	held	held
hurt	hurt	hurt
keep	kept	kept
know	knew	known
lay	laid	laid (see also **22c**)
lead	led	led
leave	left	left
lend	lent	lent
let	let	let
lie	lay	lain (see also **22c**)
light	lit, lighted	lit, lighted
lose	lost	lost
make	made	made
mean	meant	meant
meet	met	met
put	put	put
quit	quit	quit
read	read	read
ride	rode	ridden
ring	rang	rung
rise	rose	risen (see also **22c**)
run	ran	run

*Hang in the sense of "put to death" is regular: hang, hanged, hanged.

Base form	Past tense	Past participle
say	said	said
see	saw	seen
seek	sought	sought
sell	sold	sold
send	sent	sent
set	set	set (see also **22c**)
shake	shook	shaken
shine	shone	shone
shoot	shot	shot
shrink	shrank	shrunk
shut	shut	shut
sing	sang	sung
sink	sank	sunk
sit	sat	sat (see also **22c**)
slay	slew	slain
sleep	slept	slept
slide	slid	slid
slit	slit	slit
speak	spoke	spoken
spend	spent	spent
spin	spun	spun
spit	spit, spat	spit
split	split	split
spread	spread	spread
spring	sprang	sprung
stand	stood	stood
steal	stole	stolen
stick	stuck	stuck
sting	stung	stung
stink	stank (or stunk)	stunk
strike	struck	struck, stricken
swear	swore	sworn
sweep	swept	swept
swim	swam	swum
swing	swung	swung
take	took	taken
teach	taught	taught
tear	tore	torn

Base form	Past tense	Past participle
tell	told	told
think	thought	thought
throw	threw	thrown
tread	trod	trodden, trod
understand	understood	understood
upset	upset	upset
wake	woke	waked, woken
wear	wore	worn
weave	wove	woven
weep	wept	wept
win	won	won
wind	wound	wound
wring	wrung	wrung
write	wrote	written

22b Verb forms after auxiliaries

An independent clause needs a *complete verb*. Verb forms such as the *-ing* form and the past participle are not complete, because they do not show tense. They need auxiliary verbs to complete their meaning as a verb of a clause.

Auxiliary verbs	Modal auxiliary verbs	
do: does, do, did	will, would	shall, should
be: be, am, is, are, was, were, being, been	can, could	may, might, must
have: has, have, had		

Auxiliary verbs and modal auxiliary verbs can be used in combination. Whatever the combination, the verb form immediately following the final auxiliary or modal verb is fixed: base form, *-ing*, or past participle.

Which form should I use?

1. Immediately after *do, does, did,* and the nine modal verbs—*will, would, can, could, shall, should, may, might,* and *must*—use the base form.

   ▶ The gecko *can climb* on vertical surfaces.

   ▶ Unfortunately, the therapy *did* not *cure* the patient.

   ▶ The elementary school *should have* bought more art supplies.

2. After *has, have,* and *had,* use the past participle.

   ▶ The computer *has detected* a problem.

   ▶ They should *have gone* to the parade. [not "should have went"]

   In informal speech, we run sounds together, and the pronunciation may be mistakenly carried over into writing.

   ▶ She should ~~of~~ left that job last year.
   ^{have}

   The pronunciation of the contraction *should've* is probably responsible for the nonstandard form *should of.* Edit carefully for the appearance of the word *of* in place of *have* in verb phrases.

3. After *be, am, is, are, was, were,* and *been,* use the *-ing* form for active voice verbs.

   ▶ The new taxes *are penalizing* the middle class.

   ▶ The voters will *be showing* their disapproval.

   e s l *Be + -ing* Always use a *be* auxiliary before the *-ing* form. The *-ing* form alone can never be a complete verb in a clause.

   ▶ Angry crowds gathering.
   ^{are}   ■

4. After *be, am, is, are, was, were, been,* and *being,* use the past participle for the passive voice (see **22g**).

   ▶ The fossils *were removed* to a safe location.

   ▶ The corrupted file should *be quarantined.*

   ▶ His speech might have *been plagiarized.*

   e s l *Be, Been,* and *Being* *Be* requires a modal before it to form a complete verb (*could be jogging, will be closed*). *Been* requires *have, has,* or *had* (*have been driving, has been eaten*). *Being* must be preceded by *am, is, are, was,* or *were* to form a complete verb and must be followed by a past participle: *He was being followed.* ■

22c Verbs commonly confused

Give special attention to verbs that are similar in form but different in meaning. Some of them can take a direct object; these are called *transitive verbs.* Others never take a direct object; these are called *intransitive verbs.*

1. *rise:* to get up; ascend (intransitive, irregular)
   raise: to lift; to cause to rise (transitive, regular)

Base	-s	-ing	Past tense	Past participle
rise	rises	rising	rose	risen
raise	raises	raising	raised	raised

▶The sun *rose* at 5:55 a.m. today.

▶The historian *raised* the issue of accuracy.

2. *sit:* to occupy a seat (intransitive, irregular)
   set: to put or place (transitive, irregular)

sit	sits	sitting	sat	sat
set	sets	setting	set	set

▶The audience *sat* on hard wooden seats.

▶The artist *set* his sculpture in the middle of the shelf.

3. *lie:* to recline (intransitive)
   lay: to put or place (transitive)

lie	lies	lying	lay	lain
lay	lays	laying	laid	laid

lay
▶She ~~laid~~ down for an hour after her oral presentation.

lying
▶She was ~~laying~~ down when you called.

Lay
▶~~Lie~~ the map on the floor.

In addition, note the verb *lie* ("to say something untrue"), which is intransitive and regular.

Base	-s	-ing	Past tense	Past participle
lie	lies	lying	lied	lied

▶He *lied* when he said he had won three trophies.

22d Verb tenses

Tenses and time are closely related. Verbs change form to indicate present or past time. Auxiliary verbs (*be, do,* and *have*) are used with the main verb to convey completed actions (perfect forms), actions in progress (progressive forms), and actions that are completed by some specified time or event and that emphasize the length of time in progress (perfect progressive forms).

Simple present   Use the simple present tense for the following purposes:

1. To make a generalization

   ► Gardening *nourishes* the spirit.

2. To indicate a permanent or habitual activity

   ► He *works* for Sony.

   ► The directors *distribute* a financial report every six months.

3. To express future time in dependent clauses (clauses beginning with subordinating words such as *if, when, before, after, until, as soon as*) when *will* is used in the independent clause

   ► When they *arrive,* the meeting will begin.

4. To discuss literature and the arts (called the *literary present*) even if the work was written in the past, or the author is no longer alive

   ► In *Zami,* Audre Lorde *describes* how a librarian *introduces* her to the joys of reading.

   However, when you write a narrative of your own, use past tenses to tell about past actions.

   ~~~~~~~~~~~~~~~~~walked~~~~~~kissed
   ► Then the candidate ~~walks~~ up to the crowd and ~~kisses~~
   all the babies.

Present progressive   Use the present progressive to indicate an action in progress at the moment of speaking or writing.

► He *is playing* pool with his nephew.

e s l   **Verbs of Mental Activity, Appearance, Possession, and Inclusion**   Do not use progressive forms with intransitive verbs such as *believe, know, like, prefer, want, smell, own, seem, appear,* and *contain.*

~~~~~~~~~~~~~~believe
► Many people ~~are believing~~ that there may be life on other planets.   ■

Present perfect and present perfect progressive   Use the present perfect (*has* or *have* followed by a past participle) in the following instances:

1. To indicate that an action occurring at some unstated time in the past is related to present time

   ▶ They *have worked* in New Mexico, so they know its laws.

2. To indicate that an action beginning in the past continues to the present

   ▶ She *has worked* as a paralegal for three years.

   However, if you state the exact time when something occurred, use the simple past tense, not the present perfect.

   ▶ They ~~have~~ worked in Arizona four years ago.

3. To report research results in APA style

   ▶ Feynmann *has shown* that science can be fun.

Use the present perfect progressive when you indicate the length of time an action is in progress up to the present time.

▶ They *have been dancing* for three hours. [This sentence implies that they are still dancing.]

Simple past   Use the simple past tense when you specify exactly when an event occurred or when you illustrate a general principle with a specific incident in the past.

▶ World War I soldiers *suffered* in the trenches.

▶ Some bilingual schools offer intensive instruction in English. My sister *went* to a bilingual school where she *studied* English for two hours every day.

When the sequence of past events is indicated with words like *before* or *after,* use the simple past for both events.

▶ She *knew* how to write her name before she *went* to school.

Use past tenses in an indirect quotation introduced by a past tense verb.

▶ His chiropractor *told* him that the adjustments *were* over.

Past progressive   Use the past progressive for an activity in progress over time or at a specified point in the past.

▶ Abraham Lincoln *was attending* the theater when he was assassinated.

Past perfect and past perfect progressive Use the past perfect or past perfect progressive when one past event was completed before another past event occurred.

▶ The professor announced that she *had revised* the syllabus. [She revised before she announced.]

▶ Ben *had cooked* the whole meal by the time Sam arrived. [Two events occurred: Ben cooked the meal; then Sam arrived.]

▶ He *had been cooking* for three hours when his sister finally offered to help. [An event in progress—cooking—was interrupted in the past.]

22e -ed forms (past tense and past participle)

With regular verbs, both the past tense form and the past participle form end in *-ed*. This ending can cause writers trouble, since in speech the ending is often dropped—particularly when it blends into the next sound. Standard English requires the *-ed* ending in the following instances:

1. To form the past tense of a regular verb

   ▶ Her assistant ask~ed~ to take on more responsibility.

   Pay attention to the verb used to express a past habit.

   ▶ Roger Clemens use~d~ to pitch for the Yankees.

2. To form the past participle of a regular verb for use with the auxiliary *has, have,* or *had* in the active voice or with forms of *be* (*am, is, are, was, were, be, being, been*) in the passive voice (see **22g**)

   ▶ She has work~ed~ there for a long time. [Active]

   ▶ The work will be finish~ed~ tomorrow. [Passive]

3. To form a past participle used as an adjective

   ▶ The nurses rushed to help the injure~d~ toddler.

   ▶ I was surprise~d~ to read how many awards he had won.

NOTE: The following *-ed* forms are used after forms of *be* or *get: concerned, confused, depressed, divorced, embarrassed, married, prejudiced, satisfied, scared, supposed (to), surprised, used (to), worried*. See also **35e ESL**.

d
►She was confuse by the language in the mortgage application.
 ^

d
►They were suppose to call their parents.
 ^

Do not confuse the past tense and past participle forms of irregular verbs (**22a**). A past tense form occurs alone as a complete verb, and a past participle form must be used with a *have* or *be* auxiliary.

drank
►He ~~drunk~~ the liquid before his medical tests.
 ^

did
►She ~~done~~ her best to learn how to count in Japanese.
 ^

gone
►The explorers could have ~~went~~ alone.
 ^

rung
►The bell is ~~rang~~ five times for an emergency.
 ^

22f Verbs in conditional sentences, wishes, requests, demands, and recommendations

Conditions When *if* or *unless* is used to introduce a dependent clause, the sentence expresses a condition. There are four types of conditional sentences; two refer to actual or possible situations, and two refer to speculative or hypothetical ones.

KEY POINTS

Verb Tenses in Conditional Sentences

Meaning expressed	*If* clause	Independent clause
1. Fact	Simple present	Simple present

► If people *earn* more, they *spend* more.

2. Prediction/ possibility	Simple present	*will, can, should, might* + base form

► If you *turn* left here, you *will reach* Mississippi.

(Continued)

(Continued)

3. Speculation about present or future	Simple past or subjunctive *were*	*would, could, should, might* + base form

▶ If he *had* a cell phone, he *would use* it. [But he does not have one.]

▶ If she *were* my lawyer, I *might win* the case. [But she is not.]

4. Speculation about past	Past perfect (*had* + past participle)	*would have* *could have* *should have* *might have* } + past participle

▶ If they *had saved* the diaries, they *could have sold* them. [But they did not save them.]

NOTE: Do not use *would* in the conditional clause. However, *would* occurs frequently in the conditional clause in speech.

▶ If the fish fry committee ~~would show~~ ^showed^ more initiative, more people might attend the events.

▶ If the speaker ~~would have~~ ^had^ heard their criticisms, she would have been angry.

Wishes For a present wish—about something that has not happened and is therefore hypothetical and imaginary— use the past tense or the subjunctive *were* in the dependent clause. For a wish about the past, use the past perfect: *had* + past participle.

A wish about the present

▶ I wish I *had* your attitude.

▶ I wish that Shakespeare *were* still alive.

A wish about the past

▶ Some union members wish that the strike *had* never *occurred.*

Requests, demands, and recommendations After certain verbs, such as *request, command, insist, demand, move* (meaning "propose"), *propose,* and *urge,* use the base form of the verb (in the subjunctive mood) regardless of the person and number of the subject.

▶The dean suggested that students *be* allowed to vote.

▶He insisted that she *hand in* the report.

22g Passive voice

In the active voice, the grammatical subject is the doer of the action, and the sentence gives a straightforward display of "who is doing what." The passive voice tells what *is done to* the subject of the sentence. The person or thing doing the action may or may not be mentioned but is always implied: "My car was repaired" (by somebody at the garage).

Active

active voice verb
(simple past)

┌─ subject ─┐   ┌─ direct object ─┐
▶Alice Walker   wrote   *The Color Purple.*

Passive

passive voice verb
(simple past)

┌─── subject ───┐   ┌─ doer or agent ─┐
▶*The Color Purple* was written by Alice Walker.

To form the passive voice, use an appropriate tense of the verb *be* followed by a past participle. Do not overuse the passive voice. A general rule is to use the passive voice only when the doer in your sentence is unknown or unimportant or when you want to keep subjects consistent (see **16a**).

▶The pandas are rare. Two of them *will be returned* to the wild.

e s l **Passive Voice with Transitive Verbs** Use the passive voice *only* with verbs that are transitive in English. Intransitive verbs such as *happen, occur,* and *try (to)* are not used in the passive voice.

▶The ceremony ~~was~~ happened yesterday. ■

23 Subject-Verb Agreement

23a Basic principles

When you use the present tense, the subject and verb must agree in person (first, second, or third) and number (singular or plural). The ending -s is added to both nouns and verbs but in very different contexts.

🔑 **KEY POINTS**

Two Key Points about Agreement

1. Follow the *one -s rule* in the present tense. You can either put an -s on the noun to make it plural or put an -s on the verb to make it singular (note the irregular forms *is* and *has*). An -s added to both subject and verb is not Standard English.

Faulty agreement	My friends comes over every Saturday.

Possible revisions	My friend comes over every Saturday. (one friend)

	My friends come over every Saturday. (more than one)

2. Do not omit a necessary -s.

   ►Whitehead's novel deal with issues of race
     and morality. *(s added)*

   ►The ~~book~~ on my desk describe life in Tahiti. *(books)*

23b Subject separated from verb

When words separate the subject and the verb, find the verb and ask *Who?* or *What?* about it to determine exactly what the subject is. Ignore any intervening words.

►Her *collection* of baseball cards *is* much admired.
  [What is admired? The subject, *collection,* is singular.]

►The government's *proposals* about preserving the environment *cause* controversy.
  [What things cause controversy? The subject, *proposals,* is plural.]

Do not be confused by intervening words ending in *-s,* such as *always* and *sometimes.* The *-s* ending still must appear on a present tense verb if the subject is singular.

makes
►His assistant always ~~make~~ mistakes.

Phrases introduced by *as well as, along with, together with,* and *in addition to* that come between the subject and the verb do not affect the number of the verb.

wants
►His daughter, as well as his two sons, ~~want~~ him to move nearby.

23c Subject after verb

When the subject comes after the verb in the sentence, the subject and verb must still agree.

1. *Questions*   In a question, the auxiliary verb agrees with the subject, which follows the verb.

   ►*Does* the editor agree to the changes?

   ┌────────── plural subject ──────────┐
   ►*Do* the editor and the production manager agree to the changes?

2. *Initial* **here** *or* **there**   When a sentence begins with *here* or *there,* the verb agrees with the subject, which follows the verb.

   ►There *is* a reason to rejoice.

   ►There *are* many reasons to rejoice.

   e s l   *It* **with a Singular Verb**   *It* does not follow the same pattern as *here* and *there.* Sentences beginning with *it* (which is the subject) always take a singular verb.

   ►It *is* hundreds of miles away.

3. *Inverted order*   When a sentence begins not with the subject but with a phrase preceding the verb, the verb still agrees with the subject, which follows it.

   plural
   ┌prepositional phrase┐ verb ┌plural subject┐
   ►In front of the library sit two stone lions.

23d **Tricky subjects with singular verbs**

1. **Each *and* every**   *Each* and *every* may seem to indicate more than one, but grammatically they are singular words. Use them with a singular verb. See also **23f**.

   ▸ *Every change* in procedures *causes* problems.

   ▸ *Each* of the poems *employs* a different rhyme scheme.

2. ***-ing subjects***   With a noun formed from an *-ing* verb (called a *gerund*) as a subject, always use a singular verb form.

   ▸ *Speaking* in public *causes* many people as much fear as death.

3. ***Singular nouns ending in -s***   With nouns that end in *-s*, such as *politics, economics, physics, mathematics,* and *statistics,* use a singular verb to refer to the collective discipline.

   ▸ *Politics is* dirty business.

   Always use a singular verb with *news*.

4. ***Phrases of time, money, and weight***   When the subject is regarded as one unit, use a singular verb.

   ▸ *Five hundred dollars seems* too much to pay.

5. ***Uncountable nouns***   An uncountable noun (such as *furniture, money, equipment, food, advice, happiness, honesty, information, knowledge*) encompasses all the items in its class. An uncountable noun does not have a plural form and is always followed by a singular verb (**34a** ESL).

   ▸ *The information* found in the newspapers *is* not always accurate.

6. ***One of***   *One of* is followed by a plural noun and a singular verb form.

   ▸ *One of* the results *has* special significance.

7. ***The number of***   The phrase *the number of* is followed by a plural noun (the object of the preposition *of*) and a singular verb form.

   ▸ *The number of* reasons *is* growing.

However, with *a number of,* meaning "several," use a plural verb.

▶ A number of reasons *are* listed in the letter.

8. *A title of a work or a word used to refer to a word itself*
Use a singular verb with a title of a work or a word used to refer to a word itself (underlined or italicized).

▶ *Cats was* based on a poem by T. S. Eliot.

▶ In her story, the word *dudes appears* five times.

23e Collective nouns

Generally, use a singular verb form with a collective noun like *class, government, family, jury, committee, group, couple,* or *team.*

▶ The couple *returns* to Niagara Falls every other year.

Use a plural verb if you wish to emphasize differences among the individuals or if members of the group are thought of as individuals.

▶ The jury *are* from a variety of backgrounds.

You can also avoid the issue by revising the sentence.

▶ The members of the jury *are* from a variety of backgrounds.

However, with collective nouns like *police, poor, elderly,* and *young,* always use plural verbs.

▶ The elderly *deserve* our respect.

23f Compound subjects

With and   When a subject has two or more parts joined by *and,* treat the subject as plural and use a plural verb form.

▶ His daughter and his son *want* him to move to Florida.

However, if the two joined parts refer to a single person or thing, use a singular verb.

▶ The restaurant's chef and owner *makes* good fajitas.

With each *or* every   When *each* or *every* is used with a subject that has two or more parts joined by *and,* use a singular verb.

▶ Every project and essay *has* to be completed on time.

▶ Each book and lecture *addresses* the same topic.

With or *or* **nor**   With compound subjects joined by *or* or *nor*, the verb agrees with the part of the subject nearer to it.

▶ Her sister or her *parents plan* to visit her next week.

▶ Neither her parents nor her *sister drives* a station wagon.

23g Indefinite pronouns

Use a singular verb with the following indefinite pronoun subjects.

someone, somebody, something

anyone, anybody, anything

no one, nobody, nothing

everyone, everybody, everything

each, either, neither, one

▶ Nobody *knows* the answer.

▶ Someone *has* been sitting in my chair.

▶ Everyone *agrees* on the filmmaker's motives.

▶ Both films are popular; *neither contains* gratuitous violence.

23h Quantity words

Quantity words can be used alone or to modify a noun. Some are singular; some are plural; some can be used to indicate either singular or plural, depending on the noun they refer to.

Words expressing quantity

With singular nouns and verbs	With plural nouns and verbs
much	many
(a) little	(a) few (see p. 217)
a great deal (of)	several
a large amount (of)	a large number (of)
less	fewer
another	both

▶ Much *has* been accomplished.

▶ Much progress still *needs* to be made.

▶ Many *have* gained from the recent stock market rise.

▶ Many activities *let* everyone participate.

▶ Few of his fans *are* buying his recent book.

You will see and hear *less* used in place of *fewer*, but in formal writing, use only *fewer* to refer to a plural word.

▶ More *movies* have been made this year than last, but *fewer have* made money.

The following quantity words can be used with both singular and plural nouns and verbs: *all, any, half (of), more, most, neither, no, none, other, part (of), some.*

▶ You gave me *some* information. *More* is necessary.

▶ You gave me *some* facts. *More* are needed.

23i Relative clauses (*who, which, that*)

Determine subject-verb agreement within a relative (adjective) clause by asking whether the word that *who, which,* or *that* refers to (its antecedent) is singular or plural.

▶ The book that *has* been at the top of the bestseller list for weeks gives advice about health. [*Book* is the antecedent of *that*.]

▶ The books that *have* been near the top of the bestseller list for a few weeks give advice about making money. [*Books* is the antecedent of *that*.]

For more on relative pronouns, see **24e**.

24 Pronouns

A pronoun is a word that substitutes for a noun, a noun phrase, or another pronoun.

24a Personal pronouns

Personal pronouns change form to indicate person (first, second, or third), number (singular or plural), and function in a clause (case).

KEY POINTS

Forms of Personal Pronouns

Person	Subject	Object	Possessive (+ noun)	Possessive (stands alone)	Intensive and reflexive
First person singular	I	me	my	mine	myself
Second person singular and plural	you	you	your	yours	yourself/ yourselves
Third person singular	he she it	him her it	his her its	his hers its [rare]	himself herself itself
First person plural	we	us	our	ours	ourselves
Third person plural	they	them	their	theirs	themselves

In a compound subject or object with **and**   To decide which pronoun to use with a compound subject or object (*I* or *me, he* or *him,* for example), mentally recast the sentence with only the pronoun in the subject or object position.

►Jenny and ~~me~~ I volunteer in a soup kitchen. [If *Jenny* is dropped, you would have *I volunteer,* not *me volunteer.* Here you need the subject form, *I.*]

►She asked my brother and ~~I~~ me to show an ID. [If *my brother* is dropped, you would have *She asked me to show an ID.* You need the object form, *me.* The form *myself* is used to refer to the subject: *I criticized myself.*]

After a preposition   After a preposition, use an object form.

►Between you and ~~I~~ me, the company is in serious trouble.

After a linking verb   Use the subject form of the pronoun after a linking verb such as *be.*

►Sam confessed that the one to blame was ~~him~~ he. [Many would choose to revise this sentence to sound less formal: "Sam confessed that he was the one to blame."]

With an infinitive   Use an object pronoun after a verb used with an infinitive. When a sentence has only one object, this principle is easy to apply.

▶ The dean wanted *him* to lead the procession.

Difficulties occur with compound objects.

           him and me
▶ The dean wanted ~~he and~~ I to lead the procession.
                 ^
  [The dean wanted *him* to lead/*me* to lead . . .]

In appositive phrases   When using a pronoun in an appositive phrase (one that gives more specific information about a preceding noun), determine whether the noun that the pronoun refers to functions as subject or object in its own clause.

▶ The supervisor praised only two employees, Ramon

   me
 and ~~I~~.
   ^

                                    I
▶ Only two employees, Ramon and ~~me~~, received a bonus.
                                 ^

We or us before a noun   Use *us* when the noun phrase is the direct object of a verb or preposition, *we* when it is the subject.

                 us
▶ The singer waved to ~~we~~ fans.
                   ^

  We
▶ ~~Us~~ fans have decided to form a club.
  ^

In comparisons   In comparisons with *than* and *as,* decide on the subject or object form of the pronoun by mentally completing the comparison.

▶ She is certainly not more intelligent than I.   [. . . than
  I am.]

▶ Jack and Sally work together; Jack sees his boss more
  than she.   [. . . more than she does.]

▶ Jack and Sally work together; Jack sees his boss more
  than her.   [. . . more than he sees Sally.]

Possessive pronoun before an -ing form   Generally, use a possessive pronoun before an *-ing* verb form used as a noun (a *gerund*).

▶ We appreciate *your* participating in the auction.

▶ *Their* winning the marathon surprised us all.

Sometimes, though, the *-ing* form is not used as a noun. In that case, the pronoun preceding the *-ing* form should be the object form.

▶ We saw *them* giving the runners foil wraps.

No apostrophe with possessive pronouns   Even though possessive in meaning, the pronouns *yours, ours, theirs, his,* and *hers* should never be used with an apostrophe. Use an apostrophe only with the possessive form of a noun.

▶ That coat is *Maria's*.   ▶ That is *her* coat.

▶ This hat is *mine*.   ▶ That coat is *hers*.

Do not use *mines.* It is nonstandard. For the distinction between *its* and *it's,* see **27d**.

24b   Clear reference

The noun, noun phrase, or pronoun that a pronoun refers to is known as its *antecedent.*

▶ Because the Canadian skater practiced daily, *she* won the championship. [The antecedent of *she* is *skater.*]

State a specific antecedent.   Avoid using a pronoun such as *they, this,* or *it* without an explicit antecedent.

No specific   When Mr. Rivera applied for a loan, *they*
antecedent   outlined the procedures for him.

       In the preface, *it* states that the author lives
       in Kenya.

Revision   When Mr. Rivera applied to bank officials for
       a loan, *they* outlined the procedures for him.

       The preface states that the author lives in
       Kenya.

Do not make a pronoun refer to a possessive noun or to a noun within a prepositional phrase.

                                   George Orwell
▶ In ~~George Orwell's~~ "Shooting an Elephant," ~~he~~ reports an incident that shows the evil effects of imperialism.

Avoid an ambiguous reference.   Your readers should never be left wondering which *this, they,* or *it* is being discussed.

Ambiguous reference	He faced having to decide whether to move to California. This was not what he wanted to do. [We do not know what *this* refers to: having to decide? moving to California?]
Revision	He faced having to decide whether to move to California. This decision was not one he wanted to make.

24c Agreement with antecedent

A plural antecedent needs a plural pronoun; a singular antecedent needs a singular pronoun.

▶Listeners heard *they* could win free tickets. The ninth caller learned *she* was the winner.

NOTE: Demonstrative pronouns *this* and *that* are singular. *These* and *those* are the plural forms.

A generalized (generic) antecedent   Generic nouns describe a class or type of person or object, such as *a student* meaning "all students." Do not use *they* to refer to a singular generic noun, and make sure that you use *he* and *she* without gender bias (**18c**).

Faulty agreement	When *a student* writes well, *they* can go far in the business world.
Possible revision	When *a student* writes well, *he or she* can go far in the business world.
Better revisions	When *students* write well, *they* can go far in the business world.
	Students who write well often have successful careers.

Often, a plural noun is preferable as it avoids clumsy repetition of *he or she*.

▶We should judge ~~a person~~ by who ~~he or she is~~, not
   people   they are

by the color of ~~his or her~~ skin.
                  their

A collective noun   Refer to a collective noun like *class, family, jury, committee, couple,* or *team* with a singular pronoun.

▶The committee has not yet completed *its* report.

However, when the members of the group named by the collective noun are considered to be acting individually, use a plural pronoun.

▶ The committee began to cast *their* ballots in a formal vote.

An indefinite pronoun Indefinite pronouns such as *one, each, either, neither, everyone, everybody, someone, somebody, something, anyone, anybody, anything, no one, nobody,* and *nothing* are generally singular in form (**23g**). A singular antecedent needs a singular pronoun to refer to it. For many years, the prescribed form in Standard English was *he,* as in sentences such as *Everyone needs his privacy* or *Each person needs his privacy.* Now, however, such usage is regarded as biased; the alternative *he or she* is clumsy; and *they,* while used often in informal writing, is regarded by many as not accurate. Use a plural noun and pronoun instead.

Gender bias	*Everyone* picked up *his* marbles and went home.
Clumsy	*Everyone* picked up *his or her* marbles and went home.
Informal usage	*Everyone* picked up *their* marbles and went home.
Revised	*The children* picked up *their* marbles and went home.

See **18c** for more on gender bias with pronouns.

24d Appropriate use of *you*

In writing, do not use *you* for general reference to mean "people generally." Use *you* only to address the reader directly, as in "If you turn to the table on page 10, you will find. . . ."

▶ While growing up, ~~you~~ teenagers face arguments with ~~your~~ their parents.

24e Relative pronouns: *Who, whom, which, that*

When to use who, which, *or* that Use *who* (or *whom*) to refer to human beings; use *which* or *that* to refer to animals, objects, or concepts. Never use *what* as a relative pronoun.

▶ The teacher ~~which~~ who taught me algebra was strict.

When to use who **or** whom *Whom* is an object pronoun. You will often hear and read *who* in its place, but many readers prefer the standard form.

▶**Whom** [informal *who*] were they describing?

Whom used as a relative pronoun can often be omitted.

▶The players [*whom*] the team honored invited everyone to the party.

Never use *whom* in place of *who* in the subject position of a clause.

▶The dancer *who is doing the tango* is a scientist.

▶They want to know *who* we think *is in charge.*

▶The manager will hire *whoever is qualified.*

When to use which **or** that Generally, use *that* rather than *which* in restrictive clauses (ones that provide necessary rather than extra information—see **26c**). When *that* is the object of its clause, you can omit it. Use *which* when you provide extra information.

▶The book [*that*] you gave me is fascinating.

▶*War and Peace,* which I read in college, is fascinating.

25 Adjectives and Adverbs

Adjectives describe, or modify, nouns or pronouns. They do not add -s or change form to reflect number or gender. Adverbs modify verbs, adjectives, and other adverbs, as well as whole clauses.

Adjective Mr. Lee tried three *different* approaches.

Adverb His new assistant settled down *comfortably.*

25a **Correct forms of adjectives and adverbs**

Check your dictionary for information on adjective and adverb forms not covered here.

Adverb: adjective + -ly Many adverbs are formed by adding *-ly* to an adjective: *intelligent/intelligently*. Sometimes when *-ly* is added, a spelling change occurs: *easy/easily*.

Adjectives ending in -ic To form an adverb from an adjective ending in *-ic*, add *-ally* (*basic, basically; artistic, artistically*), with the exception of *public*, whose adverb form is *publicly*.

Irregular adverb forms Several adjectives do not add *-ly* to form an adverb:

Adjective	Adverb
good	well
fast	fast
hard	hard

▶He is a *good* cook.   ▶He cooks *well*.

NOTE: *Well* can also function as an adjective, meaning "healthy" or "satisfactory."

▶A *well* baby smiles often.   ▶She feels *well* today.

25b When to use adjectives and adverbs

In speech, adjectives (particularly *good, bad,* and *real*) are often used to modify verbs, adjectives, or adverbs. This is nonstandard usage.

             badly   really well
▶She plays chess ~~bad~~.   ▶I sing ~~real good~~.

    After linking verbs like *be, seem, appear,* and *become,* use an adjective (as a complement): She seems *pleasant*.

    Certain verbs, such as *appear, look, feel, smell,* and *taste,* are sometimes used as linking verbs and sometimes used as action verbs. If the modifier tells about the subject, use an adjective. If the modifier tells about the action of the verb, not the subject, use an adverb.

Adjective	She looks *confident* in her new job.
Adverb	She looks *confidently* at all the assembled partners.

Adjective	The steak smells *bad*.
Adverb	The chef smelled the lobster *appreciatively*.

25c Compound adjectives

A compound adjective needs hyphens to connect its parts. Note the form when a compound adjective is used: a hyphen, no noun plural ending, and an *-ed* ending where necessary (see also **32b**).

▶ They have a *five-year-old* daughter. [Their daughter is five years old.]

▶ He is a *left-handed* pitcher. [He pitches with his left hand.]

Many compound adjectives use the *-ed* form: *flat-footed, barrel-chested, broad-shouldered, old-fashioned, well-dressed, left-handed.*

25d Avoiding double negatives

Although some languages and dialects allow more than one negative to emphasize an idea, Standard English uses only one negative in a clause. Words like *hardly, scarcely,* and *barely* are considered negatives. The contraction *-n't* stands for the adverb *not.* Avoid double negatives.

Double negative	We *don't* have *no* excuses.
Revised	We *don't* have *any* excuses.
	We have *no* excuses.

| Double negative | City residents *can't hardly* afford the sales tax. |
| Revised | City residents *can hardly* afford the sales tax. |

25e Comparative and superlative forms

Adjectives and adverbs have *comparative* and *superlative* forms that are used for comparisons. Use the comparative form when comparing two items, people, places, or ideas; use the superlative form when comparing more than two.

	Short adjectives	
	Comparative (comparing two)	Superlative (comparing more than two)
short	shorter	shortest
pretty	prettier	prettiest
simple	simpler	simplest
fast	faster	fastest

Long adjectives and *-ly* adverbs

	Comparative	Superlative
intelligent	more intelligent	most intelligent
carefully	more carefully	most carefully

If you cannot decide whether to use an *-er/-est* form or *more/most,* consult a college dictionary. If there is an *-er/-est* form, the dictionary will say so.

NOTE: Do not use the *-er* form with *more* or the *-est* form with *most.*

▶ The first poem was ~~more~~ better than the second.

▶ Boris is the ~~most~~ fittest person I know.

Irregular forms

	Comparative	Superlative
good	better	best
bad	worse	worst
much/many	more	most
well	better	best
badly	worse	worst

25f Avoiding faulty and incomplete comparisons

Make sure that you state clearly what items you are comparing. Some faulty comparisons can give a reader the wrong idea.

▶ He likes the parrot better than his wife. *(does)*

▶ Williams's poem gives a more objective depiction of the painting than Auden*('s)*. [To compare Williams's poem with Auden's poem, you need to include an apostrophe; otherwise, you compare a poem to the poet W. H. Auden.]

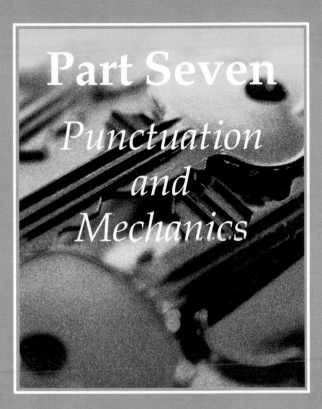

Part Seven

*Punctuation
and
Mechanics*

26 Commas

27 Apostrophes

28 Quotation Marks

29 Other Punctuation Marks

30 Italics and Underlining

31 Capitals, Abbreviations,
and Numbers

32 Hyphens

33 Online Guidelines

175

PART SEVEN Punctuation and Mechanics

26 Commas, 178

26a Comma: Yes, 178
26b Comma: No, 180
26c With extra (nonrestrictive) elements, 181
26d Special uses, 182

27 Apostrophes, 183

27a Apostrophe: Yes and no, 183
27b For possession, 184
27c In plurals, 184
27d It's and its, 185

28 Quotation Marks, 185

28a Punctuation introducing and ending a quotation, 185
28b Dialogue, 186
28c Double and single quotation marks, 187
28d Titles of short works, definitions, and translations, 187
28e When not to use, 187

29 Other Punctuation Marks, 188

29a Periods, question marks, and exclamation points, 188
29b Semicolons, 189
29c Colons, 189

29d Dashes, parentheses, slashes, and brackets, 190
29e Ellipsis dots, 192

30 Italics and Underlining, 192

30a Titles of long, whole works, 193
30b Letters, figures, words as words, and named transportation, 193

31 Capitals, Abbreviations, and Numbers, 193

31a Capitals, 193
31b Abbreviations, 194
31c Numbers, 196

32 Hyphens, 197

32a Hyphens with prefixes, 197
32b Hyphens in compound words, 197
32c Hyphens in numbers, 197
32d End-of-line hyphens, 197

33 Online Guidelines, 198

33a Punctuation in URLs, 198
33b Underlining and italics online, 198

Why do punctuation and mechanics matter? They matter because they chunk words into meaningful groups for readers. Try reading the following without the benefit of the signals a reader usually expects.

When active viruses especially those transmitted by contact can spread easily within the world health organization hard working doctors are continually collaborating to find treatments for several infectious diseases sars avian flu and hepatitis.

Conventional punctuation and mechanics clarify the meaning:

When active, viruses--especially those transmitted by contact--can spread easily; within the World Health Organization, hard-working doctors are continually collaborating to find treatments for several infectious diseases: SARS, avian flu, and hepatitis.

How Punctuation Shows Meaning

What Do You Want to Do?	Options and Further Information
Overall purpose: **To end a sentence**	
To indicate the end of a sentence, with a close connection to the next sentence	Period, question mark, or exclamation point (. ? !) **29a** Semicolon (;) **29b**
Overall purpose: **To separate**	
To separate an introductory word(s), a phrase, or a clause from an independent clause	Comma (,) **26a**, item 2
To separate independent clauses only when a connecting word (*and, but, or, nor, so, for,* or *yet*) is used	Comma (,) **26a**, item 1
To separate items (words, phrases, clauses) in a list (*x, y,* and *z*)	Comma (,) **26a**, item 5
To separate coordinate adjectives	Comma (,) **26a**, item 6
To separate items in a list that contains internal commas (*x, x; y, y;* and *z*)	Semicolon (;) **29b**
To separate a verb from a quoted statement that follows or precedes it	Comma (,) **26a**, item 7
To separate lines of poetry written as running text	Slash (/) **29d**

Overall purpose: To insert

To insert a word, words, or an "extra information" (nonrestrictive) phrase or clause into a sentence	Commas (, ,) **26c**
To give more emphasis to the insert	Dashes (- -) **29d**
To insert a change within a quotation	Square brackets [ ] **29d**
To insert explanatory information	Parentheses ( ) **29d**

Overall purpose: To delete

To indicate material deleted from a quotation	Ellipsis dots (…) **29e**

Overall purpose: To anticipate

To indicate a coming explanation or a list after an independent clause	Colon (:) **29c**

Overall purpose: To quote

To quote exact words or give the title of a story, a poem, or an article	Quotation marks (" ") **28a**
To enclose a quotation within another quotation	Single quotation marks (' ') **28c**

Overall purpose: To indicate possession

For most words	Apostrophe + s ('s) **27a, 27b**
For nouns forming the plural with s	Apostrophe after the s (s') **27a, 27b**

---

26 Commas

A comma separates parts of a sentence; it does not separate one sentence from another. To determine whether to use a comma, follow the guidelines in the boxes in **26a** and **26b**.

26a Comma: Yes

Use the following guidelines, but note that variations can occur.

KEY POINTS

Comma: Yes

1. Between two independent clauses connected by a coordinating conjunction: *and, but, or, nor, so, for,* or *yet*

   ▶The talks failed, but the union leaders held their ground.

   Comma use can be optional if the clauses are short.

   ▶He offered to help and he did.

2. After a phrase or a dependent clause occurring before the subject of the independent clause

   ▶While the guests were eating, a mouse ran across the floor.

   Note how omitting the comma can lead to a misreading.

3. Before and after extra (nonrestrictive) information inserted in a sentence ("extra commas with extra information"—see **26c**)

   ▶Her father, a computer programmer, works late at night.

4. To set off transitional expressions such as *however, therefore, for example,* and *in fact*

   ▶The ending, however, is disappointing. In fact, it is totally predictable.

5. Between items in a series of three or more

   ▶The robot vacuums, makes toast, and plays chess.

6. Between coordinate adjectives that can be reversed and connected with *and*

   ▶When people move, they often discard their worn, dilapidated furniture.

7. To separate a direct quotation from a subject and verb

   ▶"I intend to win an Oscar," she announced.

26b Comma: No

> **KEY POINTS**
>
> **Comma: No**
>
> 1. Not separating subject and verb
>
>   ▶The man in the tuxedo is her English teacher.
>
>   (However, use two commas to set off any extra material inserted between the subject and verb, as in item 3 in **26a**.)
>
> 2. Not before part of a compound structure that is not a complete independent clause
>
>   ▶She won the trophy and accepted it graciously.
>
> 3. Not *after* a coordinating conjunction (*and, but, or, nor, so, for, yet*) connecting two independent clauses, but *before* it
>
>   ▶The movie tried to be engaging, but it failed.
>
> 4. Not between two independent clauses without a coordinating conjunction, which would create a comma splice (**20**). (Use a period or a semicolon instead.)
>
>   ▶The writing had faded⨯it was hard to decipher.
>
> 5. Not separating an independent clause from a following dependent clause introduced by *after, before, because, if, since, unless, until,* or *when* (no comma either before or after the subordinating conjunction)
>
>   ▶She will continue working for the city until she has saved enough money for graduate school.
>
> 6. Not before a clause beginning with *that*
>
>   ▶Jo warned us that the speech would be long.
>
>   However, note that a comma can appear before a *that* clause when it is the second comma of a pair before and after inserted material: *He skates so fast, despite his size, that he will probably break the world record.*
>
>   *(Continued)*

(Continued)

7. Not before and after essential (restrictive) information (**26c**)

   ▸The player who scored the goal became a hero.

   Here the information is essential, answering the question "Which player?"

8. Not between a verb and its object or complement

   ▸The best gifts are food and clothes.

9. Not immediately after *such as*

   ▸Popular fast-food items, such as hamburgers and hot dogs, tend to be high in cholesterol.

10. Not separating cumulative adjectives (that modify the whole phrase that follows)

    ▸the little old stone house

26c Commas with extra (nonrestrictive) elements

Use commas to set off a phrase or clause whenever what is inserted is extra information, that is included almost as an aside or "by the way." If the insertion comes in midsentence, it needs to be set off by a pair of commas.

▸His dog, a big Labrador retriever, is afraid of thunder. [If you read "His dog is afraid of thunder," you would not necessarily need to know what type of dog he owns to understand the point of the sentence. The insert provides additional, not necessary, information.]

▸She loves her car, a red Toyota. [The insert after the comma provides additional information about her car.]

▸My supervisor, who is only twenty-five, has been promoted. [The independent clause "My supervisor has been promoted" does not lead the reader to ask, "Which supervisor?" The relative clause merely adds interesting information; it does not define or restrict the noun *supervisor*.]

Do not use commas to set off essential (restrictive) information.

►**The people who live in the apartment above mine make too much noise.** [If you read only "The people make too much noise," you would ask, "Which people?" The relative clause here restricts "the people" to a subgroup: not all people make too much noise; those in the apartment above do.]

26d Special uses of commas

- Use a comma or commas to set off a phrase that modifies the whole sentence (an absolute phrase).

  ►**The audience looking on in amusement, the valedictorian blew kisses to all her favorite instructors.**

- Use a comma or commas to set off an inserted idea, a contrast, or a conversational tag (such as *yes, no, well,* or a direct address).

  ►**Yes, the author, as he did in his previous book, has again provided inside information about Hollywood.**

  ►**The show dwelt on tasteless, not educational, details.**

  ►**Whatever you build here, Mr. Trump, will cause controversy.**

- Use a comma to separate the day from the year in a date.

  ►**On May 14, 1998, the legendary singer Frank Sinatra died.** [Note, however, that no comma is used before the year in the alternate style for dates when the day precedes the month: 14 May 1998.]

- Use a comma (never a period) to divide numbers into thousands or millions.

  ►**1,200**   ►**515,000**   ►**34,000,000**

  No commas are necessary in years (1999), numbers in addresses (3501 East 10th Street), or page numbers (page 1002).

- Use commas around a person's title or degree.

  ►**Stephen L. Carter, PhD, gave the commencement speech.**

- Use a comma to separate the parts of an address.

  ▶Alice Walker was born in Eatonton, Georgia, in 1944.

  However, do not use a comma before a ZIP code: Berkeley, CA 94704.

27 Apostrophes

Apostrophes show a possessive relationship (*the government's plans*—the plans of the government, belonging to the government). They also signal omitted letters (*wasn't*).

27a Apostrophe: Yes and no

KEY POINTS
Apostrophe: Yes

1. Use -*'s* for the possessive form of all nouns except those already ending in plural -*s: student's, reporter's, women's, boss's.*

2. Use an apostrophe alone for the possessive form of plural nouns ending in -*s: students', bosses'* (**27b**).

3. Use an apostrophe to indicate omitted letters in contracted forms such as *didn't, they're,* and *let's.* However, some readers of formal academic writing may object to such contractions.

4. Use *it's* only for "it is" or "it has": *It's a good idea; it's been a long time* (**27d**).

KEY POINTS
Apostrophe: No

1. Do not use an apostrophe to form plurals of nouns: *big bargains, coming attractions.* See **27c** for rare exceptions.

2. Never use an apostrophe before an -*s* ending on a verb: *She likes him.*

3. Do not use an apostrophe with possessive pronouns (*hers, its, ours, yours, theirs): The house lost its roof.*

(Continued)

(Continued)

4. Do not use an apostrophe to form the plurals of names *(the Browns)*, abbreviations *(VCRs)*, and decades *(the 1990s)*.

5. Do not use an apostrophe to indicate possession with names of buildings, items of furniture, and other objects; instead, use *of: the roof of the hotel, the back of the desk.*

27b Apostrophe to show possession

More than one noun   When you want to indicate separate ownership for two nouns in a sentence, make each one possessive.

▶Updike's and Roth's recent works have received glowing reviews.

For joint ownership, use only one apostrophe: *Sam and Pat's house.*

Compound nouns   Add the -'s to the last part.

▶my brother-in-law's car

Singular words ending in -s   Add -'s for the possessive.

▶Dylan Thomas's imagery

However, when a singular word ending in -s has a -z pronunciation, an apostrophe alone can also be used: *Erasmus's rhetoric* or *Erasmus' rhetoric.*

Plural nouns   If a plural noun does not end in -s, add -'s to form the possessive: *the women's tasks.* Add an apostrophe alone to a noun forming its plural with an -s: *the students' suggestions.*

27c -'s for a plural form: Two exceptions

1. Use -'s for the plural form of letters of the alphabet. Italicize (or underline) only the letter, not the plural ending.

   ▶Georges Perec wrote a novel with no *e*'s in it at all.

2. Use *-'s* for the plural form of a word used to refer to the word itself. Italicize or underline the word used as a word, but do not italicize the *-'s* ending.

▶ You have used too many *but*'s in that sentence.

NOTE: With numbers and abbreviations, MLA guidelines recommend no apostrophe: *the 1900s, CDs, FAQs.* However, you will frequently find these used with *-'s.* Just be consistent in your usage.

27d *It's* and *its*

When deciding whether to use *its* or *it's,* think about meaning. *It's* means *it is* or *it has. Its* means "belonging to it." (Use the apostrophe only if you intend *it is* or *it has.*)

▶ It's a good idea.   ▶ The committee took its time.

---

28 Quotation Marks

Double quotation marks indicate the beginning and end of a quotation or a title of a short work. The text between the quotation marks is marked off as the exact words that someone said, thought, or wrote.

28a Punctuation introducing and ending a quotation

- After an introductory verb, use a comma followed by a capital letter to introduce a direct quotation.

  ▶ Calvin Trillin says, "As far as I'm concerned, *whom* is a word that was invented to make everyone sound like a butler." —In "Whom Says So?"

- Use a colon after a complete sentence introducing a quotation, and begin the quotation with a capital letter.

  ▶ Woody Allen always makes us laugh even about serious issues like wealth and poverty: "Money is better than poverty, if only for financial reasons."   —In *Without Feathers*

When a quotation is integrated into the structure of your own sentence, use no special introductory punctuation other than the quotation marks.

▶Phyllis Grosskurth comments that "anxiety over money was driving him over the brink."

—In *Byron*

- Put periods and commas inside quotation marks, even if these punctuation marks do not appear in the original quotation.

▶When Rosovsky characterizes Bloom's ideas as "mind-boggling," he is not offering praise.

—In *The University*

However, in a documented paper, when you use a parenthetical citation after a short quotation at the end of a sentence, put the period at the end of the citation, not within the quotation. See **9b** for long quotations.

▶Geoffrey Wolff observes that when his father died, there was nothing "to suggest that he had ever known another human being" (11).

—In *The Duke of Deception*

- Put question marks and exclamation points inside the quotation marks if they are part of the original source, with no additional period. When your sentence is a statement, do not use a comma or period in addition to a question mark or exclamation point.

▶She asked, "Where's my mama?"

- Put a question mark, exclamation point, semicolon, or colon that belongs to your sentence outside the closing quotation marks. If your sentence contains punctuation that is your own, not part of the original quotation, do not include it within the quotation marks.

▶The chapter focuses on this question: Who are "the new American dreamers"?

28b Quotation marks in dialogue

Do not add closing quotation marks until the speaker changes or you interrupt the quotation. Begin each new speaker's words on a new line.

▶   "I'm not going to work today," he announced to his son. "Why should I? My boss is away on vacation. And I have a headache."

"Honey, your boss is on the phone," his wife called from the bedroom.

If a quotation from one speaker continues for more than one paragraph, place closing quotation marks at the end of only the *final* paragraph. However, place opening quotation marks at the beginning of every paragraph so that readers realize that the quotation is continuing.

28c Double and single quotation marks

Enclose quotations in double quotation marks. Use single quotation marks for a quotation or title of a short work that occurs within a quotation. (British usage is different.)

▶ Margaret announced, "I have read 'The Lottery' already."

28d Quotation marks with titles of short works, definitions, and translations

Enclose in quotation marks the title of a short work such as a short story, poem, article, song, TV program (not a series), or book chapter.

▶ Ishmael Reed's essay "America: The Multinational Society" begins with an illuminating quotation.

For titles of long works, use italics or underlining (**30a**). Enclose definitions and translations in quotation marks.

▶ The abbreviation *p.m.* means "afternoon."

28e When not to use quotation marks

- Do not use quotation marks with indirect quotations.

  ▶ One woman I interviewed said that her husband argued like a lawyer.

- Do not use quotation marks with clichés, slang, or trite expressions. Instead, revise (**18a** and **18b**).

  involvement.
  ▶ All they want is ~~"a piece of the action."~~

- Do not use quotation marks with long indented quotations. In academic writing, when you use MLA style to quote more than three lines of poetry or four typed lines of prose, indent the whole passage one inch from the left margin. Do not enclose the quoted passage in quotation marks, but retain any internal quotation marks (**9b**).

- Do not use quotation marks around—or underline—your own essay title. Use quotation marks in your title only if your title includes a quotation or the title of a short work.

  ▶The Benefits of Affirmative Action

  ▶Approaches to Education in Charles Baxter's "Gryphon"

29 Other Punctuation Marks

29a Periods, question marks, and exclamation points

Periods, question marks, and exclamation points end a sentence. The Modern Language Association (MLA), in its list of Frequently Asked Questions at <http://www.mla.org>, recommends leaving one space after a punctuation mark at the end of a sentence, but it also sees "nothing wrong with using two spaces after concluding punctuation marks." (Consult your instructor.) In a list of works cited, however, whether MLA or APA, leave only one space after each period in an entry.

Periods (.)   Use a period to end a sentence or to signal an abbreviation: *Mr., Dr., a.m.,* and so forth (see **31b**). Periods are not used in names of government agencies or organizations indicated by initials, in acronyms (abbreviations pronounced as words), or in Internet abbreviations by initials: *ACLU, IRS, NOW, URL.*

Question marks (?)   A question mark signals a direct question.

▶What is he writing?

Do not use a question mark with an indirect question (**36c** ESL).

▶Nobody asked him what he was writing.

Exclamation points (!)   An exclamation point at the end of a sentence tells the reader that the writer considers the statement amazing, surprising, or extraordinary. Avoid overuse, and never accompany an exclamation point with a period, comma, or question mark.

29b Semicolons

- Use a semicolon between two independent clauses to avoid a run-on sentence or a comma splice. Use a semicolon instead of a period when the ideas in two independent clauses are very closely connected, but do not use a capital letter to begin a clause after a semicolon.

  ▶Biography tells us about the subject; biographers also tell us about themselves.

- Use a semicolon between independent clauses when the sentence also contains a transitional expression such as *however, moreover, in fact, nevertheless, above all,* or *therefore* (see **16b** and **26a** for more on transitional expressions).

  ▶The results of the study support the hypothesis; however, further research is necessary.

- Use semicolons to separate items in a list containing internal commas. Items in a list are usually separated by commas. However, using semicolons helps avoid ambiguity in a list in which additional internal commas appear.

  ▶When I cleaned out the refrigerator, I found a chocolate cake, half-eaten; some canned tomato paste, which had a blue fungus growing on the top; and some possibly edible meat loaf.

- Do not use semicolons interchangeably with colons. A colon, not a semicolon, is used to introduce a list or an explanation.

  ▶They contributed a great deal of food: salad, chili, and dessert.

- Do not use a semicolon if a phrase or a dependent clause precedes it, even if that element is long. Use a comma instead.

  ▶Because the training period was so long and arduous for all the players, the manager allowed one visit from family and friends.

29c Colons

A colon (:) follows an independent clause and introduces information that balances or explains that clause. A colon says to a reader, "What comes next will define, illustrate, or explain what you have just read."

- Use a colon after an independent clause to introduce a list, a quotation, an explanation, or a rule.

  ►The students included three pieces of writing in their portfolios: a narrative, an argument, and a documented paper.

  ►Oscar Wilde makes the point well: "The real schools should be the streets."

Note that a capital letter is often used when a complete sentence containing an explanation or a rule follows a colon.

  ►After his cancer treatment, cyclist Lance Armstrong accomplished what many thought impossible: He won the Tour de France six times in a row.

- Use a colon in salutations, letters and memos, precise time notations, titles, and biblical citations.

  Dear Chancellor Witkin:
  To: The Chancellor
  7:20 p.m
  Lessons: A Memoir
  Genesis 37:31–35 (In this case, a period can be used in place of the colon: 37.31–35.)

- Do not use a colon directly after a verb (such as a form of *be* or *include*), a preposition, or expressions such as *for example, especially,* and *such as.*

  ►The book includes a preface, an introduction, an appendix, and an index.

  ►They packed many different items for the picnic, such as taco chips, salsa, bean salad, pita bread, and egg rolls.

  ►His taste is so varied that his living room includes, for example, antiques, modern art, and art deco lighting fixtures.

29d Dashes, parentheses, slashes, and brackets

Dashes (—)   Dashes set off material that is inserted into a sentence. Type a dash or two hyphens with no extra space before, after, or between them. (Recent software will automatically convert two hyphens to a dash as you type.)

▶Armed with one weapon—his wit—he set off.

Commas can sometimes be used to set off inserted material, too, but when the insertion itself contains commas, dashes are preferable.

▶The contents of his closet—torn jeans, frayed jackets, and suits shiny on the seat and elbows—made him reassess his priorities.

Parentheses ( )   Parentheses mark an aside or some supplementary information.

▶Everyone admired Chuck Yeager's feat (breaking the sound barrier).

At the end of a sentence, place the period inside the last parenthesis only when a complete new sentence is enclosed.

▶Chuck Yeager's feat led to competition in the space industry. (He broke the sound barrier.)

Slashes (/)   Use a slash with a space before and after it to separate lines of poetry quoted within your own text. For quoting four or more lines of poetry, see **9b**.

▶Philip Larkin asks a question that many of us relate to: "Why should I let the toad *work* / Squat on my life?"

Slashes are also used to designate word options such as *and/or* and *he/she.* Do not overuse these expressions.

Square brackets ([ ])   Square brackets indicate inserted or changed material within a quotation. Insert only words or parts of words that help the quotation fit into your sentence grammatically or that offer necessary explanation.

▶According to Ridley, information is "the key to both of these features of life [the ability to reproduce and to create order]."

Use [sic] to indicate that an error appears in the original source.

Angle brackets (< >)   Use angle brackets to enclose e-mail addresses and URLs (Web addresses), particularly in an MLA-style works-cited list. See **10c**, items 31–45.

29e Ellipsis dots

Use three ellipsis dots (...) when you omit material from the middle of a quotation (but not at the beginning or end of a quotation unless the omission of part of a sentence occurs at the beginning or end of your own sentence). See also **9b**.

▶Ruth Sidel reports that the women in her interviews "have a commitment to career ... and to independence" (27).

When the omitted material falls at the end of a quoted sentence, put a period before the three ellipsis dots, making four dots in all.

▶Ruth Sidel reports that some women "have a commitment to career, to material well-being, to success, and to independence. ... In short, they want their piece of the American Dream" (27).

To omit material at the end of a quoted sentence when the omission coincides with the end of your own sentence, use three dots, and place the sentence period after the parenthetical reference to the source.

▶Ruth Sidel reports that some women "have a commitment to career ... "(27).

When you omit a complete sentence, use three ellipsis dots after the period. To omit one line or more of poetry from a long, indented quotation, indicate the omission with a line of dots.

▶This poem is for the hunger of my mother
. . . .
who read the Blackwell's
catalogue like a menu of delights.

—Aurora Levins Morales, *Class Poem*

30　Italics and Underlining

Use italics or underlining to highlight a word, phrase, or title. Word-processing programs offer italic type. Often, though, in manuscript form, underlining is more distinctive and therefore preferred in MLA works-cited lists and in material to be graded or typeset. When writing online, use italics; underlining is used for links.

30a Italicize or underline titles of long, whole works.

Italicize or underline the titles of books, magazines, newspapers, plays, films, TV and radio series, long poems, musical compositions, software programs, works of art, and Web sites.

▸ <u>The Sun Also Rises</u>   ▸ *The Sun Also Rises*

▸ <u>Newsweek</u>   ▸ *Newsweek*

▸ <u>The Daily Show</u>   ▸ *The Daily Show*

Do not italicize or underline the names of sacred works such as the Bible, books of the Bible (Genesis, Psalms), and the Koran (Qur'an) or of documents such as the Declaration of Independence and the Constitution.

Do not italicize or underline the titles of short works. Instead, use quotation marks (**28d**). Do not use italics or quotation marks around the title of your own essay (**28e**).

30b Italicize or underline letters, figures, words used as words, and named transportation.

▸ *Mayflower*   ▸ <u>Columbia</u>

▸ a lowercase *r*   ▸ a big gold <u>5</u>

▸ *Zarf* is a useful word for some board games.

31 Capitals, Abbreviations, and Numbers

Use the following guidelines for capitalizing words.

31a Capitals

- Always capitalize the pronoun *I* and the first word of a sentence.

- Capitalize proper nouns and adjectives. Use capitals with the names of specific people, places, things, languages, and nationalities: *Albert Einstein, Hungary, the Milky Way, Golden Gate Park, the Adirondacks, the Roosevelt Memorial, Wednesday, March, the Fourth of July, the Red Cross, University of Texas, Department of English, the Civil War, the Renaissance, Buddhism, Islam, the Torah, the Koran (or the Qur'an), the Navajo, Greece, Greek, Spain, Spaniards, Spanish, Kleenex, the USS Kearsarge.*

- Use internal capitals when appropriate for online names such as *AltaVista* and *eBay*.

  NOTE: Do not capitalize general classes or types of people, places, things, or ideas: *government, jury, mall, prairie, utopia, traffic, court, the twentieth century, goodness, reason.*

- Capitalize a title before a person's name.

  ▶ The reporter interviewed Senator Thompson.

  Do not use a capital when a title does not precede a person's name.

  ▶ Each state elects two senators.

- Capitalize major words in titles. In titles of published books, journals, magazines, essays, articles, films, poems, and songs, use a capital letter for all words except articles (*the, a, an*), coordinating conjunctions (*and, but, or, nor, so, for, yet*), *to* in an infinitive (*to stay*), and prepositions unless they begin or end a title or subtitle.

  ▶ "Wrestling with the Angel: A Memoir"

- Capitalize the first word of a quoted sentence when you introduce it with a complete sentence of your own.

  ▶ Quindlen says, "This is a story about a name," and thus tells us the topic of her article.

  However, do not capitalize when you merge a quotation into your own sentence:

  ▶ When Quindlen says that she is writing "a story about a name," she is announcing her topic.

  For capital letters after colons, see **29c**.

31b Abbreviations

Use only the following types of abbreviations. Do not abbreviate words to save time and space. For example, write *through*, not *thru; night*, not *nite; chapter*, not *chap.*

- Abbreviate titles used with people's names. The following abbreviated titles appear before names: *Mr., Ms., Mrs., Prof., Dr., Gen.,* and *Sen.* The following abbreviated titles appear after names: *Sr., Jr., PhD, MD, BA,* and *DDS.* Do not use a title both before and after a name; choose one or the other.

▶ **Dr. Benjamin Spock**   ▶ **Benjamin Spock, MD**

(Sometimes titles such as *MD* appear with periods: *M.D.;* however, both MLA and *The Chicago Manual of Style* prefer not to include periods. Whichever form you use, be consistent.)

Do not abbreviate a title not attached to a name.

▶ He went to the ~~dr.~~ twice last week.
_____ ^doctor^ (above the crossed-out "dr.")

> ▶ He went to the ~~dr.~~ twice last week.

- Abbreviate names of familiar institutions (*UCLA, YMCA*), countries (*USA*), examinations (*SAT*), diplomas (*GED*), people (*FDR*), and objects (*VCR*). If you use a specialized abbreviation, first use the term in full with the abbreviation in parentheses; then use the abbreviation. See **29a** for more on periods and abbreviations.

  ▶ **The Graduate Record Examination (GRE) is required by many graduate schools. GRE preparation is therefore big business.**

  For the plural of an abbreviation, just add *-s: VCRs.*

- Abbreviate terms used with numbers. Use the abbreviations *BC, AD, AM* (or *a.m.*), *PM* (or *p.m.*), *$, mph, wpm, mg, kg,* and other units of measure only when they occur with specific numbers.

  ▶ **35 BC**   [meaning "before Christ," now often replaced with BCE, "before the common era"]

  ▶ **AD 1776**   [*anno domini*, "in the year of the Lord," now often replaced with CE, "common era," used after the date: 1776 CE]

  ▶ **2:00 AM, 2:00 A.M.,** or **2:00 a.m.** [*ante meridiem*, Latin for "before midday"; always use periods with the lower-case letters *a.m.* and *p.m.*]

  Do not use these abbreviations when no number is attached to them.

  ▶ They arrived late in the ~~p.m.~~
  _____ ^afternoon.^ (above the crossed-out "p.m.")

- Abbreviate common Latin terms such as *etc., e.g.,* and *NB,* but only in notes, parentheses, and source citations, not in the body of your text.

31c Numbers

In the humanities and in business letters

- Use words for numbers consisting of not more than two words and for fractions (*nineteen, fifty-six, two hundred, one-half*).
- Use numerals for longer numbers (*326; 5,625*).
- Use a combination of words and numerals for numbers over a million (*45 million*).

In scientific and technical writing

- Write all numbers above nine as numerals.
- Write numbers below ten as numerals only when they show precise measurement, as when they are grouped and compared with other larger numbers (*5 of the 39 participants*), or when they precede a unit of measurement (*6 cm*), indicate a mathematical function (*8%; 0.4*), or represent a specific time, date, age, score, or number in a series.
- Write fractions as words.

Numbers at the beginning of a sentence

- Spell them out.

  ▶One hundred twenty-five members voted for the new bylaws.

  ▶Six thousand fans have already bought tickets.

e s l **Number with *hundred, thousand, million*** Even after plural numbers, use the singular form of *hundred, thousand,* and *million.* Add a plural *-s* only when there is no preceding number: Hundreds *of books were damaged in the flood.* Five hundred *books were damaged in the flood.* ■

Special instances of numerals in nonscientific writing

Time and dates	6 p.m. on 31 July 2004
Decimals	20.89
Statistics	median score 35
Addresses	16 East 93rd Street
Chapters, pages, scenes, lines	Chapter 5, page 97
Abbreviations or symbols	6°C, for temperature Celsius, $21, 6'7"
Scores	The Yankees won 5–4.

For percentages and money, use the numeral and symbol (*75%, $24.67*), or spell out the expression if it is fewer than four words (*seventy-five percent, twenty-four dollars*).

Use *-s*, not *-'s*, for the plural form of numerals: *in the 1980s, 700s in the SATs*.

32 Hyphens

32a Hyphens with prefixes

Many words with prefixes are written as one word without a hyphen: *cooperate, multilingual, unnatural*. Others need a hyphen: *all-inclusive, self-indulgent*. When the main word is a numeral or a proper noun, always use a hyphen: *all-American, post-1990*. If you are unsure about whether to use a hyphen, check a dictionary.

32b Hyphens in compound words

Some compound words are written as one word (*toothbrush*), others as two words (*coffee shop*), and still others with one or more hyphens (*cross-examine, father-in-law*). Always check an up-to-date dictionary.

Use a hyphen with compound adjectives preceding a noun: *a well-organized party, a law-abiding citizen, a ten-page essay*. When the modifier follows the noun, no hyphen is necessary: *The party was well organized. Most citizens try to be law abiding. The essay was ten pages long.*

Do not use a hyphen between an *-ly* adverb and an adjective or after an adjective in its comparative (*-er*) or superlative (*-est*) form: *a tightly fitting suit, a sweeter sounding melody*.

32c Hyphens in numbers

Use hyphens in two-word numbers between twenty and ninety-nine whenever the numbers are spelled out: *Twenty-two applicants arrived early in the morning.* Also use a hyphen in spelled-out fractions: *two-thirds of a cup*.

32d End-of-line hyphens

Most word processors either automatically hyphenate words or automatically wrap words around to the next line. Choose the latter option to avoid the strange and unacceptable word division that sometimes appears with automatic hyphenation (go to Tools/Language/Hyphenation).

33 Online Guidelines

33a Punctuation in URLs

Punctuation marks communicate essential information in URLs (Uniform Resource Locators) and in e-mail addresses. Because one error can invalidate a whole address, always copy an address exactly, preferably by using Copy/Paste to duplicate it directly from your browser into your document. Some e-mail addresses are case-sensitive, so pay attention to capital and lowercase letters. In addition, pay attention to the following guidelines as you write and revise:

- Do not add a hyphen to split an address line.
- If an address includes a hyphen, do not break the line after the hyphen—a reader may not know whether the hyphen is part of the address.
- Do not insert any spaces into an online address.
- Split a URL across lines only after a slash (in MLA style) or before a punctuation mark such as a period.
- Do not split the protocol *http://* across lines.
- In MLA style, enclose a URL in angle brackets. If URLs appear in your paper underlined and with hotlinks, go to Tools/AutoCorrect/Auto Format as You Type and uncheck the box to replace "Internet and network paths with hyperlinks." This will get rid of the underlining under the URL and allow you to insert angle brackets.

33b Underlining and italics online

In Web pages, underlining indicates a link to another part of the document or to a new document. When you write online, therefore, use italics in instances when you might use underlining in hard copy, such as for titles of large works.

However, some plain-text e-mail providers do not support text features such as italics or underlining. In such cases, use single underscore marks to indicate underlining (James Joyce's_Ulysses_) and asterisks for emphasis (They were *noticeably* antagonistic).

Part Eight

For Multilingual/ ESL Writers

34 *A, An,* and *The*

35 Infinitive, *-ing,* and *-ed* Forms

36 Sentence Structure and Word Order

34 *A, An,* and *The*, 200

34a What you need to know about nouns, 200

34b Four basic questions about article use, 201

34c Basic rules, 202

34d *The* for a specific reference, 203

35 Infinitive, *-ing,* and *-ed* Forms, 204

35a Verb followed by infinitive, 204

35b Verb followed by *-ing,* 205

35c Preposition + *-ing,* 205

35d Verb followed by infinitive or *-ing,* 206

35e *-ing, -ed* adjectives, 206

36 Sentence Structure and Word Order, 207

36a Basic rules, 207

36b Direct and indirect object, 208

36c Direct and indirect questions, 209

36d *Although* and *because* clauses, 209

If English is not your first language, you will probably make some errors as you write, especially when you are grappling with new subject matter and difficult topics. For a guide to the specific types of errors commonly made by speakers of different languages, visit the *Keys for Writers* Web site at <http://college.hmco.com/keys.html> and go to *ESL Center.* This Web site also provides you with links to sites specifically designed for multilingual students.

34 *A, An,* and *The*

To decide whether to use *a, an, the,* or no article at all before a noun, first determine the type of noun.

34a What you need to know about nouns

Nouns fall into two categories.

Proper nouns A proper noun names a unique person, place, or thing and begins with a capital letter: *Walt Whitman, Lake Superior, Grand Canyon, Vietnam Veterans Memorial.*

Common nouns A common noun does not name a unique person, place, thing, or idea: *bicycle, furniture, plan, daughter, home, happiness.* Common nouns can be further categorized into two types, countable and uncountable:

- A *countable noun* can have a number before it (*one, two,* and so on); it has a plural form. Countable nouns frequently add *-s* to indicate the plural: *picture, pictures; plan, plans.* Singular countable nouns can be used after *a, an, the, this, that, each, every.* Plural countable nouns can be used after *the, these, those, many, a few, both, all, some, several.*

- An *uncountable noun* has no plural form: *furniture, equipment, advice, information, scenery, happiness.* Uncountable nouns can be used after *the, this, that, much, some, any, no, a little, a great deal of,* or a possessive such as *my* or *their.* They can never be used after a number or a plural quantity word such as *several* or *many.* Never use an uncountable noun after *a* or *an.*

  ▶My country has ⱥ lovely scenery.

NOTE: You can use an uncountable noun in a countable sense—that is, indicate a quantity of it—by adding a word or phrase that indicates quantity, but the noun itself always remains singular: three pieces of *furniture,* two bits of *information,* many pieces of *advice.*

Some nouns can be countable in one context and uncountable in another.

▶He loves *chocolate.* [All chocolate, applies to the class: uncountable]

▶She gave him *a chocolate.* [One piece of candy from a box: countable]

34b Articles: Four basic questions

Ask four basic questions about a noun to decide whether to use an article and, if so, which article to use.

KEY POINTS

Articles at a Glance: Four Basic Questions

1. PROPER OR COMMON NOUN?
   ↓
   Singular; no
       article (zero article)
   Plural: *the*

   2. SPECIFIC OR NONSPECIFIC REFERENCE?
      ↓
      the (see **34d**)

(Continued)

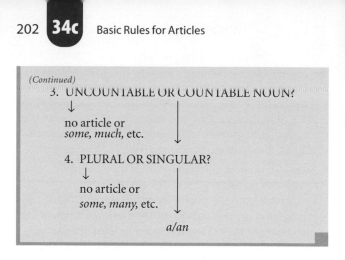

(Continued)

3. UNCOUNTABLE OR COUNTABLE NOUN?
↓

no article or
some, much, etc.

4. PLURAL OR SINGULAR?
↓

no article or
some, many, etc.

a/an

Using the questions: a sample Answering the four questions can help you decide which article, if any, to use with the noun *jacket* in the following sentence.

▶The motorcyclist I saw on the street was carrying ___?___ jacket and wearing black leather pants.   article

1. *Jacket* is a common noun.

2. *Jacket* is not identified in the text as one specific jacket in the same way that *motorcyclist* is (the one the writer saw on the street).

3. *Jacket* is a countable noun.

4. *Jacket* is singular and begins with a consonant sound (*a* is used before a consonant sound, *an* before a vowel sound as in *an egg, an honest man*).

▶The motorcyclist I saw on the street was carrying *a* jacket and wearing black leather pants.

34c Basic rules for articles

1. Use *the* whenever a reference to a common noun is specific and unique for writer and reader (see **34d**).

   the
   ▶He loves ˄house that she bought.

2. Do not use *a/an* with plural countable nouns.

   ▶They cited a̸ reliable surveys.

3. Do not use *a/an* with uncountable nouns.

   ▶He gave a̸ helpful advice.

4. To make generalizations about countable nouns, do one of the following:

   • Use the plural form: *Lions are majestic.*

   • Use the singular with *a/an*: *A lion is a majestic animal.*

   • Use the singular with *the* to denote a classification: *The lion is a majestic animal.*

5. A countable singular noun can never stand alone. Make sure that a countable singular noun is preceded by an article or by a demonstrative pronoun (*this, that*), a numeral, a singular word expressing quantity (see **23h**), or a possessive.

   A (Every, That, One, Her) nurse
   ▶ ~~Nurse~~ has a difficult job.

6. In general, though there are many exceptions, use no article with a singular proper noun (*Mount Everest*), and use *the* with a plural proper noun (*the Himalayas*).

34d *The* for a specific reference

When you write a common noun that both you and the reader know refers to one or more specific persons, places, things, or concepts, use the article *the*. The reference can be specific in two ways: outside the text or inside it.

Specific reference outside the text

▶ I study the earth, the sun, and the moon. [The ones in our solar system]

▶ She closed the door. [Of the room she was in]

▶ Her husband took the dog out for a walk. [The dog belonging to the couple]

Specific reference inside the text

▶ *The* kitten that her daughter brought home had a distinctive black patch above one eye. [The kitten is identified in the text as the specific one that her daughter brought home.]

▶Her daughter found *a* kitten. When they were writing a
lost and found ad that night, they realized that *the*
kitten had a distinctive black patch above one eye. [The
second mention is of a specific kitten identified earlier—
the one her daughter found.]

The *with a superlative*

▶He bought *the most expensive* bicycle in the store.

---

35 Infinitive, -*ing*, and -*ed* Forms

35a Verb followed by an infinitive

Some verbs are followed by an infinitive (*to* + base form):
His father wanted to rule the family. Verbs commonly followed by an infinitive include

agree	choose	fail	offer	refuse
ask	claim	hope	plan	venture
beg	decide	manage	pretend	want
bother	expect	need	promise	wish

Note any differences between English and your own language. In Spanish, for example, the word for *refuse* is followed by the equivalent of an -*ing* form.

▶He refused ~~criticizing~~ the system.
  ^to criticize

Position of a negative   In a verb + infinitive pattern, the position of the negative affects meaning. Note the difference in
meaning that the position of a negative (*not, never*) can create.

▶He did *not decide* to buy a new car. His wife did.

▶He decided *not to buy* a new car. His wife was
  disappointed.

Verb + noun or pronoun + infinitive   Some verbs are followed by a noun or pronoun and then an infinitive.

▶The librarian *advised them to use* a better database.

Verbs that follow this pattern are *advise, allow, ask, encour-
age, expect, force, need, order, persuade, cause, command, con-
vince, remind, require, tell, urge, want, warn.*

Spanish and Russian use a *that* clause after verbs like *want*. In English, however, *want* is followed by an infinitive, not by a *that* clause.

▶Rose *wanted* ~~that her son would~~ become a doctor.
     ^{her son to}

Make, let, *and* have   After these verbs, use a noun or pronoun and a base form of the verb (without *to*).

▶He *made his son practice* for an hour.

▶They *let us leave* early.

▶She *had her son-in-law wash* the car.

35b   Verb followed by *-ing* (gerund)

▶I can't help *singing* along with Norah Jones.

The *-ing* form of a verb used as a noun is known as a *gerund*. The verbs that are systematically followed by an *-ing* form make up a relatively short and learnable list.

admit	consider	enjoy	miss	resist
appreciate	delay	finish	postpone	risk
avoid	deny	imagine	practice	suggest
be worth	discuss	keep	recall	tolerate
can't help	dislike			

▶We considered ~~to invite~~ his parents.
      ^{inviting}

▶Most people dislike ~~to hear~~ cell phones at concerts.
          ^{hearing}

Note that a negation comes between the verb and the *-ing* form.

▶During their vacation, they enjoy *not* getting up early every day.

35c   Preposition + *-ing*

After a preposition, use the *-ing* form that functions as a noun (the gerund).

▶They congratulated him *on winning* the prize.

▶He ran three miles *without stopping*.

▶The cheese is the right consistency *for spreading*.

NOTE: Take care not to confuse *to* as a preposition with *to* used in an infinitive. When *to* is a preposition, it is followed by a noun, a pronoun, a noun phrase, or an *-ing* form, not by the base form of a verb.

▶They want *to adopt* a child. [infinitive]

▶They are looking forward *to adopting* a child.
   [preposition + *-ing* form]

See Glossary of Usage, page 221 for forms used after *used to* and *get used to*.

35d Verb followed by an infinitive or *-ing*

Some verbs can be followed by either an infinitive or an *-ing* form (a gerund) with almost no discernible difference in meaning: *begin, continue, hate, like, love, start*.

▶She loves *cooking*.   ▶She loves *to cook*.

  With a few verbs (*forget, remember, try, stop*), however, the infinitive and the *-ing* form signal different meanings.

▶He *remembered to mail* the letter. [intention]

▶He *remembered mailing* the letter. [past act]

35e *-ing* and *-ed* forms as adjectives

Adjectives can be formed from both the present participle *-ing* form and the past participle form of verbs (*-ed* ending for regular verbs). Each form has a different meaning: The *-ing* adjective indicates that the word modified produces an effect; the past participle adjective indicates that the word modified has an effect produced on it.

▶The boring cook served baked beans yet again. [The cook produces boredom. Everyone is tired of baked beans.]

▶The bored cook yawned as she scrambled eggs. [The cook felt the emotion of boredom as she did the cooking, but the eggs could still be appreciated.]

Produces an effect	Has an effect produced on it
amazing	amazed
amusing	amused

annoying	annoyed
confusing	confused
depressing	depressed
disappointing	disappointed
embarrassing	embarrassed
exciting	excited
interesting	interested
satisfying	satisfied
shocking	shocked
worrying	worried

NOTE: Do not drop the *-ed* ending from a past participle. Sometimes in speech it blends with a following *t* or *d* sound, but in writing the *-ed* ending must be included.

▶ I was surprise͜ to see her wild outfit.
             d

▶ The researchers were ~~worry~~ that the results were contaminated.
               worried

36 Sentence Structure and Word Order

36a Basic rules of order

- Always include the subject of a clause, even a filler subject *it* or *there*.

  ▶ The critics hated the movie because was too sentimental.
              it

  ▶ When the company lost money, were immediate effects on share prices.
              there

- Do not put an adverb or a phrase between the verb and its object.

  ▶ The quiz show host congratulated |many times| the winner.

  ▶ He saw |yesterday| the movie.

- Position a long descriptive phrase after, not before, the noun it modifies.

  ▶I would go to known only to me places.

- Stick to the order of subject-verb-direct object.

  ▶~~Good grades received~~ every student in the class received good grades.

- Do not use a pronoun to restate the subject.

  ▶Visitors to the Statue of Liberty ~~they~~ have worn the steps down.

- Do not include a pronoun that a relative pronoun has replaced.

  ▶The house that I lived in ~~it~~ for ten years has been sold.

36b Direct and indirect object

Some verbs can be followed by both a direct object and an indirect object. (The indirect object is the person or thing to whom or to what, or for whom or for what, something is done.) *Give, send, show, tell, teach, find, sell, ask, offer, pay, pass,* and *hand* are some verbs that take indirect objects. The indirect object follows the verb and precedes the direct object.

▶He gave his mother some flowers.

▶He gave her some flowers.

An indirect object can also be replaced with a prepositional phrase that *follows* the direct object.

▶He gave some flowers to his mother.

NOTE: Some verbs—such as *explain, describe, say, mention,* and *open*—are never followed by an indirect object. However, they can be followed by a direct object and a prepositional phrase with *to* or *for*.

►She explained ~~me~~ ^to me^ the election process.

►He described ~~us~~ ^to us^ the menu.

36c Direct and indirect questions

When a direct question is reported indirectly, it loses the quotation marks, the word order of a question, and the question mark. Sometimes changes in tense are also necessary after an introductory verb in the past tense (see **22d**).

Direct question	The buyer asked, *"Are the goods* ready to be shipped?"
Indirect question	The buyer asked if *the goods were* ready to be shipped.

Direct question	*"Why did you send* a letter instead of a fax?" my boss asked.
Indirect question	My boss asked why *I [had] sent* a letter instead of a fax.

Use only a question word or *if* or *whether* to introduce an indirect question. Do not also use *that*.

►My boss wondered ~~that~~ why I had left early.

Avoid shifts between direct and indirect quotations (**21d**).

36d *Although* and *because* clauses

In some languages, a subordinating conjunction (such as *although* or *because*) can be used along with a coordinating conjunction (*but, so*) or a transitional expression (*however, therefore*) in the same sentence. In English, only one is used.

Faulty	*Although* he loved his father, *but* he did not visit him.
Possible revisions	*Although* he loved his father, he did not visit him.
	He loved his father, *but* he did not visit him.

Faulty   *Because* she loved children, *therefore* she became a teacher.

Possible revisions   Because she loved children, she became a teacher.

She loved children, *so* she became a teacher.

She loved children; *therefore,* she became a teacher.

See **26a** for punctuation with *therefore* and other transitional expressions.

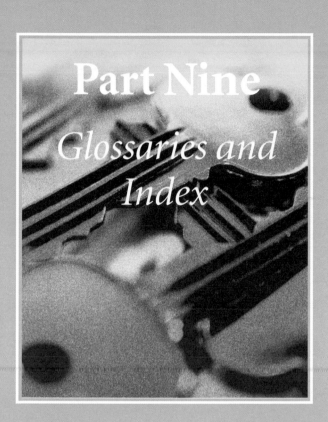

Part Nine

Glossaries and Index

37 Glossary of Usage

38 Glossary of Grammatical Terms

Index

211

37 Glossary of Usage, 212

38 Glossary of Grammatical Terms, 221

Index, 231

37   Glossary of Usage

accept, except, expect   *Accept* is a verb: *She accepted the salary offer. Except* is usually a preposition: *Everyone has gone home except my boss. Expect* is a verb: *They expect to visit New Mexico on vacation.*

adapt, adopt   *Adopt* means "to take into a family" or "to take up and follow": *The couple adopted a three-year-old child. The company adopted a more aggressive policy. Adapt* means "to adjust" and is used with the preposition *to*: *We need some time to adapt to work after college.*

advice, advise   *Advice* is a noun: *Take my advice and don't start smoking. Advise* is a verb: *He advised his brother to stop smoking.*

affect, effect   In their most common uses, *affect* is a verb, and *effect* is a noun. To *affect* is to have an *effect* on something: *Pesticides can affect health. Pesticides have a bad effect on health. Effect,* however, can be used as a verb meaning "to bring about": *The administration hopes to effect new health care legislation. Affect* can also be used as a noun in psychology, meaning "a feeling or emotion."

all ready, already   *All ready* means "totally prepared": *The students were all ready for their final examination. Already* means "by this time": *He has already written the report.*

all right, alright   *Alright* is nonstandard. *All right* is standard.

all together, altogether   *Altogether* is an adverb meaning "totally," often used before an adjective: *His presentation was altogether impressive. All together* is used to describe acting simultaneously: *As soon as the boss appeared, the managers spoke up all together.*

allude, elude   *Allude* means "to refer to": *She alluded to his height. Elude* means "to avoid": *He eluded her criticism by leaving the room.*

allusion, illusion   *Allusion* means "reference to": *Her allusions to his height made him uncomfortable. Illusion* means "false idea": *He had no illusions about being Mr. Universe.*

almost, most   Do not use *most* to mean *almost: Almost* (not *Most*) *all of my friends are computer literate.*

a lot, alot, lots *Alot* is nonstandard. *A lot of* and *lots of* are regarded by some as informal for *many* or *a great deal of: They have performed many research studies.*

ambiguous, ambivalent *Ambiguous* is used to describe a phrase or act that has more than one meaning: *The ending of the movie is ambiguous; we don't know if the butler really committed the murder. Ambivalent* describes lack of certainty and the coexistence of opposing attitudes and feelings: *The committee is ambivalent about the proposal for restructuring the company.*

among, between Use *between* for two items, *among* for three or more: *I couldn't decide between red or blue. I couldn't decide among red, blue, or green.*

amoral, immoral *Amoral* can mean "neither moral nor immoral" or "not caring about right or wrong," whereas *immoral* means "morally wrong": *Some consider vegetarianism an amoral issue, but others believe eating meat is immoral.*

amount, number *Number* is used with countable plural expressions: *a large number of people, a number of attempts. Amount* is used with uncountable expressions: *a large amount of money, work,* or *information.*

anyone, any one *Anyone* is a singular indefinite pronoun meaning "anybody": *Can anyone help me? Any one* refers to one from a group and is usually followed by *of* + plural noun: *Any one* (as opposed to *any two*) *of the suggestions will be considered acceptable.*

anyplace The standard *anywhere* is preferable.

anyway, anywhere, nowhere; anyways, anywheres, nowheres *Anyway, anywhere,* and *nowhere* are standard forms. The others, ending in *-s,* are not.

apart, a part *Apart* is an adverb: *The old book fell apart.* But *I'd like to be a part of that project.*

as, as if, like See *like, as, as if.*

as regards, in regard to See *in regard to, as regards.*

at Avoid including *at* at the end of a question: *Where's the library?* not *Where's the library at?*

awful, awfully Avoid using these words to mean "bad" (*It's an awful story*) or "very" (*They are awfully rich*).

a while, awhile *While* is a noun: *a while ago; in a while. Awhile* is an adverb meaning "for some time": *They lived awhile in the wilderness.*

bad, badly　*Bad* is an adjective, *badly* an adverb. Use *bad* after linking verbs (such as *am, is, become, seem*); use *badly* to modify verbs: *They felt bad after losing the match. They had played badly.*

barely　Avoid creating a double negative (such as *can't barely type*). *Barely* should always take a positive verb: *She can barely type. They could barely keep their eyes open.* See *hardly.*

because, because of　*Because* is used to introduce a dependent clause: *Because it was raining, we left early. Because of* is a preposition that is followed by an object: *We left early because of the rain.*

being as, being that　Avoid. Use *because* instead: *Because* (not *Being as*) *I was tired, I didn't go to class.*

belief, believe　*Belief* is a noun: *She has radical beliefs. Believe* is a verb: *He believes in an afterlife.*

beside, besides　*Beside* is a preposition meaning "next to"; *besides* is a preposition meaning "except for": *Sit beside me. He has no assistants besides us. Besides* is also an adverb meaning "in addition": *I hate horror movies. Besides, there's a long line.*

better　See *had better.*

between　See *among.*

breath, breathe　The first is a noun, the second a verb: *Take three deep breaths. Breathe in deeply.*

can't hardly　This expression is nonstandard. See *hardly.*

cite, site, sight　*Cite* means "to quote or mention"; *site* is a noun meaning "location"; *sight* is a noun meaning "view": *She cited the page number in her paper. They visited the original site of the abbey. The sight of the skyline from the plane produced applause from the passengers.*

complement, compliment　As verbs, *complement* means "to complete or add to something," and *compliment* means "to make a flattering comment about someone or something": *The wine complemented the meal. The guests complimented the hostess on the fine dinner.* As nouns, the words have meanings associated with the verbs: *The wine was a fine complement to the meal. The guests paid the hostess a compliment.*

compose, comprise　*Compose* means "to make up"; *comprise* means "to include." *The conference center is composed of twenty-five rooms. The conference center comprises twenty-five rooms.*

conscience, conscious　*Conscience* is a noun meaning "awareness of right and wrong." *Conscious* is an adjective meaning "awake" or "aware." *Her conscience troubled her after the accident. The victim was still not conscious.*

continual, continuous *Continual* implies repetition while *continuous* implies lack of a pause. *The continual interruptions made the lecturer angry. Continuous rain for two hours stopped the game.*

could care less This expression used without a negative is not standard. In formal English, use it only with a negative: *They couldn't care less about their work.*

credible, creditable, credulous *Credible* means "believable": *The jurors found the accused's alibi to be credible, and so they acquitted her. Creditable* means "deserving of credit": *A B+ grade attests to a creditable performance. Credulous* means "easily taken in or deceived": *Only a child would be so credulous as to believe that the streets are paved with gold.* See also *incredible, incredulous.*

custom, customs, costume *Custom* means "habitual practice or tradition." *Customs* refers to a government agency that collects taxes on imports or to the procedures for inspecting items entering a country. A *costume* is a style of dress: *a family custom; go through customs at the airport; a Halloween costume.*

dairy, diary The first noun is associated with cows and milk, the second with daily journal writing.

desert, dessert *Desert* can be pronounced two ways and can be a noun with the stress on the first syllable *(the Mojave Desert)* or a verb, pronounced the same way as the noun *dessert: When did he desert his family?* As a noun, *desert* means "a dry, often sandy, environment." As a verb *desert* means "to abandon." *Dessert* (with the stress on the second syllable) is the sweet course at the end of a meal.

different from, different than Standard usage is *different from: She looks different from her sister.* However, *different than* appears frequently in speech and informal writing, particularly when *different from* would require more words: *My writing is different than* (in place of *different from what*) *it was last semester.*

disinterested, uninterested *Disinterested* means "impartial or unbiased": *The mediator was hired to make a disinterested settlement. Uninterested* means "lacking in interest": *He seemed so uninterested in his job that his boss wondered what to do about him.*

do, due *Do* is a verb. Do not write "*Do* to his absences, he lost his job"; instead, use the two-word preposition *due to* or *because of.*

due to Use *due to,* not *because of,* after a noun plus a form of *be: The Yankees' win was due to Jeter's fielding.* See also *because, because of.*

due to the fact that, owing to the fact that Wordy. Use *because* instead: *They stopped the game because* (not *due to the fact that*) *it was raining.*

each, every These are singular pronouns; use them with a singular verb. See also **23d** and **23g**.

each other, one another Use *each other* with two, *one another* with more than two: *The twins love each other. The triplets all love one another.*

effect See *affect.*

e.g. In the body of a formal text, use *for example* or *for instance* in place of this Latin abbreviation.

elicit, illicit *Elicit* means "to get or draw out": *The police tried in vain to elicit information from the suspect's accomplice. Illicit* is an adjective meaning "illegal": *Their illicit deals landed them in prison.*

elude See *allude, elude.*

emigrate, immigrate *Emigrate from* is "to leave a country"; *immigrate to* is "to move to another country": *They emigrated from Ukraine and immigrated to the United States.* The noun forms *emigrant* and *immigrant* are derived from the verbs.

eminent, imminent *Eminent* means "well known and noteworthy": *an eminent lawyer; imminent* means "about to happen": *an imminent disaster.*

etc. This abbreviation for the Latin *et cetera* means "and so on." Do not let a list trail off with *etc.* Rather than writing *They took a tent, a sleeping bag, etc.,* write *They took a tent, a sleeping bag, cooking utensils, and a stove.*

every, each See *each, every.*

everyday, every day *Everyday* as one word is an adjective meaning "usual": *Their everyday routine is to break for lunch at 12:30. Every day* is an adverbial expression of frequency: *I get up early every day.*

except, expect See *accept, except, expect.*

explicit, implicit *Explicit* means "direct": *She gave explicit instructions. Implicit* means "implied": *A tax increase is implicit in the proposal.*

farther, further Both can apply to distance: *She lives farther (further) from the campus than I do.* But only *further* is used to mean "additional" or "additionally": *The management offered further incentives. Further, the union proposed new work rules.*

female, male Use these words as adjectives, not as nouns replacing *man* and *woman: There are only three women* (not *females*) *in my class. We are discussing female conversational traits.*

few, a few Use *a few* for *some*; use *few* for *hardly any: She has a few days off to relax. She has few friends and is lonely.*

fewer, less Formal usage demands *fewer* with plural countable nouns *(fewer holidays), less* with uncountable nouns *(less money).* However, in informal usage, *less* with plural nouns commonly occurs, especially with *than: less than six items, fifty words or less.* In formal usage, *fewer* is preferred.

get married to, marry These expressions can be used interchangeably: *She will marry her childhood friend next month. He will get married to his fiancée next week.* (The noun form is *marriage: Their marriage has lasted thirty years.*)

had better Include the *had* in standard English, although it is often omitted in advertising and in speech: *You had better* (not *You better*) *try harder.*

hardly This is a negative word. Do not use it with another negative: *He could hardly walk* (not *He couldn't hardly walk*) *after the accident.*

hisself Nonstandard; use *himself.*

illicit, elicit See *elicit, illicit.*

illusion, allusion See *allusion, illusion.*

immigrate, emigrate See *emigrate, immigrate.*

imminent, eminent See *eminent, imminent.*

implicit See *explicit, implicit.*

imply, infer *Imply* means "to suggest in an indirect way": *He implied that further layoffs were unlikely. Infer* means "to guess" or "to draw a conclusion": *I inferred that the company was doing well.*

incredible, incredulous *Incredible* means "difficult to believe": *The violence of the storm was incredible. Incredulous* means "skeptical, unable to believe": *They were incredulous when he told them about his daring exploits in the whitewater rapids.*

in regard to, as regards Use one or the other. Do not use the nonstandard *in regards to.*

install, instill To *install* is to "set in position for use" or "establish." To *instill* is to "implant": *She would not have been able to install the fixture if her parents hadn't instilled in her a sense of craftsmanship.*

irregardless Avoid this nonstandard form and use *regardless* instead: *He selected history as a major regardless of its relevance would give him for a business career.*

it's, its The apostrophe in *it's* signals not a possessive but a contraction of *it is* or *it has*. *Its* is the possessive form of the pronoun *it*: *The city government agency has produced its final report. It's available upon request.* See also **27d.**

kind, sort, type In the singular, use with *this* and a singular noun. Use them in the plural with *these* and a plural noun: *this kind of book, these kinds of books.*

kind of, sort of Do not use these to mean "somewhat" or "a little": *The pace of the baseball game was somewhat* (not *kind of*) *slow.*

lend, loan *Lend* is a verb, but *loan* is ordinarily used as a noun: *Our cousins offered to lend us some money, but we refused the loan.*

less, fewer See *fewer, less.*

like, as, as if *As* and *as if* introduce a dependent clause with a subject and verb: *She walks as her father does. She looks as if she could eat a big meal. Like* is a preposition followed by a noun or pronoun, not by a clause: *She looks like her father.* In speech, however, *like* is often used where formal usage dictates *as* or *as if: She walks like her father does. He looks like he needs a new suit.* Formal usage requires *He looks as if he needs a new suit.*

literally Avoid overuse: *literally* is an adverb meaning "actually" or "word for word" and should not be used in conjunction with figurative expressions such as *she was driving me crazy* or *he was bouncing off the walls. Literally* should be used only when the words describe exactly what is happening: *He was so scared his face literally went white.*

loan See *lend, loan.*

loose, lose *Loose* is an adjective meaning the opposite of *tight: This jacket is comfortable because it is so loose. Lose* is a verb, with the past tense and past participle form *lost: Many people lose their jobs in a recession.*

lot, alot, lots See *a lot, alot, lots.*

marital, martial *Marital* is associated with marriage, *martial* with war.

may be, maybe *May be* consists of a modal verb followed by the base form of the verb *be; maybe* is an adverb meaning "perhaps." If you can replace the expression with *perhaps*, make it one word: *They may be there already, or maybe they got caught in traffic.*

most, almost See *almost, most.*

myself Use only as a reflexive pronoun (*I told them myself*) or as an intensive pronoun (*I myself told them*). Do not use *myself* as a subject pronoun; use *My sister and I won* (not *My sister and myself won*).

nowadays All one word. Make sure you include the final -*s*.

nowhere, nowheres See *anyway*.

number, amount See *amount, number*.

off, off of Use only *off*, not *off of*: *She drove the car off* (not *off of*) *the road.*

OK, O.K., okay Reserve these forms for informal speech and writing. Choose another word in a formal context: *Her performance was satisfactory* (in place of *Her performance was OK*).

one another See *each other, one another.*

owing to the fact that See *due to the fact that.*

passed, past *Passed* is a past tense verb form: *They passed the deli on the way to work. He passed his exam. Past* can be a noun (*in the past*), an adjective (*in past times*), or a preposition (*She walked past the bakery*).

personal, personnel *Personal* is an adjective meaning "individual", *personnel* is a noun referring to employees or staff: *It is my personal belief that a company's personnel should be treated like family.*

plus Do not use *plus* as a coordinating conjunction or a transitional expression. Use *and* or *moreover* instead: *He was promoted and* (not *plus*) *he received a bonus.* Use *plus* as a preposition meaning "in addition to": *His salary plus his dividends placed him in a high tax bracket.*

precede, proceed *Precede* means "to go or occur before": *The Roaring Twenties preceded the Great Depression. Proceed* means "to go ahead": *After you have paid the fee, proceed to the examination room.*

pretty Avoid using *pretty* as an intensifying adverb. Omit it or use a word like *really, very, rather,* or *quite: The stew tastes very* (not *pretty*) *good.*

principal, principle *Principal* is a noun (*the principal of a school*) or an adjective meaning "main": *His principal motive was greed. Principle* is a noun meaning "standard or rule": *He always acts on his principles.*

quite, quiet Do not confuse the adverb *quite*, meaning "very," with the adjective *quiet* ("still" or "silent"): *We felt quite relieved when the audience became quiet.*

quote, quotation   *Quote* is a verb. Do not use it as a noun; use *quotation: The quotation* (not *quote*) *from Walker tells the reader a great deal.*

real, really   *Real* is an adjective; *really* is an adverb. Do not use *real* as an intensifying adverb: *She acted really* (not *real*) *well.*

reason is because   Avoid *the reason is because.* Instead, use *the reason is that* or rewrite the sentence. See **21g.**

regardless   See *irregardless.*

respectable, respectful, respective   *Respectable* means "presentable, worthy of respect": *Wear some respectable shoes to your interview. Respectful* means "polite or deferential": *Parents want their children to be respectful to adults. Respective* means "particular" or "individual": *The friends of the bride and the groom sat in their respective seats in the church.*

respectfully, respectively   *Respectfully* means "showing respect": *He bowed respectfully when the queen entered. Respectively* refers to items in a list and means "in the order mentioned": *Horses and birds gallop and fly, respectively.*

should (could, might, etc.) of   Nonstandard for *should have: should have* tried; *might have* seen. See **22b.**

since   Use only when time or reason is clear: *Since you insist on helping, I'll let you paint this bookcase.* Unclear: *Since he got a new job, he has been happy.*

site, sight, cite   See *cite, site, sight.*

sometimes, sometime, some time   *Sometimes* means "occasionally": *He sometimes prefers to eat lunch at his desk. Sometime* means "at an indefinite time": *I read that book sometime last year.* The expression *some time* is the noun *time* modified by the quantity word *some: I worked for Honda for some time—about five years, I think.*

sort, type, kind   See *kind, sort, type.*

sort of, kind of   See *kind of, sort of.*

stationary, stationery   *Stationary* means "not moving" *(a stationary vehicle);* you use *stationery* when you write letters.

than, then   *Then* is a time word; *than* must be preceded by a comparative form: *bigger than, more interesting than.*

their, there, they're   *They're* is a contracted form of *they are; there* indicates place or is used as a filler in the subject position in a sentence; *their* is a pronoun indicating possession: *They're over there, guarding their luggage.*

theirself, theirselves, themself   Nonstandard; use *themselves.*

to, too, two   Do not confuse these words. *To* is a sign of the infinitive and a common preposition; *too* is an adverb; *two* is a number: *She is too smart to agree to report to two bosses.*

uninterested, disinterested   See *disinterested, uninterested.*

unique   The adjective *unique* means "the only one of its kind" and therefore should not be used with qualifying adjectives like "very" or "most": *His recipe for chowder is unique* (not *most unique* or *quite unique*).

used to, get (become) used to   These expressions share the common form *used to.* But the first, expressing a past habit that no longer exists, is followed by a base form of the verb: *He used to wear his hair long.* (Note that after *not,* the form is *use to: He did not use to have a beard.*) In the expression *get (become) used to, used to* means "accustomed to" and is followed by a noun or an *-ing* form: *She couldn't get used to driving on the left when she was in England.*

way, ways   Use *way* to mean "distance": *He has a way to go. Ways* in this context is nonstandard.

weather, whether   *Weather* is a noun; *whether* is a conjunction: *The weather will determine whether we go on the picnic.*

whose, who's   *Whose* is possessive: *Whose goal was that? Who's* is a contraction of *who is* or *who has: Who's the player whose pass was caught?*

your, you're   *Your* is a pronoun used to show possession. *You're* is a contraction for *you are: You're wearing your new shoes today, aren't you?*

38 Glossary of Grammatical Terms

absolute phrase   A phrase consisting of a noun followed by a participle (*-ing* or past participle) and modifying an entire sentence: *The flags blowing in the wind,* the stadium looked bleak. **26d.**

active voice   Attribute of a verb when its grammatical subject performs the action: The dog *ate* the cake. See also *passive voice.*

adjective   A word that describes or limits (modifies) a noun or pronoun: A *happy* child. The child is *happy.* **25.** See also *comparative, coordinate adjective, superlative.*

adjective clause   See *relative clause.*

adverb   A word that modifies a verb, an adjective, or another adverb. Many adverbs end in *-ly:* She ran *quickly.* He is *really* successful. The children were *well* liked. **25.** See also *comparative, superlative.*

adverb clause   A dependent clause that modifies a verb, an adjective, or an adverb and begins with a subordinating conjunction: He left early *because he was tired.*

agreement   The grammatical match in person, number, and gender between a verb and its subject or a pronoun and the word it refers to (its *antecedent*): The *benefits continue; they are* pleasing. The *benefit continues. It is* pleasing. **23, 24c.**

antecedent   The noun that a pronoun refers to or replaces: My sons found a *kitten. It* was black and white. **24b, 24c.**

appositive phrase   A phrase occurring next to a noun and used to describe it: His father, *a factory worker,* is running for office. **24a.**

article   *A, an* (indefinite), or *the* (definite article). **34 ESL.**

auxiliary verb   A verb that joins with another verb to form a complete verb. Auxiliary verbs are forms of *do, be,* and *have* as well as the modal auxiliary verbs. **22a, 22b.** See also *modal auxiliary verb.*

base form   The form of a verb with no endings; the dictionary form, used in an infinitive after *to: see, eat, go, be.* **22a.**

clause   A group of words that includes a subject and a verb. See also *independent clause; dependent clause.* **19b, 20, 26a, 26b.**

cliché   An overused, predictable expression: *as cool as a cucumber.* **18a.**

collective noun   A noun naming a group of people, places, objects, or ideas that are regarded as a unit: *society, jury, family.* **23e, 24c.**

comma splice   An error caused by connecting two independent clauses with only a comma. **20.**

common noun   A noun that does not name a unique person, place, or thing. **34a ESL.** See also *proper noun.*

comparative   The form of an adjective or adverb used to compare two people or things: *bigger, more interesting.* **25e.**

complement   A *subject complement* is a word or group of words used after a linking verb to refer to and describe the subject: Harry looks *happy.* An *object complement* is a word or group of words used after a direct object to complete its meaning: They call him a *liar.* **25b.**

complete verb   A verb that shows tense. Some verb forms, such as present *(-ing)* participles and past participles, require an auxiliary verb or verbs to make them complete verbs. *Going* and *seen* are not complete verbs; *are going* and *has been seen* are complete. **22a.**

compound adjective   An adjective formed of two or more words, used as one unit, and often connected with hyphens: a *well-constructed* house. **25c.**

compound noun   A noun formed of two or more words: *toothbrush, merry-go-round.* **32b.**

compound predicate   A predicate containing two or more verbs and their objects, complements, and modifiers: He *whistles* and *sings in the morning.* **19c, 26b.**

compound subject   Two or more subjects with the same predicate that are connected by words such as *and, or,* and *nor: My uncle and my aunt* are leaving soon. **23f.**

conditional clause   A clause introduced by *if* or *unless,* expressing conditions of fact, prediction, or speculation: *If we earn more, we spend more.* **22f.**

conjunction   A word or words like *and* and *because* that connect sentences or sentence elements. See also *coordinating conjunction, subordinating conjunction.* **19c, 20b.**

contraction   A word or words abbreviated by replacing one or more letters with an apostrophe: *can't* (for *cannot*), *he's* (for *he is* or *he has*), or *they're* (for *they are*). **27a, 27d.**

coordinate adjective   One of two or more evaluative adjectives modifying the same noun or pronoun. When coordinate adjectives appear in a series, their order can be reversed, and they can be separated by *and.* Commas are used between coordinate adjectives: the *comfortable, expensive car.* **26a.** See also *cumulative adjective.*

coordinating conjunction   The seven coordinating conjunctions are *and, but, or, nor, so, for,* and *yet.* They connect sentence elements that are parallel in structure: He couldn't call, *but* he wrote a letter. **20b, 26a, 26b.**

countable noun   A common noun that has a plural form and can be used after a plural quantity word (*many, three,* and so on); one *book,* three *stores,* many *children.* **34a ESL.**

cumulative adjective   An adjective modifying other adjectives before a noun. Cumulative adjectives occur in a set order with no comma separating them: *a new red plastic bench.* **26b.** See also *coordinate adjective.*

dangling modifier   A modifier that does not modify the missing noun or pronoun it is intended to modify. *Turning the corner,* the lights went out. (Corrected: *Turning the corner, we* saw the lights go out.) **21c.**

demonstrative pronoun   *This, that, these,* or *those: That* is my glass. **24c.**

dependent clause A clause that cannot stand alone as a complete sentence and needs to be attached to an independent clause. A dependent clause begins with a subordinating word such as *because, if, when, although, who, which,* or *that: When it rains,* we can't take the children outside. **19b.**

diction Choice of appropriate words and tone. **18.**

direct object The person or thing that receives the action of a verb or verb form: They ate *cake* and *ice cream.* **36b ESL.**

direct quotation A person's words, reproduced exactly by a writer and placed in quotation marks: *"I won't be home until noon,"* she said. **8a, 21d, 26a, 36c ESL.**

double negative Using two negative words in the same sentence is nonstandard usage: I do *not* know *nothing.* (Corrected: I do not know anything.) **25d.**

dummy subject See *filler subject.*

ellipsis Omission of words from a quotation, indicated by three dots (an *ellipsis mark*): "I pledge allegiance to the flag . . . and to the republic for which it stands. . . ." **8a, 29e.**

faulty predication A construction in which subject and verb do not fit logically: The *decrease* in stolen cars *has diminished* in the past year. (Corrected: The *number* of stolen cars *has decreased* in the past year.) **21e.**

filler (or dummy) subject *It* or *there* used in the subject position of a clause, followed by a form of *be: There are* two elm trees on the corner. **15b, 23c.**

first person The person speaking or writing: *I* or *we.* **24a.**

fragment A group of words that is punctuated as a sentence but is grammatically incomplete because it lacks a subject or a complete verb or lacks an independent clause: *Because it was a sunny day.* **19.**

fused sentence See *run-on sentence.*

gender Classification of a noun or pronoun as masculine *(my uncle, he),* feminine *(Ms. Torez, she),* or neuter *(book, it).* **18c, 24c.**

generic noun A noun referring to a general class or type of person or object: A *student* has to write many papers. **24c.**

gerund A form, derived from a verb, that ends in *-ing* and functions as a noun: *Walking* is good for your health. **23d, 24a, 35b ESL, 35c ESL.**

helping verb See *auxiliary verb.*

indefinite pronoun A pronoun that refers to a nonspecific person or object: *anybody, something.* **23g**.

independent clause A clause containing a subject and a complete verb, not introduced by a subordinating word. An independent clause stands alone grammatically: *Birds sing. The old man was singing a song.* Hailing a cab, *the woman used a silver whistle.* **19, 20, 26a, 26b**.

indirect object The person or thing to whom or what, or for whom or what, an action is performed. It comes between a verb and a direct object: He gave his *sister* some flowers. **36b** ESL.

indirect question A reported question with no quotation marks: They asked *if we would help them.* **36c** ESL.

indirect quotation A presentation or paraphrase of the words of another speaker or writer, integrated into a writer's own sentence. He said *that they were making money.* **21d**.

infinitive The base form, or dictionary form, of a verb, preceded by *to: to see, to steal.* **21b, 24a, 35a** ESL, **35d** ESL.

intransitive verb A verb that is not followed by a direct object: Exciting events *have occurred.* He *fell.* **22c, 22d, 22g**. See also *transitive verb.*

irregular verb A verb that does not form its past tense and past participle with *-ed: sing, sang, sung.* **22a**.

linking verb A verb connecting a subject to its complement. Typical linking verbs are *be, become, seem,* and *appear:* He *seems* angry. A linking verb is intransitive; it does not take a direct object. **24a, 25b**.

mental activity verb A verb not used in a tense showing progressive aspect: *prefer, want, understand.* He *wants* to leave (*not* He *is wanting*). **22d**.

misplaced modifier An adverb (particularly *only* and *even*) or a descriptive phrase or clause positioned in a sentence in such a way that it appears to modify the wrong word or words: She showed the doll to her sister *that her aunt gave her.* **21b**.

mixed structure A sentence with two or more types of structures that do not match grammatically: *By doing* her homework at the last minute *caused* Meg to make many mistakes. **21a**.

modal auxiliary verb An auxiliary verb used with the base form of the main verb. Modal auxiliaries are seldom used alone and do not change form. The modal auxiliaries are *will, would, can, could, shall, should, may, might,* and *must.* **22b**.

modifier A word or words describing a noun, verb, phrase, or whole clause: He is a *happy* man. He is smiling *happily.* **21b, 25**.

mood The mood of a verb tells whether it states a fact (*indicative:* She *goes* to school); gives a command (*imperative: Come* back soon); or expresses a condition, wish, or request (*subjunctive:* I wish you *were* not leaving). **22f**.

nonrestrictive phrase or clause A phrase or clause, set off with commas, that adds nonessential information to a sentence: His report, *which he gave to his boss yesterday,* received enthusiastic praise. Also called *nonessential phrase* or *clause.* **24e, 26c**.

noun A word that names a person, place, thing, or idea. Nouns can be proper or common and, if common, countable or uncountable. **34a** ESL. See also the following entries on the various types of nouns: *collective noun, common noun, compound noun, countable noun, generic noun, proper noun, uncountable noun.*

number The indication of a noun or pronoun as singular (one person, place, thing, or idea) or plural (more than one). **23a, 24a**.

object of preposition A noun or pronoun (along with its modifiers) following a preposition: on *the beach.* **35c** ESL.

paragraph A group of sentences, usually on one topic, set off in a text. **1, 4a, 16b.**

parallelism The use of coordinate structures that have the same grammatical form: She likes *swimming* and *playing* tennis. **21f**.

participle phrase A phrase beginning with a present participle (-*ing*) or a past participle: The woman *wearing a green skirt* is my sister. *Baffled by the puzzle,* he gave up. **21c, 22a**.

passive voice Attribute of a verb when its grammatical subject is the receiver of the action that the verb describes: The book *was written* by my professor. **15c, 22g**. See also *active voice.*

past participle A form of a verb, ending in -*ed* for regular verbs and having various forms for irregular verbs. The past participle needs an auxiliary verb or verbs in order to function as a complete verb of a clause: *has chosen, was cleaned, might have been told.* It can also function alone as an adjective. **22a, 22e, 22g, 35e** ESL.

perfect progressive verb tense forms Verb tenses that show actions in progress up to a specific point in present, past, or future time. For active voice verbs, use a form of the auxiliary *have been* followed by the -*ing* form of the verb: *has/have been living, had been living, will have been living.* **22d**.

perfect verb tense forms Verb tenses that show actions completed by present, past, or future time. For active voice verbs, use forms of the auxiliary *have* followed by the past participle of the verb: *has/have arrived, had arrived, will have arrived.* **22d**.

person   The form of a pronoun or verb that indicates whether the subject is doing the speaking (first person, *I* or *we*); is spoken to (second person, *you*); or is spoken about (third person, *he, she, it,* or *they*). **24a, 24b**.

phrase   A group of words that does not contain a subject and a verb but that functions as a noun, verb, adjective, or adverb: *under the tree, to work hard.* **19c**. See also *absolute phrase, appositive phrase,* and *participle phrase.*

possessive   The form of a noun or pronoun that indicates ownership (such as *my, his, their,* and *theirs*). The possessive form of a noun is indicated by an apostrophe or an apostrophe and *-s: Mario's* car, the *children's* nanny, the *birds'* nests. **24a, 27a, 27b**.

predicate   The part of a sentence that contains the verb and its modifiers and that comments on or makes an assertion about the subject. **21e**.

preposition   A word used before a noun or pronoun to indicate time, space, or some other relationship (such as *in, to, for, about, during*). **35c** ESL.

present participle   The *-ing* form of a verb, showing an action in progress or as continuous: They are *sleeping.* Without an auxiliary, the *-ing* form cannot be a complete verb, but it can be used as an adjective: *searing* heat. **22a, 35e** ESL.

progressive verb tense forms   Verb tenses that show actions in progress at a certain point or over a period of time in past, present, or future time. They use a form of *be* + the *-ing* form of the verb: They *are working;* he *will be writing.* **22a**.

pronoun   A word used to represent a noun or a noun phrase. Pronouns are of various types: personal *(I, they)*; possessive *(my, mine, their, theirs)*; demonstrative *(this, that, these, those)*; intensive or reflexive *(myself, herself)*; relative *(who, whom, whose, which, that)*; interrogative *(who, which, what)*; and indefinite *(anyone, something).* **23g, 24, 36a** ESL.

pronoun reference   The connection between a pronoun and its antecedent. Reference should be clear and unambiguous: The *lawyer* picked up *his* hat and left. **24b**.

proper noun   The capitalized name of a specific person, place, or thing: *Golden Gate Park, University of Kansas.* **31a, 34a** ESL.

quantity word   A word expressing the idea of quantity (such as *each, several, some, many,* or *much*). Subject-verb agreement is important with quantity words: *Each* of the students *has* a different assignment. **23h**. See also *agreement*.

reflexive pronoun   A pronoun ending in *-self* or *-selves* and referring to the subject of a clause. Standard forms are *himself* and *themselves*. See *hisself* in **Glossary of Usage**, page 217.

regular verb   Verb with *-ed* in past tense and past participle forms. **22a**.

relative clause   Also called an *adjective clause,* a relative clause is a dependent clause beginning with a relative pronoun *(who, whom, whose, which,* or *that)* and modifying a noun or pronoun: The writer *who won the prize* was elated. **23i, 24e**.

relative pronoun   Pronoun that introduces a relative clause: *who, whom, whose, which, that.* **23i, 24e**.

restrictive phrase or clause   A phrase or clause that provides information necessary to the meaning of the word or phrase it modifies. A restrictive phrase or clause is not set off with commas: The book *that is first on the bestseller list* is a memoir. Also called *essential phrase or clause.* **24e, 26c**.

run-on sentence   Two independent clauses not separated by a coordinating conjunction or by any punctuation. Also called *fused sentence: The dog ate the meat the cat ate the fish.* (Corrected: *The dog ate the meat; the cat ate the fish.*) **20**.

second person   The person addressed: *you.* **24a, 24d**.

shifts   Inappropriate switches in grammatical structure such as from one tense to another, between statement and command, or between indirect and direct quotation: Joan asked *whether I was warm enough and did I sleep well.* (Corrected: . . . *and had slept well.*) **21d**.

split infinitive   An infinitive with a word or words inserted between *to* and the base form of the verb: *to successfully complete.* Some readers may object to this structure. **21b**.

Standard English   "The variety of English that is generally acknowledged as the model for the speech and writing of educated speakers."—*American Heritage Dictionary.* **23**.

subject   The noun or pronoun that performs the action of the verb in an active voice sentence or receives the action of the verb in a passive voice sentence. Every sentence needs a subject and a verb. **15a, 16a, 19, 19c, 21c, 21e, 23**.

subjunctive   See *mood.*

subordinate clause   See *dependent clause.*

subordinating conjunction A word (such as *because, if, when, although, since, while*) used to introduce a dependent adverb clause. **19b, 26b.**

superlative The form of an adjective or adverb used to compare three or more people or things: *biggest, most unusual, least effectively.* **25e.**

tense The form of a verb that indicates time. Verbs change form to distinguish present and past time: He *goes;* he *went.* Auxiliary verbs indicate progressive and perfect actions. **22d.** See also *perfect, progressive,* and *perfect progressive verb tense forms.*

third person The person or thing spoken about: *he, she, it, they,* or nouns. **24a.**

transitional expression A word or phrase (usually followed by a comma) used to connect two independent clauses. Typical transitional expressions are *for example, however,* and *similarly:* We were able to swim today; *in addition,* we took the canoe out on the river. **16b, 20, 26a, 29b.**

transitive verb A verb that has an object, a person or thing that receives the action (in the active voice): Dogs *chase* cats. Transitive verbs can be used in the passive voice (in which case the subject receives the action of the verb): Cats *are chased* by dogs. **22c, 22g.** See also *intransitive verb.*

uncountable noun A common noun that cannot follow a plural quantity word (such as *several* or *many*) is never used with *a* or *an,* is used with a singular third person verb, and has no plural form: *furniture, happiness, information.* **23d, 23h, 34a** ESL, **34b** ESL, **34c** ESL.

verb A word that expresses action or being and that tells what the subject of the clause is or does. A complete verb of a clause might require auxiliary or modal auxiliary verbs to complete its meaning. **22.** See also the following entries for more specific information.

active voice	mental activity	perfect verb tense
agreement	verb	forms
auxiliary verb	modal auxiliary	predicate
base form	verb	present participle
complete verb	mood	progressive verb
compound	passive voice	tense forms
predicate	past participle	regular verb
infinitive	perfect progressive	tense
intransitive verb	verb tense	transitive verb
irregular verb	forms	voice
linking verb		

voice Transitive verbs (those followed by an object) can be used in the active voice *(He is painting the door)* or the passive voice *(The door is being painted).* **22g.**

zero article The lack of an article *(a, an,* or *the)* before a noun. Uncountable nouns are used with the zero article when they make no specific reference. **34b** ESL, **34c** ESL.

Text Credits

Part 1: Page 14 (top), *A Nation Online: How Americans Are Expanding Their Use of the Internet*, Feb. 2002: 28. Data taken from Table 2-3, <http://www.ntia.gov/ntiahome/dn/anationonline2.pdf>.

Page 14 (bottom), Insurance Institute for Highway Safety, *The New York Times*, 22 Apr. 2003: A16 (figure "Danger on the Road"). Copyright © 2003 by The New York Times Co. Reprinted with permission.

Page 15 (top), College Board, *Trends in College Pricing 2002: Annual Survey of Colleges* (New York: College Board, 2002) (figure "Average Tuition and Fee Charges (Enrollment Weighted) in Constant (2002) Dollars, 1971–1972 to 2002–2003"). <http://www.collegeboard.com>. Copyright © 2002 by College Entrance Examination Board. Reprinted with permission. All rights reserved.

Page 15 (bottom), L. J. Sax, Jr., *The American Freshman: National Norms for Fall 2002.* Los Angeles Higher Education Research Institute, University of California at Los Angeles, 2003 <http://gseis.ucla.edu/heri/norms_charts.pdf>. Reprinted by permission of The Higher Education Research Institute.

Page 16 (bottom), National Telecommunications and Information Administration, *A Nation Online: How Americans Are Expanding Their Use of the Internet* , Feb. 2002: 28. Data taken from Table 2-3, <http://www.ntia.gov/ntiahome/dn/anationonline2.pdf>.

Page 17, James A. Davis, Tom W. Smith, and Peter V. Marsden, *General Social Survey, 1972–2002* [cumulative file] [computer file], 2nd ICPSR version (Chicago: National Opinion Research Center [producer], 2003. Storrs, CT: Roper Center for Public Opinion Research, University of Connecticut / Ann Arbor, MI: Inter-University Consortium for Political and Social Research, 1972–2002.

Part 2: Page 46, From *http://www.reclaimdemocracy.org/ independent_business/dead_malls.html*. Reprinted by permission.

Part 4: Page 80 (top and bottom), © EBSCO Publishing, 2004. All rights reserved.

Part 7: Page 191, The quotation from "Toads" by Philip Larkin is reprinted from *The Less Deceived* by permission of The Marvell Press, England and Australia.

Page 192, Aurora Levins Morales, "Class Poem," in Aurora Morales and Rosario Morales, eds., *Getting Home Alive* (Ithaca, NY: Firebrand), 45-47. Copyright 1986 by Aurora Levins Morales. Used with permission from Firebrand Books, Ithaca, N.Y.

Part 9: Page 228, definition for "Standard English," copyright © 2000 by Houghton Mifflin Company. Reproduced by permission from *The American Heritage Dictionary of the English Language,* 4th edition.

Index

Note: An asterisk (*) refers to a page number in the Glossary of Grammatical Terms.

a, an, the
  article use and, 201–203
  nouns and, 200–204
  specific references and, 203–204
Abbreviations
  in CBE style, 58
  guidelines for, 194–195
  plural forms of, 195
Abrupt shifts, 144
Absolute phrases, 102, 221*
Abstracts
  APA citation style for, 100, 103
  APA sample of, 106
  Chicago citation style for, 112
  MLA style for citing, 76
  online, 103
accept, except, expect, 212
Action checks, 124–125
Active voice, 152, 159, 221*
adapt, adopt, 212
Adjective clauses. *See* Relative clauses
Adjectives
  commas between, 179
  comparative and superlative, 173–174
  compound, 173, 197, 223*
  coordinate, 223*
  correct forms of, 171–172
  cumulative, 223*
  explanation of, 221*
  -ing and *-ed* forms as, 206–207
  past participles as, 156
  when to use, 172
adopt, adapt, 212
Adverb clauses, 141, 222*

Adverbs
  comparative and superlative, 173–174
  correct forms of, 171–172
  explanation of, 221*
  irregular forms of, 172
  when to use, 172
Advertisements, MLA citation style for, 88
advice, advise, 212
a few, few, 217
affect, effect, 212
Afterwords
  APA citation style for, 99–100
  MLA citation style for, 73
Age references, 131
Agreement
  explanation of, 222*
  subject-verb, 160–165
all ready, already, 212
all right, alright, 212
all together, altogether, 212
allude, elude, 212
allusion, illusion, 212
almost, most, 212
a lot, alot, lots, 213
already, all ready, 212
alright, all right, 212
AltaVista, 26
although clauses, 209–210
altogether, all together, 212
ambivalent, ambiguous, 213
American Psychological Association (APA) style. *See* APA (American Psychological Association) style
among, between, 213
amoral, immoral, 213
amount, number, 213
and/or, 191

Angle brackets, 77, 79, 191, 198

Antecedents
explanation of, 222*
with pronouns, 168–170

Anthology citations
APA style for, 94, 98–99
Chicago citation style for, 111
MLA style for, 64, 71

anyone, any one, 213

anyway, anywhere, nowhere, anyways, anywheres, nowheres, 213

APA (American Psychological Association) style
for articles, 100–102
basic features of, 92
for books, 97–100
colored type and, 12
for electronic and Internet sources, 102–104
formatting and presenting papers in, 11, 12, 13
for in-text citations, 92–96
key points for, 96–97
for long quotations, 54–55
for multimedia and miscellaneous sources, 105
sample paper in, 105–107
tense use and, 155

apart, a part, 213

Apostrophes
explanation of, 183
in *it's* vs. *its,* 185
in possessive pronouns, 168
to show possession, 183, 184
use of, 183–185

Appositive phrases
explanation of, 222*
pronouns with, 167

Architecture sources, 29

Arguments
audience and, 9
features of good, 7
formulating claims in, 7–8
providing reasons and support for, 8–9
writing, 6–9

Aristotle, 9

Articles (grammar)
basic questions about, 201–202
basic rules for, 202–203
explanation of, 222*

Articles (reference)
APA citation style for, 100–102
CBE citation style for, 118–120
Chicago citation style for, 111–112
evaluating, 41
MLA citation style for, 74–76, 82
scholarly vs. nonscholarly, 39–40

Art sources, 29

Art works
italicizing or underlining titles of, 193
MLA citation style for, 87–88

as, as if, like, 213, 218

as regards, in regard to, 213, 217

Asterisks, 198

at at the end of questions, 213

Audience
appeals to, 9
considering, 9

Author citations
APA style for, 93–96
CBE style for, 118–119
Chicago style for, 108–109
MLA style for, 56, 63–65, 70–74
for online sources, 78

An asterisk (*) refers to a page number in the Glossary of Grammatical Terms.

Auxiliary verbs
    explanation of, 147, 222*
    modal, 147, 151–152, 225*
    use of, 151–152
awful, awfully, 213
a while, awhile, 213

bad, badly, 213
barely, 214
Bar graphs, 15–16
Base form, 222*
because, because of, 213
because clauses, 209–210
being as, being that, 214
belief, believe, 214
beside, besides, 214
better, 214
between, 214
Biased language, 130–132
Bible citations
    colons in, 190
    italics or underlining and,
        193
    MLA style for, 68, 74
Bibliographies, 28
    Chicago style for, 109–110,
        114–115
    working, 38–39
Biology sources, 29
Blogs, 42
    MLA style for, 84–85
Bookmarks, 28, 39
Books
    APA citation style for,
        97–100
    CBE citation style for,
        118–119
    Chicago citation style for,
        109–111
    evaluating, 40–41
    MLA citation style for,
        69–74
    MLA citation style for
        online, 81
Boolean searching, 26
Brackets
    angle, 77, 79, 191, 198
    square, 54, 191

breath, breathe, 214
Business research sources, 30
Business sources. *See*
        Organizations or
        corporations as sources

can't hardly, 214
Capital Community College
        site, 7
Capitalization
    in MLA Works Cited list, 69
    rules for, 193–194
Cartoons, MLA citation style
        for, 88
CBE/CSE (Council of Biology
        Editors/Council of
        Science Editors) style
    abbreviations in, 58
    for articles, 118–120
    for author citations, 118–119
    basic features of, 117
    for books, 118–119
    for databases, 119–120
    discussion lists, 120
    for electronic sources,
        119–120
    formatting papers in, 11,
        13, 115–116, 120
    headings in, 13
    indentation in, 109
    in-text citations in, 117
    list of references in, 117–118
    paper formatting in, 120
    title pages in, 11
CD-ROMs
    Chicago citation style for, 114
    MLA citation style for, 85
Charts
    MLA citation style for, 86
    for reading Web sites, 44–46
Chemistry sources, 30
Chicago Manual of Style style,
        58
    basic features of, 108
    for bibliographies, 114–115
    for endnotes, 108–114
    formatting and presenting
        papers in, 11

Chicago Manual of Style style
(*continued*)
  for in-text citations, 108
  paper formatting in,
    115–116
  title pages in, 11
Citations. *See also specific*
  styles for
  indicating boundaries of,
    49–51
  paraphrases and, 52–53
  plagiarism and, 51–52
  for quotations, 56
cite, site, sight, 214
Classical works
  APA citation style for, 96
  Chicago citation style for,
    111
Classics sources, 31
Clauses
  adverb, 141, 222*
  because and *although,*
    209–210
  conditional, 157–158, 223*
  dependent, 135–136, 179,
    189, 224*
  explanation of, 222*
  independent, 135–138, 179,
    189, 225*
  nonrestrictive, 179, 181, 226*
  relative, 165, 182, 228*
  restrictive, 171, 182, 228*
Clichés, 128, 187, 222*
Collective nouns
  explanation of, 222*
  pronouns with, 169
  subject-verb agreement
    and, 166
Colons
  correcting run-on sentences
    with, 140
  with quotations, 185, 186
  using, 189–190
Commas
  correcting run-on sentences
    with, 140

  guidelines for using,
    179–181
  with independent clauses,
    138
  with inserted material, 191
  with quotations, 185, 186
  semicolons vs., 189
  when not to use, 180–181
Comma splices
  correcting, 138–139
  explanation of, 172, 222*
Common ground, in
  arguments, 9
Communications sources, 21
Comparatives
  explanation of, 222*
  pronouns with, 167
complement, compliment,
  214
Complements, 172, 181, 222*
Complete verbs, 222*
Compose, comprise, 214
Compound adjectives
  explanation of, 223*
  hyphens with, 197
  using, 173
Compound nouns
  apostrophes with, 184
  explanation of, 223*
  hyphens with, 197
Compound predicates, 137,
  223*
Compound subjects
  explanation of, 223*
  pronouns with, 166
  subject-verb agreement
    and, 163–164
Compound verbs, 146
Computer science research
  sources, 31–32
Computer software
  APA citation style for, 105
  italicizing or underlining
    titles of, 193
Conditional clauses, 157–158,
  223*

Conjunctions
    coordinating, 138, 179, 180,
        223*
    explanation of, 223*
    subordinating, 135–136,
        138–139, 200*, 209–210
Connections, 125–127
conscience, conscious, 214–215
Consistency, 126
    on tone, 127–128
continual, continuous, 215
Contractions, 223*
Coordinate adjectives, 223*
Coordinating conjunctions
    commas with, 179, 180
    explanation of, 223*
    independent clauses with,
        138
Copyright law, 52
Corporate sources
    APA citation style for, 95,
        99
    MLA citation style for, 72
could care less, 215
Countable nouns
    articles with, 201–203, 202
    explanation of, 201, 223*
Course pages, 84
Court cases
    MLA citation style for, 68,
        88
credible, creditable, credulous,
    215
Cultural differences, 52
Cumulative adjectives
    explanation of, 223*
custom, customs, costume,
    215

dairy, diary, 215
Dangling modifiers, 143–144,
    223*
Dashes, 190–191
    correcting run-on sentences
        with, 140
Databases
    accessing, 28
    APA citation style for, 102

CBE citation style for,
    119–120
MLA citation style for, 82
Definitions
    the reason is in, 145–146
    when/where in, 145–146
Demands, verb forms with,
    159
Demonstrative pronouns,
    223*
Dependent clauses
    commas with, 179, 180
    explanation of, 224*
    semicolons with, 189
    sentence fragments and,
        135–136
desert, dessert, 215
Dialogue, 186–187
Diction, 224*
Dictionaries, 28
    MLA citation style for
        entries in, 66
different from, different than,
    215
Direct objects
    explanation of, 224*
    word order and, 208–209
Direct questions, 209
Direct quotations
    commas with, 179, 185
    explanation of, 224*
    shifts with, 144
Disabilities, unbiased language
    and, 132
Discussion lists, 42
    APA citation style for, 104
    CBE citation style for, 120
    Chicago citation style for,
        114
    MLA style for, 84–85
disinterested, uninterested,
    215
*Dissertation Abstracts
    International,* 74
Dissertations
    APA citation style for, 100
    MLA citation style for, 74
do, due, 215

Documentation, 57–58
Document design, 10–21
    APA style for, 11, 12, 13
    CBE style for, 11, 13, 120
    Chicago style for, 11,
        115–116
    for essays, 10–11
    image analysis and, 18–19
    image partnerships with
        text in, 19–21
    MLA style for, 11, 12, 13,
        88–90
    visuals in, 13–17
Dogpile, 26
Double negatives, 173, 224*
due, do, 215
due to, 215
*due to the fact that, owing to
    the fact that*, 216
Dummy subjects. *See* Filler
    subjects

each, every, 216
each other, one another, 216
E-books, *Chicago* citation
    style for, 114
Economics research sources,
    32
-*ed* forms, 156–157
Editor citations
    APA style, 94, 98–99
    Chicago style for, 111
    MLA style, 64, 70–71
Editorials, APA citation style
    for, 102
Education research sources, 32
effect, affect, 212
e.g., 216
Electronic sources
    APA citation style for, 96,
        102–104
    CBE citation style for,
        119–120
    Chicago citation style for,
        112–114
    MLA citation style for, 67

elicit, illicit, 216
Ellipses
    explanation of, 224*
    with quotations, 54
    using, 192
elude, allude, 212
E-mail
    angle brackets with
        addresses for, 191
    APA citation style for, 96,
        104
emigrate, immigrate, 216
eminent, imminent, 216
Emotional appeals, 9
Encyclopedias, 27
    MLA citation style for, 71
    MLA citation style for
        entries in, 66
Endnotes, 58
    in APA style, 92
    Chicago style for, 108–114
    MLA style for, 62
Engineering research sources,
    32–33
Environmental studies
    research sources, 33
ESL writers. *See*
    Multilingual/ESL writers
Essay format, 10–11
-*est* forms, hyphens with, 197
et al., 64
etc., 216
Ethical appeals, 9
Ethnicity, unbiased language
    and, 131
Ethnic studies research
    sources, 33
Evaluating Web Resources, 43
every, each, 216
everyday, every day, 216
Evidence, for arguments, 9
except, accept, expect, 212
Exclamation points
    quotation marks and, 186
    quotations and, 63
    using, 188

An asterisk (*) refers to a page number in the Glossary of Grammatical Terms.

Exclusionary language, 130–132
expect, accept, except, 212
explicit, implicit, 216

farther, further, 216
Faulty predication, 144, 224*
female, male, 217
few, a few, 217
fewer, less, 217
Field research, 24–25
Filler subjects, 224*
Films
  APA citation style for, 105
  Chicago citation style for,
    114
  italicizing or underlining
    titles of, 193
  MLA citation style for, 86
First person, 224*
Fonts, 12
  colored, 12
  for essays, 11
Footnotes, 62, 92, 108
Forewords
  APA citation style for,
    99–100
  MLA citation style for, 73
Formulaic phrases, 123
Forwarded documents, MLA
  style for, 84–85
Fragments, 224*. *See also*
  Sentence fragments
Frames, 45
further, farther, 217
Fused sentences. *See* Run-on
  sentences

Gender, 224*
Gender bias, 130–132
Generic nouns, 169, 224*
Geography research sources,
  28, 33
Geology research sources, 34
Gerunds, 224*
  as adjectives, 206–207
  possessives with, 167–168
  subject-verb agreement
    with, 162

verbs followed by, 205
verbs followed by infinitives
  or, 206
verbs followed by
  prepositions and,
  205–206
get married to, marry, 217
Google, 12, 26, 40
Government publications
  APA citation style for, 95,
    99
  Chicago citation style for,
    111
  MLA citation style for, 65
  research using, 28
Grammar checking programs,
  4
Graphs, 13–17
  bar, 15–16
  line, 14–15
  MLA citation style for, 86
  pie, 17
  using, 17

had better, 217
hardly, 217
Headings, document design
  and, 13
Health, unbiased language
  and, 132
Helping verbs. *See* Auxiliary
  verbs
he/she, 191
hisself, 217
Historical documents, MLA
  citation style for, 68
History research sources, 34
Hotbot, 26
http://, 198
Humanities documentation,
  57–58
Hyphens, 197
  in Internet addresses, 198
  for repeated author name in
    MLA Works Cited list, 69

ibid., 110
illicit, elicit, 216

illusion, allusion, 212
I, me, 24a
immigrate, emigrate, 216
imminent, eminent, 217
immoral, amoral, 213
implicit, explicit, 217
imply, infer, 217
incredible, incredulous, 217
Indefinite pronouns
   explanation of, 225*
   pronoun reference and, 169
   subject-verb agreement
      and, 164
Indentation
   in APA references list, 97
   in CBE style, 109
   in MLA Works Cited list, 69
Independent clauses
   comma splices and,
      138–139
   commas with, 179, 180
   explanation of, 225*
   run-on sentences and,
      138–139
   semicolons with, 189
   sentence fragments and,
      135–138
Indexes, 28
Indirect objects, 208–209, 225*
Indirect questions, 209, 225*
Indirect quotations
   explanation of, 225*
   past tense with, 155
   quotations marks with, 187
   shifts with, 144
infer, imply, 217
Infinitives
   explanation of, 225*
   personal pronouns with,
      167
   split, 143, 228*
   verbs followed by, 204–205
Infomine, 28
-ing forms. *See* Gerunds
in regard to, as regards, 213,
   217

install, instill, 217
instill, install, 217
Internet. *See also* Online
   sources
   capitalization in addresses
      for, 198
   search engines, 25–28
Internet Public Library, 28
Internet sources
   APA citation style for, 96,
      102–104
   CBE citation style for,
      119–120
   Chicago citation style for,
      112–114
   MLA citation style for, 65,
      66, 67, 77–85
Interviews
   APA citation style for, 96,
      105
   Chicago citation style for, 114
   MLA citation style for, 67,
      85–86
In-text citations
   APA style for, 93–96
   CBE style for, 117
   MLA style for, 63–68
Intransitive verbs
   explanation of, 225*
   passive voice and, 159
   tense and, 154
   using, 152–153
Introductions
   APA citation style for,
      99–100
   MLA citation style for, 73
irregardless, 218
Irregular verbs
   explanation of, 147, 225*
   list of, 148–151
   past participles with,
      148–151, 157
it, there, 124–125
Italics
   explanation of, 192
   Internet sources and, 198

An asterisk (*) refers to a page number in the Glossary of Grammatical Terms.

in MLA Works Cited list,
69
for titles, 192–193
it's, its, 185, 218

Jargon, 129–130

Keyword searches
explanation of, 25–28
for online sources, 28
kind, sort, type, 218
kind of, sort of, 218

Latin abbreviations, 195
Lectures
Chicago citation style for,
114
MLA citation style for, 67
Legal documents
MLA citation style for, 68,
88
lend, loan, 218
less, fewer, 217, 218
Letters
APA citation style for, 96,
105
as letters, 193
MLA citation style for, 67,
76, 86
Letters (alphabet), *'s* with,
184
Letters to the editor
APA citation style for, 102
Chicago citation style for,
112
Librarians, 25
*Librarians' Index to the
Internet,* 28
Library of Congress, 28
lie, lay, 153
like, as, as if, 213, 218
Line graphs, 14–15
Linguistics research sources,
34
Linked sites
in essays, 11
Linking verbs
adjectives with, 172

explanation of, 225*
personal pronouns with,
166
Lists, 12–13
literally, 218
Literature
APA citation style for, 96
Chicago citation style for,
111
MLA citation style for,
67–68
research sources on,
34–35
Live performances, MLA
citation style for, 87
loan, lend, 218
Logical sequence after
subjects, 144
loose, lose, 218
lots, a lot, alot, 213
-ly forms, hyphens with, 197

Magazines
APA citation style for, 101
CBE citation style for, 119
Chicago citation style for,
112
MLA citation style for, 75,
82
online, 82
male, female, 217
Maps
MLA citation style for, 86
Margins
for college essays, 10
marital, martial, 218
marry, get married to, 217
Mathematics research sources,
35
may be, maybe, 218
Media research sources, 31
MEGO reaction, 122
Mental activity verbs, 154,
225*
MetaCrawler, 26
Meta search engines, 26
Microfiche citations
MLA style for, 74, 76

Microfilm citations
  MLA style for, 74, 76
Microform citations
  MLA style for, 74, 76
Misplaced modifiers
  explanation of, 225*
  using, 142–143
Mixed structure
  correcting, 141–142
  explanation of, 225*
*MLA Handbook for Writers of
  Research Papers*
  (Gibaldi), 62
MLA (Modern Language
  Association) style
  angle brackets in, 191
  for articles, 74–76
  for author/page in-text
    citations, 63–65
  basic features of, 62
  for books, 69–74
  for citations, 56
  colored type and, 12
  for dictionary or
    encyclopedia entries, 66
  for electronic sources, 67
  for end punctuation,
    187–188
  explanation of, 68–69
  formatting and presenting
    papers in, 11, 12, 13
  headings in, 13
  for Internet sources, 65, 66,
    67, 77–85
  italics vs. underlining in,
    192
  key points about, 68–69
  for long quotations, 54
  for miscellaneous sources,
    86–88
  for online or electronic
    sources, 66, 77–85
  page numbers not available
    or relevant and, 66
  for paper formatting and
    presenting, 88–90

  publication dates in, 57–58
  unnamed author citations
    in, 65–66
  URLs in, 198
Modal auxiliary verbs
  explanation of, 147, 225*
  using, 151–152
Modern Language
  Association. *See* MLA
  (Modern Language
  Association) style
Modifiers
  dangling, 143–144, 223*
  explanation of, 226*
  misplaced, 142–143, 225*
Money phrases, 162
Mood, 226*
MOOs (multiuser domains,
  object-oriented), MLA
  style for, 85
most, almost, 212
MUDs (multiuser domains),
  MLA style for, 85
Multilingual/ESL writers
  a, an, the and, 200–204
  infinitive, *-ing,* and *-ed*
    forms and, 204–207
  it as subject and, 125
  language use and, 3
  sentence structure/word
    order and, 207–210
Multivolume works
  APA citation style for, 99
  MLA citation style for, 72
Music research sources, 35
myself, 219

Negatives
  double, 173, 224*
  position of, 204–205
Newspapers
  APA citation style for, 101,
    102, 103
  CBE citation style for, 119
  Chicago citation style for,
    112

MLA citation style for, 75, 83
online, 83, 102, 103
Nonprint source citations. *See
also* Internet; World Wide
Web
MLA style for, 67
Nonrestrictive phrases or
clauses
commas with, 181–182
explanation of, 226*
normal, unbiased language
and, 132
Nouns
collective, 163, 169–170, 222*
common, 200, 201, 222*
compound, 158, 197, 223*
countable, 201–203, 223*
explanation of, 226*
generic, 169, 224*
pronouns with possessive,
167–168
proper, 193, 200, 201, 227*
subject-verb agreement
and, 162
uncountable, 162, 201–203,
229*
nowadays, 219
*nowhere, anyway, anywhere,
anyways, anywheres,
nowheres,* 213
number, amount, 213
Numbers, spelling out vs.
numerals for, 196–197
Nursing research sources,
35–36

Objects
direct, 208–209, 224*
indirect, 208–209, 225*
of prepositions, 226*
pronouns with compound,
166
off, off of, 219
OK, O.K., okay, 219
Omissions
ellipses to signal, 54, 192,
224*
from quotations, 54

one another, each other, 216
Online sources
APA citation style for, 96
basics for citing, 77
CBE citation style for, 120
course pages, 84
dates for, 78–79
difficulties with, 46
discussion lists and blogs,
42
evaluating, 25, 41–43, 42–43
frames in, 45
home pages, 120
how to read, 44–46
indexes, 28
internal capitalization in
names of, 194
italics and underlining and,
193, 198
links on, 43
MLA citation style for, 66,
77–85
publishers/sponsors of, 46
recognizing scholarly
articles in, 40
recording information
from, 45
search engines, 25–28
special considerations with,
78–79
subscription services or
databases, 41, 79–81
titles of, 78, 193
URL punctuation and, 198
Web-based journals and
magazines, 41
Web sites, 42
only, 142–143
Order. *See* Word order
Organization of papers, 56–57
Organizations or corporations
as sources
APA citation style for, 95,
99
MLA citation style for, 65,
72
Outlining supporting points,
5–6

*owing to the fact that, due to
    the fact that,* 216

Papers
    APA style for, 105–107
    CBE style for, 115–116
    Chicago style for, 115–116
    MLA style for, 88–90
    organization of, 56–57
Paper types, 10
*Paradigm Online Writing
    Assistant,* 7
Paragraphs, 226*
    connecting, 126–127
Parallelism, 145, 226*
Paraphrases, 52–53
Parentheses, 191
Participle phrases, 226*
passed, past, 210
Passive voice
    avoiding, 125
    explanation of, 226*
    past participles with, 152,
        159
    using, 159
Past participles
    explanation of, 147, 226*
    irregular verbs with,
        148–151, 157
    passive voice with, 152, 159
    regular verbs with,
        156–157
Past perfect progressive tense,
    156
Past perfect tense, 156
Past progressive tense, 155
Past tenses
    for irregular verbs,
        148–151, 157
    past perfect, 156
    past perfect progressive,
        156
    past progressive, 155
    regular verbs and, 417
    verb forms and, 156–157
Percentages, 17

Perfect progressive verb tense,
    226*
Perfect verb tense, 154–155,
    226–227*
Periods
    after quotations, 63
    with ellipses, 192
    in MLA Works Cited list, 69
    with parenthetical citations
        in long quotations, 55
    with quotation marks, 186
    spaces with, 11
    using, 188
Person, 165, 227*
personal, personnel, 219
Personal communications
    APA citation style for, 96,
        105
    MLA citation style for, 67
Personal pronouns
    antecedents with, 168–169
    explanation of, 227*
    forms of, 165–166
    using, 166–168
Philosophy research sources,
    36
Photographs
    MLA citation style for,
        87–88
    text with, 20
Phrase fragments, 135
Phrases. *See also* specific types
        of phrases
    absolute, 182, 221*
    explanation of, 227*
    formulaic, 123
Physics research sources, 36
Pie graphs, 17
Plagiarism
    checklist for avoiding, 51–52
    copying and pasting and, 25
    definition of, 48–49
    guidelines for avoiding,
        51–52
    knowing what to cite and,
        49

An asterisk (*) refers to a page number in the Glossary of Grammatical Terms.

paraphrasing and, 52–53
summarizing or
    paraphrasing and, 52–53
plus, 219
Poetry
    italicizing or underlining
        titles of, 193
    MLA citation style for, 67,
        82
    omissions from, 192
    online, 82
Point of view, shifts in, 144
Political references, unbiased
    language and, 131
Political science research
    sources, 36–37
Possessive pronouns, 166,
    167–168
Possessives
    apostrophes with, 183, 184
    explanation of, 227*
precede, proceed, 219
Predicates, 227*
Prefaces
    APA citation style for,
        99–100
    MLA citation style for, 73
Prefixes, hyphens with, 197
Prepositional phrases, 168
Prepositions
    explanation of, 227*
    pronouns with, 166
    verbs followed by, 205–206
Present participles, 147, 227*
Present perfect progressive
    tense, 154–155
Present perfect tense,
    154–155
Present tenses
    present perfect, 154–155
    present perfect progressive,
        154–155
    present progressive, 154
    simple, 154
    subject-verb agreement in,
        160
Pretentious language, 127–128
pretty, 219

principal, principle, 219
Progressive tenses
    explanation of, 227*
    past, 155
    past perfect, 156
    present, 154
    present perfect, 154–155
Pronouns
    agreement with antecedent
        and, 169–170
    clear reference in use of,
        168–169, 227*
    demonstrative, 223*
    explanation of, 165, 227*
    gender bias in use of, 131
    indefinite, 164, 170, 225*
    personal, 165–171
    possessive, 167–168
    reflexive, 228*
    who, whom, which, that,
        170–171
    you, 170
Proper nouns
    articles and, 201
    capitalization of, 193–194
    explanation of, 200, 227*
Psychology research sources,
    37
Public Agenda Online, 28
*Publication Manual of the
    American Psychological
    Association,* 92. *See also*
    APA (American
    Psychological
    Association) style
Publisher's imprints, MLA
    citation style for, 73
Punctuation. *See also specific
    punctuation marks*
    angle brackets, 191
    apostrophes, 183–185
    colons, 189–190
    commas, 178–183
    dashes, 190–191
    ellipsis dots, 192
    exclamation points, 188
    how to show meaning with,
        177–178

Punctuation *(continued)*
  importance of, 176–177
  parentheses, 191
  periods, 188
  question marks, 188
  quotation marks, 185–188
  semicolons, 189
  slashes, 191
  square brackets, 191
  in URLs, 198

qtd. in, 64–65
Quantity words, 164–165,
    227–228*
Question marks
  correcting run-on sentences
      with, 140
  with quotation marks, 186
  in quotations, 63
  using, 188
Questions
  direct, 209
  at at the end of, 185
  indirect, 209, 225*
  subject-verb agreement in,
      161
quite, quiet, 219
Quotation marks
  with dialogue, 186–187
  double and single, 187
  long passages and, 54–55
  with quotations, 185–186
  for titles of short works,
      187, 188
  when not to use, 187–188
Quotations
  adding to or changing
      words in, 54
  capitalization in, 194
  direct, 144, 179, 185, 224*
  guidelines for using, 53–55
  indented, 188
  indirect, 144, 185, 187, 225*
  introducing, 55–56
  punctuation with, 185–186
quote, quotation, 220

Racial affiliation, 131
Radio programs
  APA citation style for, 105
  italicizing or underlining
      titles of, 193
  MLA citation style for, 86–87
Rational appeals, 9
real, really, 220
reason is . . . , 146, 120
Reasons, supporting
    arguments with, 8–9
Recommendations, verb forms
    with, 159
References to your intentions,
    124
Reflexive pronouns, 228*
Regional language, 129
Regular verbs
  explanation of, 147, 228*
  past participles with,
      156–157
Relative clauses
  explanation of, 228*
  subject-verb agreement
      and, 165
Relative pronouns, 165,
    170–171, 228*
Religion research sources, 37
Religious references, unbiased
    language and, 131
Republished books
  APA citation style for, 100
  MLA citation style for, 73
Requests, verb forms with,
    159
Research. *See also* Sources
  field, 24–25
  finding sources in, 24–39
  focus in, 24
  keyword searches and,
      25–27
  online, 25–28
Research Quickstart, 28
*respectable, respectful,
    respective,* 220
respectfully, respectively, 220

An asterisk (*) refers to a page number in the Glossary of Grammatical Terms.

Restrictive phrases or clauses, 171, 181, 228*

Reviews
  APA citation style for, 101
  Chicago citation style for, 112

Reviews, citing, 76

rise, raise, 153

Run-on sentences
  correcting, 138–139
  explanation of, 138, 228*

Sacred text citations, 68
  colons in, 190
  italics or underlining with, 193

Sacred texts
  Chicago citation style for, 111
  MLA citation style for, 74

Scientific Style and Format: The CBE Manual for Authors, Editors, and Publishers (Council of Biology Editors), 116

Search engines, 25–28

Searches, keyword, 25–28

Second person, 166–167, 171, 228*

Semicolons
  with independent clauses, 138, 139, 189
  in lists with commas, 189
  with quotation marks, 186
  using, 189

Sentence fragments
  dependent clause fragments and, 135–136
  explanation of, 135
  identifying and correcting, 135
  intentional, 137–138
  missing verbs or subjects, 137
  phrase fragments and, 135

Sentence problems
  abrupt shifts, 144
  adjectives and adverbs, 171–174

compound structures and comparisons, 146
  dangling modifiers, 143–144
  definitions, 145–146
  logical sequence, 144
  misplaced modifiers, 142–143
  mixed constructions, 141–142
  parallel structures, 145
  pronouns, 165–171
  run-ons and comma splices, 138–139, 222*
  subject-verb agreement, 160–165
  verb problems, 160–165

Series, MLA citation style for, 73

Sexual orientation, unbiased language and, 132

Shifts, 144, 228*

should have, 152, 220

sic, 191

Simple past tense, 155

Simple present tense, 154

since, 220

sit, set, 153

site, sight, cite, 214

Slang, 129, 187

Slashes, 191

Slides
  Chicago citation style for, 114
  MLA citation style for, 87–88

Sociology research sources, 37–38

Software. *See* Computer software

sometimes, sometime, some time, 220

sort, kind, type, 218

sort of, kind of, 218

Sound recordings
  Chicago citation style for, 114
  MLA citation style for, 87

Sources
   evaluating, 25, 40–46
   indicating boundaries of
      citations of, 49–51
   introducing cited material
      from, 55–56
   keeping track of, 38–39
   key points about, 38–39
   online, 25–28
   plagiarism and, 47–58
   quoting from, 53–55
   scholarly and nonscholarly,
      39–40
   searching for, 24–39
   for specific subjects,
      28–38
Spacing, for essays, 11
Specific words, 128–129
Speeches
   Chicago citation style for,
      114
   MLA citation style for, 86
Spelling checkers, 4
Split infinitives, 143, 228*
Square brackets, 191
   adding to or changing
      words in quotations and,
      54
Standard English, 228*
stationary, stationery, 220
Statistics research sources, 35
*Stephen's Guide to the Logical
   Fallacies,* 7
Stereotypes, 131
Subjects
   compound, 164, 166, 223*
   consistent use of, 125
   explanation of, 228*
   filler, 224*
   it as, 125
   logical sequence after, 144
   sentence fragments and, 137
   verb use with, 124
Subject-verb agreement
   basic principles of, 160

collective nouns and, 163
compound subjects and,
   164
indefinite pronouns and,
   164
quantity words and,
   164–165
relative clauses and, 165
subject after verb and,
   161
tricky singular subjects and,
   162–163
words between subject and
   verb and, 160–161
Subjunctive. *See* Mood
Subordinate clauses. *See*
   Dependent clauses
Subordinating conjunctions
   comma splice correction
      with, 139
   correcting run-on sentences
      with, 140
   explanation of, 229*
   sentence fragments and,
      135–136
   using, 209–210
Subscription services, 79–81
   APA citation style for,
      102
   MLA citation style for,
      79–81
Summaries, 52–53
Superlatives
   of adjectives and adverbs,
      173–174
   explanation of, 229*
Supporting points, 5–6
   for arguments, 8–9
Synchronous communication
   citations, 85

Tables, 13–17
Tangled construction, 142
Technical reports, APA
   citation style for, 100

Television programs
    APA citation style for, 105
    italicizing or underlining
        titles of, 193
    MLA citation style for, 86–87
Tenses. *See also* specific tenses
    explanation of, 229*
    past perfect, 156
    past perfect progressive, 156
    past progressive, 155
    present perfect, 154–155
    present perfect progressive,
        154–155
    present progressive, 154
    simple past, 155
    simple present, 154
than, then, 220
that, 170–171
the, a, an, 200–204
their, there, they're, 220
theirself, theirselves, themself,
    220
there, it, 124–125
the reason is, 145–146, 220
Theses
    confident stance on, 127
    deriving from topics, 4–5
    elements of good, 5
    formulating arguable, 7–8
    providing reasons and
        support for, 8–9
    statement of, where to
        place, 5
*Thinking Critically about
    World Wide Web
    Resources,* 43
Third person, 165–166, 229*
Time phrases, subject-verb
    agreement and, 162
Title pages
    for essays, 11
    italics or underlining for,
        192–193
    personal, 194–195
    quotation marks with, 187,
        188
    within titles, 73

to, too, two, 221
Tone
    commitment to, 127–128,
        128–129
Transitional expressions
    comma splices and, 139
    commas with, 179
    connecting with, 126–127
    explanation of, 229*
    semicolons with, 189
Transitive verbs
    explanation of, 229*
    in passive voice, 159
    using, 153
Translated books
    APA citation style for, 99
    MLA citation style for, 72
Transportation vehicles,
    names of, 164
Trite expressions, 187
type, sort, kind, 218

Uncountable nouns
    articles and, 201, 202, 203
    explanation of, 201, 229*
    subject-verb agreement
        and, 162
Underlining
    guidelines for, 192–193
    Internet use and, 198
    in MLA Works Cited list, 69
Uniform Resource Locators.
    See URLs (Uniform
    Resource Locators)
uninterested, disinterested, 215
unique, 221
URLs (Uniform Resource
    Locators)
    angle brackets with, 79, 191
    copying and pasting, 79
    domain names in, 42
    .edu sources and, 42–43
    evaluating, 42–43
    MLA citation style for, 77
    MLA style for, 84–85
    narrowing searches by
        domains in, 27

URLs (Uniform Resource
    Locators) *(continued)*
  narrowing searches with, 27
  for online books, 81
  punctuation in, 198
  for subscription services
    and databases, 79–81
used to, get (become) used to,
    221
Usenet news group citations,
    MLA style for, 84–85

Verbs. *See also* Subject-verb
    agreement
  auxiliary, 147, 151–152, 222*
  complete, 223*
  compound, 146
  in conditional sentences,
    157–158
  explanation of, 147, 229*
  followed by infinitives,
    204–205
  followed by *-ing,* 205
  followed by preposition and
    -ing, 205–206
  intransitive, 152–153, 159,
    225*
  irregular, 148–151, 157,
    225*
  linking, 166, 200, 225*
  mental activity, 154, 225*
  modal auxiliary, 147,
    151–152, 225*
  regular, 147, 228*
  with requests, demands, and
    recommendations, 159
  sentence fragments and,
    137
  transitive, 152–153, 159,
    229*
  using correctly, 124–125
  with wishes, 158–159
Verb tenses
  explanation of, 153–154
  past perfect, 156

past perfect progressive, 156
past progressive, 155
present perfect, 154–155
present perfect progressive,
    154–155
present progressive, 154
simple past, 155
simple present, 154
Videos
  Chicago citation style for,
    114
  MLA citation style for, 86
Visual materials, 13–17
  creating in word processing
    programs, 13–14
  image analysis and, 18–19
  text with, 19–21
Vivid words, 128–129
Voice
  active, 152, 221*
  explanation of, 230*
  passive, 125, 152, 159, 226*

way, ways, 221
weather, whether, 221
Web. *See* World Wide Web
Web directories, 26
Weight phrases, 162
when, where, 145–146
which, 170–171
who, 170–171
whom, 170–171
whose, who's, 221
Widener Library Web site, 43
Wildcard characters, 26
Women's studies research
    sources, 38
Word choice
  biased language and,
    130–132
  tone and, 127–128
Wordiness, 123
Word order
  although and *because*
    clauses and, 209–210

An asterisk (*) refers to a page number in the Glossary of Grammatical Terms.

basic rules of, 207–210
direct and indirect objects
    and, 208–209
direct and indirect
    questions and, 209
Words, splitting at ends of
    lines, 197
Words, used as words, 193
World Wide Web. *See also*
    Online sources
    bookmarking sites on, 28,
        39
    corporate, governmental, or
        organizational authors
        on, 65
    evaluating sources on, 25,
        41–43
    research using, 25–28
    search engines, 25–28
    URL punctuation and, 198
Writing process
    for argument, 6–9
    document design and,
        10–21

organization of papers in,
    56–57
thesis statement and
    support and, 4–6
writing and revising in,
    2–4
Writing style
    action checks to improve,
        124–125
    audience and, 9
    committing to improve,
        127–128
    connecting to improve,
        125–127
    cutting to improve,
        122–124
    word choice in, 128–132
WWW Virtual Library, The, 28

Yahoo!, 26
you, 170
your, you're, 221

Zero article, 201, 230*

Key Points Boxes

Part One, The Writing Process

A Good Working Thesis, 5
The Features of a Good Argument, 7
Using Graphs, 17
On Using Visuals, 21

Part Two, Researching and Using Sources

Keyword Searching, 26
Recording the Information You Need, 38
Developing Your Junk Antennae for Web Sites, 42

Part Three, Steering Clear of Plagiarism

What to Cite, 49
Ways to Avoid Plagiarizing, 51

Part Four, Documenting Sources

Two Basic Features of MLA Style, 62
Setting Up the MLA List of Works Cited, 68
Beyond the Basics: Special Considerations of
    Online Documentation, 78
Two Basic Features of APA Style, 92
Setting Up the APA List of References, 96
Two Basic Features of the *Chicago* Endnote
    Style, 108
Setting Up *Chicago* Endnotes and Footnotes, 108
Two Basic Features of CBE/CSE Citation-Sequence
    Style, 117
Setting Up the CBE/CSE List of References, 117

Part Six, Common Sentence Problems

Options for Editing a Run-on or Comma
    Splice, 138
Verb Tenses in Conditional Sentences, 157
Two Key Points about Agreement, 160
Forms of Personal Pronouns, 166

Part Seven, Punctuation and Mechanics

Comma: Yes, 179
Comma: No, 180
Apostrophe: Yes, 183
Apostrophe: No, 183

Part Eight, For Multilingual/ESL Writers

Articles at a Glance: Four Basic Questions, 201

Common Correction and Editing Marks

Note: Numbers refer to sections in the book.

Abbreviation	Meaning
ab or abbr	abbreviation, **31b**
adj	adjective, **25**
adv	adverb, **25**
agr	agreement, **23, 24c**
art	article, **34**
awk	awkward, **15, 16, 21**
bias	biased language, **18c, 24c**
case	case, **24a**
cap (t̲o̲m)	use a capital letter, **31a**
comp	comparison, **21a, 25e, 25f**
coord	coordination, **16c, 26a**
cs	comma splice, **20**
dic	diction, **18**
db neg	double negative, **25d**
dm	dangling modifier, **21c**
doc	documentation, **10–13**
-ed	error in *-ed* ending, **22e**
frag	sentence fragment, **19**
fs	fused sentence, **20**
hyph	hyphenation, **32**
inc	incomplete, **21h, 36a**
ind quot	indirect quotation, **21d, 22d, 36c**
-ing	*-ing* error, **35**
ital	italics/underlining, **30, 33b**
jar	jargon, **18b**
lc (M̸e)	use a lowercase letter, **31a**
mix *or* mixed	mixed construction, **21a**
mm	misplaced modifier, **21b**
ms	manuscript form, **4a, 10d, 11d, 12d, 12e, 13d**
num	faulty use of numbers, **31c**

Abbreviation	Meaning
p	punctuation error, **26–29, 33**
pass	ineffective passive voice, **15c, 22g**
pron	pronoun error, **24**
quot	quotation error, **9b**
ref	pronoun reference error, **24b**
rel cl	relative clause, **24e, 26c**
rep	repetitive, **14a**
-s	error in *-s* ending, **23a**
shift	needless shift, **21d**
sp	spelling, **1**
s/pl	singular/plural error, **23a, 34a**
sub	subordination, **16c, 26a, 26b, 36d**
sup	superlative, **25e**
s-v agr	subject-verb agreement, **23**
trans	transition, **16b, 16d, 20b**
und	underlining/italics, **30, 33b**
usg	usage error, **37**
vb	verb error, **22**
vt	verb tense, **22d**
wdy	wordy, **14**
wo	word order, **36**
ww	wrong word, **18**

Symbol	Meaning
??	unclear
¶ or par	new paragraph
no ¶	no new paragraph
//	parallelism
⌒	close up space
#	add space
∧	insert
ℓ	delete
∽	transpose
x	obvious error
⊙∧	needs a period
stet	do not change

Table of Contents

1 The Writing Process

1 Writing and Revising, 2
2 Stating a Thesis and Organizing Support, 4
3 Writing an Argument, 6
4 Document Design, Visuals, and Multimedia Texts, 10

2 Researching and Using Sources

5 Searching for Sources, 24
6 Recognizing a Scholarly Article, 39
7 Evaluating Sources, 40

3 Steering Clear of Plagiarism

8 Avoiding Even the Suspicion of Plagiarism, 48
  8a What is plagiarism?, 48
  8b Knowing what to cite, 49
  8c Boundaries of a citation, 49
  8d List: Avoid plagiarism, 51

9 Using/Integrating Source Material, 52
  9a Paraphrasing, 52
  9b Quoting, 53
  9b Introducing/integrating source material, 55
  9d Organizing with ideas, not sources, 56
  9e Fitting documentation to your discipline, 57

4 Documenting Sources

10 MLA Style, 60
  10a Basic features, 62
  10b In-text citations, 63
  10c MLA works cited, 68
  10d MLA paper, 88

11 APA Style, 91
  11a Basic features, 92
  11b In-text citations, 93
  11c APA references, 96
  11d APA paper, 105

12 *The Chicago Manual of Style*, 108
  12a Basic features, 108
  12b In-text citations, 108
  12c *Chicago* endnotes, 108
  12d *Chicago* bibliography, 114
  12e *Chicago* paper, 115

13 CBE/CSE Style, 116
  13a Basic features, 117
  13b In-text citations, 117
  13c CBE/CSE references, 117
  13d CBE/CSE paper, 120

5 The 5 C's of Style

14 First C: Cut, 122
  14a Wordiness, 123
  14b Formulaic phrases, 123
  14c References to your intentions, 124

15 Second C: Check for Action ("Who's Doing What?"), 124
  15a "Who's doing what?" in subject and verb, 124
  15b Sentences beginning with *there* or *it*, 124
  15c Unnecessary passive voice, 125

16 Third C: Connect, 125
  16a Consistent subjects, 125
  16b Transitional words and expressions, 126
  16c Variety in connecting and combining, 126

17 Fourth C: Commit, 127
  17a Confident stance, 127
  17b Consistent tone, 127

18 Fifth C: Choose Vivid, Appropriate, and Inclusive Words, 128
  18a Vivid, specific words, 128
  18b Avoiding slang, regionalisms, and jargon, 129
  18c Avoiding biased and exclusionary language, 130

6 Common Sentence Problems

19 Sentence Fragments, 135
  19a Identifying/Correcting, 135
  19b Dependent clause, 135
  19c Phrase fragments, 136
  19d Intentional fragments, 137

20 Run-ons and Comma Splices, 138
  20a Identifying, 138
  20b Correcting, 138